Water Management and Climate Change

To plan successfully and manage the increased uncertainties posed by likely future climate change, knowledge needs to advance much more for the water profession beyond what is now available. Meeting these challenges does not depend exclusively on advances in climatological-hydrologic models. Policies for adaptation and strategies for mitigation measures have to be formulated on the basis of what are likely to be the potential impacts. These will have to be regularly fine-tuned and implemented according to changing needs as more reliable knowledge and data become available. Even more challenging will be the politics of policy making and implementation, which will require a quantum leap from current policy-making and implementation processes. One can even say that, in addition to the development of more reliable models, the politics of climate change and water management remains one of the greatest uncertainties for the water profession.

This book addresses water management practices and how these should and could be modified to cope with climatic and other related uncertainties over the next two to three decades; the types of strategies and good practices that may be available or have to be developed to cope with the current and expected uncertainties in relation to climate change; and the types of knowledge, information and technological developments needed to incorporate possible future climate change impacts within the framework of water resources management. Decision making in the water sector under changing climate and related uncertainties, and societal water security under altering and fluctuating climate are also discussed. Several case studies are included from several basins, cities, regions and countries in both developed and non-developing countries.

This book was originally published as a special issue of the *International Journal of Water Resources Development*.

Cecilia Tortajada is the President of the Third World Centre for Water Management, Mexico.

Asit K. Biswas is a Distinguished Visiting Professor at the Lee Kuan Yew School of Public Policy in Singapore.

Avinash Tyagi is Secretary General, International Commission on Irrigation and Drainage (ICID), India.

Routledge Special Issues on Water Policy and Governance

Edited by:

Cecilia Tortajada (IJWRD) – Third World Centre for Water Management, Mexico
James Nickum (WI) – International Water Resources Association, France

Most of the world's water problems, and their solutions, are directly related to policies and governance, both specific to water and in general. Two of the world's leading journals in this area, the *International Journal of Water Resources Development* and *Water International* (the official journal of the International Water Resources Association), contribute to this special issues series, aimed at disseminating new knowledge on the policy and governance of water resources to a very broad and diverse readership all over the world. The series should be of direct interest to all policy makers, professionals and lay readers concerned with obtaining the latest perspectives on addressing the world's many water issues.

Water Pricing and Public-Private Partnership
Edited by Asit K. Biswas and Cecilia Tortajada

Water and Disasters
Edited by Chennat Gopalakrishnan and Norio Okada

Water as a Human Right for the Middle East and North Africa
Edited by Asit K. Biswas, Eglal Rached and Cecilia Tortajada

Integrated Water Resources Management in Latin America
Edited by Asit K. Biswas, Benedito P. F. Braga, Cecilia Tortajada and Marco Palermo

Water Resources Management in the People's Republic of China
Edited by Xuetao Sun, Robert Speed and Dajun Shen

Improving Water Policy and Governance
Edited by Cecilia Tortajada and Asit K. Biswas

Water Quality Management
Present Situations, Challenges and Future Perspectives
Edited by Asit K. Biswas, Cecilia Tortajada and Rafael Izquierdo

Water, Food and Poverty in River Basins
Defining the Limits
Edited by Myles J. Fisher and Simon E. Cook

Asian Perspectives on Water Policy
Edited by Cecilia Tortajada and Asit K. Biswas

Managing Transboundary Waters of Latin America
Edited by Asit K. Biswas

Water and Security in Central Asia
Solving a Rubik's Cube
Edited by Virpi Stucki, Kai Wegerich, Muhammad Mizanur Rahaman and Olli Varis

Water Policy and Management in Spain
Edited by Francisco González-Gómez, Miguel A. García-Rubio and Jorge Guardiola

Water Quality Policy and Management in Asia
Edited by Cecilia Tortajada

Water Resources and Decision-Making Systems
Edited by Cecilia Tortajada and Kevin Parris

The Future of Public Water Governance
Has Water Privatization Peaked?
Edited by Christopher A. Scott and Bernard de Gouvello

Restoring Communities Resettled After Dam Construction in Asia
Edited by Mikiyasu Nakayama and Ryo Fujikura

The Private Sector and Water Pricing in Efficient Urban Water Management
Edited by Cecilia Tortajada, Francisco González-Gómez, Asit K. Biswas and Miguel A. García-Rubio

Water for Food Security
Challenges for Pakistan
Edited by Claudia Ringler and Arif Anwar

Water Management and Climate Change
Dealing with Uncertainties
Edited by Cecilia Tortajada, Asit K. Biswas and Avinash Tyagi

Water Management and Climate Change

Dealing with Uncertainties

Edited by
**Cecilia Tortajada, Asit K. Biswas
and Avinash Tyagi**

Routledge
Taylor & Francis Group

LONDON AND NEW YORK

First published 2015
by Routledge

2 Park Square, Milton Park, Abingdon, Oxon OX14 4RN
711 Third Avenue, New York, NY 10017, USA

Routledge is an imprint of the Taylor & Francis Group, an informa business

First issued in paperback 2016

British Library Cataloguing in Publication Data
A catalogue record for this book is available from the British Library

ISBN 13: 978-1-138-80916-1 (hbk)
ISBN 13: 978-1-138-69303-6 (pbk)

Typeset in Times New Roman
by RefineCatch Limited, Bungay, Suffolk

Publisher's Note
The publisher accepts responsibility for any inconsistencies that may have
arisen during the conversion of this book from journal articles to book chapters,
namely the possible inclusion of journal terminology.

Disclaimer
Every effort has been made to contact copyright holders for their permission to
reprint material in this book. The publishers would be grateful to hear from any
copyright holder who is not here acknowledged and will undertake to rectify
any errors or omissions in future editions of this book.

Contents

Citation Information   ix

1. Introduction   1
   Cecilia Tortajada and Asit K. Biswas

2. Adapting to climate change: towards societal water security in
   dry-climate countries   3
   Malin Falkenmark

3. Australian water policy in a climate change context: some reflections   17
   James Horne

4. Characterizing the water extremes of the new century in the US
   South-west: a comprehensive assessment from state-of-the-art
   climate model projections   32
   *Aleix Serrat-Capdevila, Juan B. Valdes, Francina Dominguez and
   Seshadri Rajagopal*

5. Impacts of climate change on the hydrological cycle in Mexico   52
   Felipe I. Arreguín-Cortés and Mario López-Pérez

6. Climate change projections of streamflow in the Iberian peninsula   64
   Domingo F. Rasilla, Carolina Garmendia and Juan Carlos García-Codron

7. Downscaled climate change projections over Spain: application to
   water resources   81
   P. Ramos, E. Petisco, J.M. Martín and E. Rodríguez

8. The application of hydrological planning as a climate change adaptation
   tool in the Ebro basin   99
   Miguel Ángel García-Vera

9. Measures against climate change and its impacts on water resources
   in Greece   117
   Evangelos A. Baltas

10. Water and disasters: a review and analysis of policy aspects   130
    Chennat Gopalakrishnan

11. Managing drought risk in water supply systems in Europe: a review   152
    Giuseppe Rossi and Antonino Cancelliere

Index   171

Citation Information

The chapters in this book were originally published in the *International Journal of Water Resources Development*, volume 29, issue 2 (June 2013). When citing this material, please use the original page numbering for each article, as follows:

Chapter 1
Editorial
Cecilia Tortajada and Asit K. Biswas
International Journal of Water Resources Development, volume 29, issue 2 (June 2013)
pp. 121–122

Chapter 2
Adapting to climate change: towards societal water security in dry-climate countries
Malin Falkenmark
International Journal of Water Resources Development, volume 29, issue 2 (June 2013)
pp. 123–136

Chapter 3
Australian water policy in a climate change context: some reflections
James Horne
International Journal of Water Resources Development, volume 29, issue 2 (June 2013)
pp. 137–151

Chapter 4
Characterizing the water extremes of the new century in the US South-west: a comprehensive assessment from state-of-the-art climate model projections
Aleix Serrat-Capdevila, Juan B. Valdes, Francina Dominguez and Seshadri Rajagopal
International Journal of Water Resources Development, volume 29, issue 2 (June 2013)
pp. 152–171

Chapter 5
Impacts of climate change on the hydrological cycle in Mexico
Felipe I. Arreguín-Cortés and Mario López-Pérez
International Journal of Water Resources Development, volume 29, issue 2 (June 2013)
pp. 172–183

Chapter 6

Climate change projections of streamflow in the Iberian peninsula
Domingo F. Rasilla, Carolina Garmendia and Juan Carlos García-Codron
International Journal of Water Resources Development, volume 29, issue 2 (June 2013)
pp. 184–200

Chapter 7

Downscaled climate change projections over Spain: application to water resources
P. Ramos, E. Petisco, J.M. Martín and E. Rodríguez
International Journal of Water Resources Development, volume 29, issue 2 (June 2013)
pp. 201–218

Chapter 8

The application of hydrological planning as a climate change adaptation tool in the Ebro basin
Miguel Ángel García-Vera
International Journal of Water Resources Development, volume 29, issue 2 (June 2013)
pp. 219–236

Chapter 9

Measures against climate change and its impacts on water resources in Greece
Evangelos A. Baltas
International Journal of Water Resources Development, volume 29, issue 2 (June 2013)
pp. 237–249

Chapter 10

Water and disasters: a review and analysis of policy aspects
Chennat Gopalakrishnan
International Journal of Water Resources Development, volume 29, issue 2 (June 2013)
pp. 250–271

Chapter 11

Managing drought risk in water supply systems in Europe: a review
Giuseppe Rossi and Antonino Cancelliere
International Journal of Water Resources Development, volume 29, issue 2 (June 2013)
pp. 272–289

Please direct any queries you may have about the citations to
clsuk.permissions@cengage.com

INTRODUCTION

Water management and climate change, their numerous interlinkages and the extent of their hydrologic, economic, social and environmental impacts over time and space are complex issues that can be predicted at our present state of knowledge only with a great deal of uncertainty. Lack of scientific understanding of the complex and interacting interrelationships and absence of reliable data are only two of the factors which prevent our forecasting likely future multidimensional and multisectoral impacts with any degree of accuracy. This, in turn, makes proper planning and investment decisions in a cost-effective and timely manner a most challenging task, even under the best of circumstances.

It is widely recognized that at the present state of knowledge, there are a number of important uncertainties in predicting the impacts of climate change in the water sector. These include but are not necessarily limited to: estimating future emission scenarios; analyzing them for greenhouse gas concentrations; predicting how these are likely to affect future global, regional and local rainfall patterns; interpreting their overall impacts on the hydrologic cycle at different scales; and assessing their impacts.

At present, it is still not possible to predict even how the annual average temperature in various regions of the world may change, let alone the rainfall pattern. Additionally, the latest generation of models to forecast average rainfall at the river basin and sub-basin levels have to be considerably improved before they can be used for water resources planning and management purposes. For water management, the problem becomes far more complex, because it must deal not only with the average changes in annual rainfall on the basin or sub-basin scale but also, and more importantly, with extreme rainfall events like serious floods and extended drought. The magnitude of the uncertainties increases several-fold when attempts are made to forecast extreme rainfall events based on increases in annual average temperatures, and even more when rainfalls have to be translated into river flows. In spite of these uncertainties, however, the overall perception is that climate change is responsible for nearly every serious flood or drought the regions and countries have witnessed in recent years.

In the final analysis, efficient water management over the long term requires reliable data and information, as well as understanding – both of the present and of expected events in the future. Historically, water infrastructure has been designed, and will continue to be designed (at least for the next several decades), on the basis of forecasts of future extreme rainfall and river-flow events that will continue to require past data and historical information. In the absence of better and more reliable estimates of expected future extreme rainfall events than the ones now available, the objective may have to be to continue constructing all types of new water infrastructure with the best knowledge available, and maintain and operate existing structures more efficiently in the event of prolonged droughts or serious floods.

To plan successfully and manage the increased uncertainties posed by likely future climate change, knowledge needs to advance much more for the water profession beyond what it is now available. Meeting these challenges does not depend exclusively on advances in climatological-hydrologic models. Policies for adaptation and strategies for mitigation measures have to be formulated on the basis of what are likely to be the potential impacts. These will have to be regularly fine-tuned and implemented according to changing needs and as more reliable knowledge and data become available. Even more challenging will be the politics of policy making and implementation, which will require a quantum leap from current policy-making and implementation processes. One can even say that, in addition to the development of more reliable models, the politics of climate change and water management remains one of the greatest uncertainties for the water profession.

To address the challenges and uncertainties related to water management and climate change, the Aragon Water Institute and the International Centre for Water and Environment of the then Ministry of Environment of Aragon, the Third World Centre for Water Management in Mexico and the International Water Resources Association jointly organized a meeting on "Water Management and Climate Change: Dealing with Uncertainties", held in Zaragoza, Spain, from 28 February to 2 March 2011.

Well-known international experts in the field of water management and climate change were specially invited to discuss future-oriented issues such as: water management practices and how these should and could be modified to cope with climatic and other related uncertainties over the next two to three decades; the types of strategies and good practices that may be available or have to be developed to cope with the current and expected uncertainties in relation to climate change; and the types of knowledge, information and technological developments needed to incorporate possible future climate change impacts within the framework of water resources management. Decision making in the water sector under changing climate and related uncertainties, and societal water security under altering and fluctuating climate, were two matters that were also discussed in depth. Several case studies were presented from basins, cities, regions and countries, such as the Ebro Basin and the Himalayas; the Aragon and Catalonia regions in Spain and the state of Gujarat in India; the city of Zaragoza; and countries such as Australia, Greece, Mexico, Singapore, Spain and the Netherlands. The session also addressed the implications climate change may have for agriculture in India and in OECD countries.

The papers were extensively reviewed by the authors and are now included in this thematic issue. Nevertheless, with the objective to give them further dissemination, these papers have been available on-line for several months on the journal's website: http://www.tandfonline.com/toc/cijw20/current. To further contribute to global discussions on climate-related topics, this thematic issue also includes two state-of-the-art reviews. One of them addresses water and disasters and provides an in-depth review and analysis of the policy aspects; the second focuses on management of drought risks in European water-supply systems.

Finally, we would like to once again invite the academic, research, policy and water and development communities to further question, debate and challenge prevailing wisdom; we believe this is the only way to promote the advancement of knowledge.

Cecilia Tortajada and Asit K. Biswas
Editors-in-chief

Adapting to climate change: towards societal water security in dry-climate countries

Malin Falkenmark

SIWI and Stockholm Resilience Center, Stockholm, Sweden

Water security needs priority in adaptation to global change. Most vulnerable will be the semi-arid tropics and subtropics, home of the majority of poor and undernourished populations. Policies have to distinguish between dry spells, interannual droughts and long-term climate aridification. Four contrasting situations are distinguished with different water-scarcity dilemmas to cope with. Some countries, where the climate is getting drier, will have to adapt their water policy to sharpening water shortage. In many developing countries it will be wise to go for win-win approaches by picking the low-hanging fruit, i.e. taking measures needed in any case. A fundamental component of adaptive management will be social learning to help people recognize their interdependence and differences. Rethinking will be needed regarding how we manage water for agricultural production, integrating solutions with domestic, industrial and environmental uses. Adaptation to global change will benefit from basin management plans, defining medium- and long-term objectives. Conceptual clarity will be increasingly essential. Water – so vital in the life support system – needs to be entered into climate change convention activities.

> Political stability, economic equity and social solidarity are very closely related to water, its management and governance. Hence the future should be viewed through a "water" lens.
>
> Global Water System Project (GWSP, 2011, p. 6)

Introduction

At the Second World Water Forum, in The Hague in 2000, the Ministerial Declaration declared a goal of providing water security in the twenty-first century, in the sense of "ensuring that freshwater, coastal and related ecosystems are protected and improved; that sustainable development and political stability are promoted, that every person has access to enough safe water at an affordable cost to lead a healthy and productive life, and that the vulnerable are protected from the risks of water-related hazards" (quoted in GWSP, 2011, p. 3). Safeguarding societal water security has two basic dimensions: on the one hand to meet water needs in their relation to socio-economic production; and on the other to limit water-related risk, primarily in situations of flood and drought, to an acceptable level.

Large-scale emission of greenhouse gases has been warming the atmosphere, increasing sea evaporation and thereby exacerbating the warming through the additional greenhouse effect from increased atmospheric water vapour (GWSP, 2011). This has lead to changes in precipitation patterns, increasing their intensity and variability. Global warming is in other words speeding up the hydrological cycle, while land use changes alter the rainwater partitioning at the land surface between the blue and green branches, i.e. what goes to rivers and groundwater as opposed to what goes to the vegetation. The outcome is alteration of all the different hydrological elements: precipitation, evaporation, river flow, lake levels and groundwater recharge.

However, the real challenge is not the proceeding climate change alone but coping with global change after also incorporating other fundamental driving forces: the ongoing population growth that adds some 80 million people every year to the world population; the effects of socio-economic development and the increasing water expectations that it involves. In terms of its implications for water requirements and pressure on the available water, Vörösmarty, Green, Salisbury, and Lammers (2000) have shown that population growth dominates greatly over climate change as a driving force towards water scarcity. One should also remember that most of the population added will in fact be living in urban areas, as a consequence not only of population growth as such but of rural push and urban migration of poor rural inhabitants, leading to greater demands on water services, changing diets, etc. All these changes are in reality moving targets and interlinked in a nexus of ongoing change that policy makers have to navigate.

Achieving water security involves the twin goals of reducing the destructive potential of water and increasing its productive potential (Gray & Sadoff, 2007). How will global change influence the water management situations in different parts of the world? What main differences are there in vulnerability predicaments? And what steps are there to take for a country in adapting to the ongoing climate change and safeguarding their particular water security?

This paper will have its focus on climate change implications as regards the role of water deficiency for water security, and how to cope with them. Special care will be taken in terms of the distinction between water scarcity and drought, in line with the recent Dakar recommendation (INBO, 2011).

Critical vulnerability differences

Fundamental differences in exposure

Hydroclimate exposure differences

Most critical in terms of life support conditions, besides temperature, is the relation between precipitation and atmospheric uptake capacity (potential evapotranspiration). Figure 1 illustrates core differences in water balance between three main climatic zones: the temperate zone, where most of the advanced industrial economies have developed; the semi-arid zone, where the majority of poor and undernourished live (approximately one billion, of which around 450 million depend on rainfed agriculture); and the humid tropics, which host a series of emerging economies. All the zones are exposed to increased rainfall variability. Most exposed to water deficiencies, however, will be the semi-arid tropical zone, in view of the large water requirements for food production.

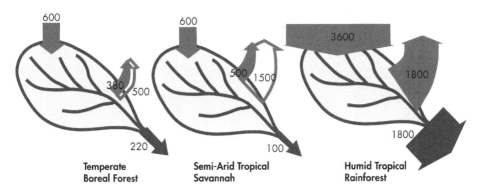

Figure 1.   Fundamental water balance contrasts between three different hydroclimatic zones (units are mm/yr).

The Ministerial Declaration at The Hague referred to earlier reflects the insight that basic water security is vital for a country to be able to enter the path towards socio-economic development. Already at early development stages, countries strive for water storages to compensate for their sensitivity to drought. Gray and Sadoff (2007) have observed vital differences between those that have *harnessed* their hydrology by water storages etc. (see Figure 7, described later), i.e. mainly industrial countries; those that are *hampered* by their hydrology (Lundqvist, 2010), partly by flood events, droughts and water pollution, i.e. mainly emerging economies; and those that remain *hostages* of their hydrology, mainly poor developing economies with particularly challenging climatic conditions and low ability to improve their water security through water resources management.

Water security calls for the ability to meet water dependence through adequate water management efforts. Differences in ability have in fact coloured the global situation considerably, as pointed out by Vörösmarty et al. (2010) in their demonstration of contrasts between basic human security and achieved water security. They indicated that rich countries have been able to lower their exposure to what they refer to as incidental threats to human security through technological and management investments for an overall population of 850 million, while minimal investments in developing countries have left 3400 million with high vulnerability. Currently, about one-third of humanity is estimated to remain excluded from what we call progress (GWSP, 2011). These different observations in terms of fundamental differences in both exposure and ability to secure adequate water security suggest that the third group – those hampered by difficult hydrological phenomena – is especially important to analyze and discuss from a climate change perspective.

Agricultural exposure to climate variability

Agricultural exposure to climate variability is particularly large in regions where the effects of rainfall fluctuations can seriously impact political stability, i.e. countries in the semi-arid tropical region, where agriculture dominates the national income. CGIAR's recent comparative research of a number of catchments in different developing situations demonstrated a strong correlation between the dominance of agriculture and early stages of the development trajectory (Kemp-Benedict et al., 2011; see Figure 2). It is therefore fair to assume that in such countries rural small-scale farmers are particularly exposed to the increasing rainfall variability, and the implications of continuing population growth are most pronounced.

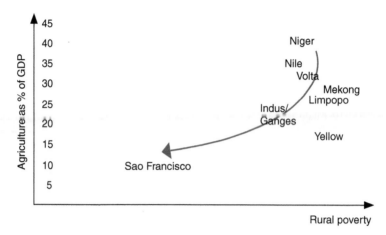

Figure 2.   Dominance of agriculture in early stages of the development trajectory. (Redrawn with kind permission from Kemp-Benedict et al., 2011).

Blue-water competition and closeness to limits

But some dry-climate countries like Australia have been able to make their way to higher positions on the development trajectory. There, water scarcity shows up as high levels of demand-driven water stress (Figure 3). In so doing, such countries have reached a level of development complexity that makes them particularly vulnerable to disturbances related to increased unpredictability and variability in blue-water availability (mainly river flow).

Figure 3 further clarifies different types of water scarcity predicament in terms of different modes of blue-water scarcity: demand-driven water scarcity along the vertical axis and population-driven scarcity along the horizontal axis. Two limits are of particular interest here: the *environmental flow reserve* in view of the need to leave some 30% of the

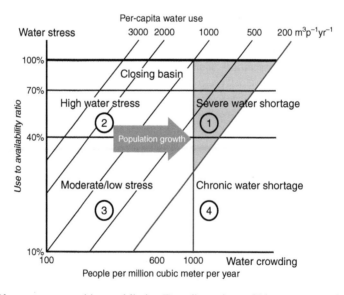

Figure 3.   Blue water competition and limits. Two dimensions of blue water scarcity. Horizontal axis shows population-related shortage (water crowding), vertical axis demand-related shortage (water stress). Diagonal lines show per capita water use.

available flow for aquatic ecosystem health; and *societal water supply requirements* for municipal and industrial needs – some 200 m^3 per person per year (Falkenmark & Lundqvist, 1997). This means that particularly vulnerable are basins close to (a) the 70% horizontal level, and (b) the 200 m^3 per person per year diagonal line. Most critical from a water shortage perspective are basins in the severe-water-shortage triangle.

Four different vulnerability situations

It is clarifying to compare four contrasting situations with rather different water scarcity dilemmas (see Figure 3).

Region 1 refers to the vulnerable triangle beyond the water crowding level of 1000 people per 10^6 m^3 per year (chronic water shortage) and above the diagonal line for water use of 200 m^3 per person per year, which is often referred to as what is needed for urban and industrial water supply (Falkenmark & Lundqvist, 1997). This is a region sensitive to both climate aridification and droughts, where competing water demands will be particularly challenging.

Region 2 refers to the upper left-hand corner of the graph, where many well-developed countries with high levels of water use, primarily irrigated agriculture, lie. For them, the dominating challenge is long periods of drought years when irrigation water needs cannot be met and policy makers start preparing for reduced allocations but social acceptance is hard to secure.

Region 3 refers to the area low or moderate in both directions, i.e. in the lower left-hand part of the diagram, where many of the poor developing countries still remain highly sensitive to rainfall variability and green-water problems.

Region 4 refers to the lower right-hand area, where some poor and highly crowded countries may be found with very low water security.

For our further analysis we can seek illustrations of basins in these different predicament categories based on official data from various sources for precipitation, evaporation and water use for domestic and industrial water supply and irrigation. In Category 1 we find large irrigated river basins in North China and India with severe water shortages and very low per capita water availability even compared to modest water demands (500–700 m^3 per person per year). Population growth will push these basins closer to the diagonal line for 200 m^3 per person per year, where most water is needed for municipal and industrial use. Category 3 represents the predicament of many poor and semi-arid countries dependent on dry-land agriculture. By their lack of financial resources, many such countries have not been able to develop their rivers to provide agricultural water security through irrigation – this is called 'economic water scarcity' by the IWMI (Molden et al., 2007) (see also Figure 7, described later). This is the predicament typical for many African countries.

In Category 2 we find rich countries with advanced, irrigation-dependent economies with high water demand (more than 2000–3000 m^3 per person per year) and large-scale export of agricultural products playing a core role in the national economy, like Australia or California. Since per capita water use is quite high, water demand management stands out as an essential policy mode. In Category 4, finally, we find exceptionally water-short and overpopulated basins, one example being the transnational Limpopo Basin in Southern Africa.

From the perspective of climate change vulnerability, we may conclude that it will be necessary for countries to be better prepared for exacerbated hydrological complications but that, depending on the type of water-scarcity predicament, climate change adaptation

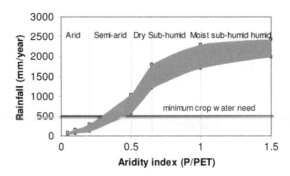

Figure 4.   Rainfall variability as a function of aridity index. Horizontal line shows crop water need. From Molden et al. (2007), IWMI.

will take rather different forms. In Categories 1 and 2, vulnerability is related to blue-water problems in terms of aridification (see also Figure 4, described later), depleted blue-water sources (Falkenmark & Molden, 2008), and difficulty in meeting water demands from municipalities, industry and irrigation projects. In Category 3, climate change problems will involve mainly green-water problems, hitting rainfed agriculture on millions of small-holder farms and reaching the poor rural strata of the population. Critical will be strategies to cope with increasing rainfall variability and its link to agricultural production, which is the dominating economic activity in many countries in the semi-arid zone, where drought sensitivity is large and economic ability to cope small. Long-term rainfall deficiency may play havoc with farmers' water security, as will be further discussed below.

In Table 1 we have structured these fundamental differences into four different categories with rather different water-deficiency challenges to address. Categories 1 and 2 are exposed to mainly blue-water problems, while Categories 3 and 4 as regards food production have mainly to address green-water problems. Category 1 is the most exposed, in the sense that irrigation – the backbone of agriculture – may be severely threatened. Category 2 will be able to manage by securing increased irrigation water use efficiency. Category 3 contains many African counties where agriculture is threatened by increasing rainfall variability. Category 4 will be particularly severely exposed due to chronic water shortage and will have to plan for a future without irrigation.

Climate change adaptation: coping with water deficiencies

Considering these four contrasting situations in terms of water predicament, we now turn attention to differences in the two particular types of water deficiencies that have to be

Table 1.   Four climate change exposure categories in drought-sensitive countries.

		Water crowding	
		Low	High
Relative water use	High	2 Low water crowding/ Large-scale irrigation	1 High water crowding/ Large-scale irrigation
	Low	3 Low water crowding/ Mainly rainfed agriculture	4 High water crowding/ Mainly rainfed agriculture

coped with to improve societal water security: increasing rainfall variability versus alterations in climate aridity (when climate zones may start to shift).

Temporary as opposed to long-term climatic water deficiency

Even if the atmospheric circulation exhibits relatively stable long-term patterns as represented by overall rainfall, the variability and unpredictability of rainfall is considerable and constitutes a major challenge for a country's meteorological services. Although variability of rainfall is expected to intensify and therefore constitute a formidable challenge, rainfall variability is nothing new. Faurès, Bernardi, and Gommes (2010) illustrate this by the monthly rainfall at Beira, Mozambique for the years 1908-2009 (see Figure 1 in their paper). Winter rainfall was anything between 0 and 400 mm/month, and summer rainfall anything between 0 and 190 mm/month.

The vulnerability to increasing rainfall fluctuation can easily be seen in Figure 4, which shows the current relation between rainfall variability and climate aridity (plus or minus one standard deviation). Most vulnerable to climate change is the zone where the horizontal line indicating the minimum rainfall required for a crop to mature intersects the rainfall curve. Evidently the semi-arid and dry sub-humid tropics and subtropics are the most vulnerable from this perspective.

We are used to drawing attention to drought episodes in terms of *absence of water*, rather than what can be done in terms of livelihood improvements by benefiting from the *presence of water* (Falkenmark & Rockström, 2008). However, it is important to distinguish between different drought origins: climate-related *meteorological* water deficiencies; runoff generation responses in terms of *hydrological* deficiencies; and so-called *agricultural* water deficiencies, which may be linked not only to climate but also to land mismanagement influencing rain partitioning at the soil surface. In terms of meteorological droughts it is helpful to distinguish between three categories: intraseasonal dry spells, interannual droughts, and aridification. While agricultural droughts are reflected in green-water shortage and therefore crop production problems, hydrological problems are reflected in blue-water shortages, i.e. low water flow and therefore water supply and irrigation problems, for instance.

Coping with intraseasonal dry spells

Rainfall variability generates dry spells almost every rainy season in the semi-arid and sub-humid regions (Barron, Rockström, Gichuki, & Hatibu, 2003). Poor water management is often reflected in an inability to bridge such water deficiency episodes and is the reason for most of the yield reductions commonly ascribed to droughts (Rockström & Karlberg, 2010). This means that much of the yield reduction could be avoided with better water management – in fact a great opportunity for agriculture in tropical drylands.

Dry spells may be influenced by climate change. Although they have meteorological origins, the effects may be increased by soil degradation and mismanagement, reducing the possibility for the rain to infiltrate.

On small-holder farms, dry spells tend to be reflected in huge water losses in dryland agriculture (Rockström, Karlberg, & Falkenmark, 2011) – blue-water losses because rain does not infiltrate, and green-water losses because plants cannot take up the green water in the root zone, having been damaged during dry spells (Figure 5). Management responses aim at increasing water use efficiency, i.e. essentially reducing both the blue-water losses (through soil management to address infiltrability of rainfall and water-holding capacity) and the green-water losses (by improving the water uptake capacity of the roots by

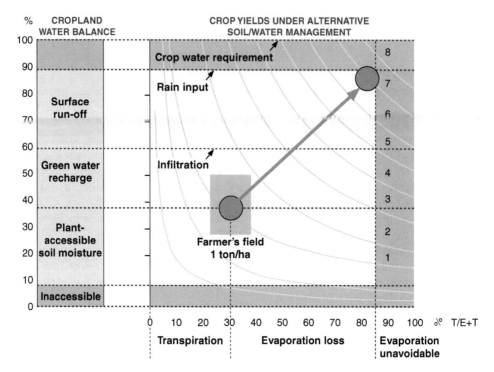

Figure 5. Actual crop yield (rounded curves) as a function of water losses suffered on the farmer's field outside Niamey, Niger. Left hand column shows water balance in percentage of crop water requirement. Grey rectangle indicates measured situation. Source: data from Rockström (1997).

protecting from dry-spell damage through supplementary irrigation and water harvesting) (Falkenmark & Rockström, 2008). Barron, Enfors, Cambridge, & Moustapha (2010) analyzed ways of coping with the consequences of rainfall in the Sahel, where dry spells shorter than 14 days are currently on the order of one to two events per season in 7 years out of 10, an occurrence that has increased since 1960. By adding a marginal input of fertilizers, they showed that millet yields could be increased fivefold.

Coping with interannual droughts

Interannual droughts complicate life considerably in the semi-arid climate regions. In 1876–78, failure of both monsoons caused the so-called Great Famine in the Bhavani Basin in Tamil Nadu, India. Not less than two-thirds of the rainy seasons were seen as unfavourable for agriculture by the start of the twentieth century (Lannerstad, 2009). Figure 6 illustrates the implications of interannual variability, both for rainfall (a) and river flow (b). The former shows that in Zimbabwe the recent deficiencies in rainfall tend to be more pronounced as compared with previous drought periods. The latter shows the combined result of a decreasing average flow (reflecting a possible climate change superimposed on increasing water use upstream) and interannual fluctuations between wet years and dry years in periods of about seven years.

Interannual droughts are difficult to predict as the result of large-scale atmospheric fluctuations of both semi-periodic and more irregular character. Examples of the former are the El Nino Southern Oscillation (ENSO) and the North Atlantic Oscillation (NAO).

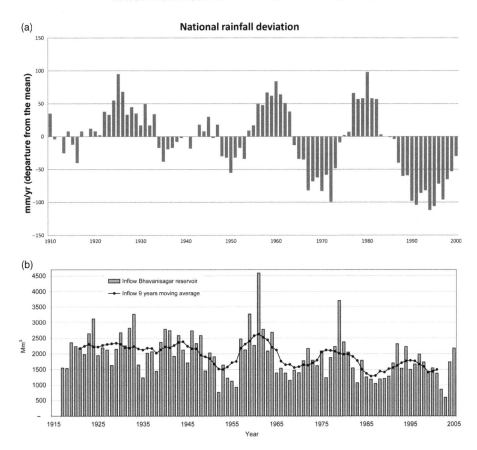

Figure 6.   Inter-annual droughts may be short or long. (a) National rainfall deviations from the long-term mean, Zimbabawe, 1910–2000 (source: Zimbabwe Department of Meteorological Service at http://weather.utande.co.zw/climate/climatchange.htm. Credit to P.Rekacewicz.UNEP/Grid-Arendal. (b) Flow at the LBP Reservoir in Bhavani basin (source: Lannerstad, 2009).

Fluctuations are reflected in sea-surface temperature variations, which are used as input in efforts to simulate probable outcomes (Faurès et al., 2010). Typical water management responses to interannual hydroclimatic variations include, besides warnings, infrastructure for water storage. While rich and emerging economies have been able to store massive amounts of water, poorer countries have lacked the ability required, as shown in Figure 7. Management responses to exacerbated interannual floods will most probably include new dams to alleviate the societal effects of droughts and to control floods to reduce inundations.

Coping with aridification

An even more challenging problem of global warming is increasing hydroclimatic aridity, in the sense of extension of the arid tropics to higher latitudes, i.e. moving to the left along the horizontal axis in Figure 4 with rainfall below minimum crop water needs. Most vulnerable are – as indicated earlier – regions where rainfall is of the same order as the green-water requirements of the crops. In such regions, rainfed agriculture may cease to be realistic, except during wet years or very locally. In a real situation, however, it will be difficult to decide whether a series of drought years reflects only an interannual drought

11

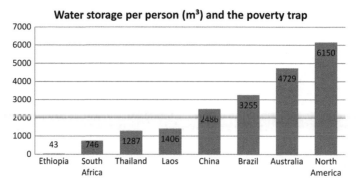

Figure 7. Water storages help to withstand water deficiency shock. Source: Redrawn from http://www.sadcwateraccounting.org/indicators/4.5PerCapitaWaterStorage.aspx?print = 1, ©SADC.

episode or in fact signals that the climate is turning more arid. Under climate change the frequency and degree of interannual droughts may be expected to change gradually. This means that there will not necessarily be any sharp frontier announcing what we think of as altered aridity calling for altered policies. A scientifically based distinction will not be possible until after a long enough delay to allow strict analysis based on good enough statistical data.

The Murray-Darling Basin in Australia offers an interesting example of the difficulties met in responding to aridification (Pittock & Cornell, 2010). It corresponds to Category 2 in Figure 3. Because it is located in a semi-arid region of the world, economic development there has been based on irrigation-supported agriculture and pasture. Climate change in terms of aridification therefore implies a serious threat to large sectors of the regional economy. Sensitivity to aridification is therefore high, especially as water is already overallocated, but so is adaptive capacity through for instance water allocation changes and water conservation measures (Turall, Burke, & Faurès, 2011). The societal problems encountered in implementing an altered water policy based on a new basin plan were described by Pittock & Connell (2010).

Conclusions

Although we tend to think about the climate through a lens of averages, physical reality and therefore also social and economic phenomena tend to reflect variability around those averages (Lundqvist & Falkenmark, 2010). The savannas constitute a critical global hotspot for several reasons: because of desertification processes and low land productivity; because these areas host an estimated 40% of the world population; and because vulnerability to climate change is high in terms of impacts on water management in agricultural systems (Falkenmark & Rockström, 2008; Turall et al., 2011).

One of the first consequences of climate change will be the increasing frequency and impact of extreme hydrological phenomena. Effects of climate change will however be superimposed on the effects of demographic growth, urbanization and globalization. The altered water situation will operate as a moving target, with implications also reflecting other driving forces such as demographic change, altered patterns of water demand due to urbanization, economic development and globalization. Rainfall variability is nothing new, but the extremes can be expected to be more frequent. As an adaptation to such global change it will be essential to achieve basic water security and protect both populations and national economies from its more or less serious effects.

Coping with rainfall variability varies with the type of hydroclimatic change – whether intraseasonal dry spells, interannual droughts or more permanent hydroclimatic aridification. When it comes to adaptation challenges, the effects of population growth and demographic changes tend to dominate in the short time perspective. Most vulnerable will be semi-arid tropics and subtropics, which are also home to the majority of poor and undernourished populations.

Some countries, where the climate is getting drier, will have to adapt their altered water policy to a sharpening water shortage, especially basins in Category 1 in Table 1 and Figure 3. Irrigation-dependent countries in the semi-arid tropics with already high water stress are more or less close to the carrying capacity of the water resources of the country, in other words in Category 2, and will have to alter their policies. They will have to find ways towards more efficient water use through reuse of urban waste water, or even efficient irrigation, maybe seeking alternative raw water sources for their large cities, etc.

Adaptive resource management

In GWSP (2011, p. 9) it is claimed that "climate change should not be seen as a driver but rather as a catalyzer for often long overdue water governance reforms". Hence uncertainties related to climate change predictions should not be used as excuse for postponing action. In view of all the uncertainties involved and the moving-target property, management responses will have to advance through a 'trial and error'–based approach continually adapted to changes experienced. Recently, more organized principles for such an approach have been developed under the term 'adaptive water management', to cope with the many kinds of uncertainties involved: lack of knowledge in water availability and variability; poor understanding of the water system behaviour; and the type of potential shocks to be encountered (Lannerstad & Molden, 2009). A fundamental component of adaptive management is *social learning*, to help people recognize their interdependence and differences, enabling collective action and the resolution of conflicts. It may also help to overcome barriers and open up possibilities for new, innovative technologies and practices.

Critical policy responses

With so much undone in terms of achieving an acceptable level of water security, it will evidently be wise to go for win-win approaches by picking the low-hanging fruit, i.e. taking measures that are needed in any case to improve national water security. Evidently, critical response activities will vary between countries with easy as opposed to difficult hydrology, between economically advanced as opposed to poor countries where agriculture still dominates as the source of the national economy. Since the Copenhagen meeting in 2009, international organizations that have been increasingly active in analyzing water policies related to climate change adaptation include the Food and Agriculture Organization (FAO) of the United Nations (Turall et al., 2011), the International Water Management Institute (IWMI, 2011) and the International Network of Basin Organizations (INBO, 2011). Merging the outcome of this study with those messages gives the following overview.

The FAO stresses that important responses will be to include both (blue) water-oriented activities such as storages, water use efficiency improvements, water accounting and data gathering, and (green-water-oriented) activities on croplands such as soil/water management and supplementary irrigation based on rainwater harvesting. They stress that crop patterns could be altered, crop breeding further developed, and crop storage from good to bad years implemented. Hydrometry will be increasingly essential, based on data gathering, compilation and analysis as a base for realistic assessments. Water accounting will be a desirable basis for water allocation modification, distinguishing between throughflow-based water uses and uses that are consumptive, depleting the water availability for those downstream. Water storages of different scales will be needed to protect users from large fluctuations due to droughts. Surface water, soil moisture and groundwater storages will be needed. For quick solutions, surface storages may benefit from small reservoirs and natural wetlands. Soil moisture can be managed through improved farming practices like soil management, conservation tillage, and rainwater harvesting. And groundwater storage can be improved by intentional recharge arrangements. Rainfed farmers are often the first ones impacted during droughts. and could be encouraged to develop rainwater-based supplementary irrigation to reduce the risk of crop yield reduction and starvation. For irrigation-based farming systems, water use efficiency should be improved by measures that reduce the often large water losses.

The INBO stresses the need for long-term efforts to develop comprehensive, integrated and consistent management of water resources, based on realistic assessments of water availability and socio-economic, cultural and political realities. Basin management should rely on integrated information systems incorporating water availability, water use, polluting pressures and dependent ecosystems, but paying adequate attention to land use changes. Adaptation to global change would benefit from basin management plans defining medium- and long-term objectives. The basin planning process should rely on integrated information systems as an objective basis for dialogue, negotiation, decision making and evaluation. Protection against both floods and droughts may be improved through a coordinated basin approach and an understanding of the 'upstream-downstream' common cause on the scale of basins and sub-basins. In transboundary basins, cooperation between riparian states has to be promoted.

The IWMI, citing the reality of increased water scarcity and variability, particularly stresses the need to seriously rethink how we manage water for agricultural production and to integrate these solutions with domestic, industrial and environmental uses. What will be essential is to change the way we think about water, where it comes from, how it is benefitted from, and what happens to water after its use. Conceptual clarity is increasingly essential, distinguishing between green water in the soil, originating from infiltrated rain, and liquid blue water in rivers, lakes and aquifers, generated through water partitioning at the land surface and in the root zone. Adapting to altered hydrological extremes makes it useful to distinguish between dry spells, interannual droughts and long-term aridification of the climate in an area. The INBO (2011) stresses the need to distinguish between drought and water scarcity. The latter is a result of imbalance between resources and abstractions. This imbalance may have two origins: it can be demand driven or population driven.

Final remarks

The very close link between climate change, water and food production makes the IWMI particularly clear in its statements:

> Water is the unifying element in our system. Our climate is the visible expression of the complex interactions of air, water and land driven by the power of the sun. Global warming is affecting those interactions. Our climate is changing and those changes will affect the

quantity and quality of water available to us all. It will affect the quality of life on our planet. What is less visible but no less alarming, is the growing threat to our capacity to produce enough food under new and uncertain climate conditions. Food production and food prices are pillars of social stability. If we compromise the ability of hundreds of millions of small farmers to grow enough food to feed us all, we are courting a grim future. Let's not go there.

IWMI, 20 June 2011

This paper has shown that there are many reasons that water should be entered into climate change convention activities. Past experience, however, shows that widespread conceptual barriers have been effective in obstructing the achievement of this goal: many politicians and policy makers tend to see water through a sectoral lens, claiming that water is just one of many sectors and has therefore to be kept out of convention negotiations. What they seem not to have understood is that water is the basis for human existence on this planet and in fact the very bloodstream of the biosphere.

References

Barron, J., Enfors, E., Cambridge, H., & Moustapha, A. (2010). Coping with rainfall variability in semiarid agro-ecosystems: Implications on catchment scale water balances by dryspell mitigation strategies among smallscale farmers in Niger. *International Journal of Water Resources Development, 16*(4), 543–559.

Barron, J., Rockström, J., Gichuki, F., & Hatibu, N. (2003). Dry spell analysis and maize yields for two semi-arid locations in east Africa. *Agricultural and Forest Meteorology, 117*, 23–37.

Falkenmark, M., & Lundqvist, J. (1997). *World freshwater problems: Call for a new realism* (Comprehensive Assessment of the Freshwater Resources of the World, Background Report 1). Stockholm: Stockholm Environment Institute.

Falkenmark, M., & Molden, D. (2008). Wake up to realities of river basin closure. *International Journal of Water Resources Development, 24*(2), 201–215.

Falkenmark, M., & Rockström, J. (2008). Building resilience to drought in desertification-prone savannas in Sub-Saharan Africa: The water perspective. *Natural Resources Forum, 32*, 93–102.

Faurès, J. M., Bernardi, M., & Gommes, R. (2010). There is no such thing as an average: How farmers manage uncertainty related to climate and other factors. *International Journal of Water Resources Development, 26*(4), 523–542.

Food and Agricultural Organization (FAO). (2009). *Mozambique: PRO-IRRI farming systems project. Farming systems assessment and perspectives in Sofala and Manica*. Rome: FAO.

Grey, D., & Sadoff, C. (2007). Sink or swim? Water security for growth and development. *Water Policy, 9*, 545–571.

GWSP. (2011). *Water security, Challenges for science and policy. Interconnected problems of a changing world: Call for sustainable solutions*. Bonn: Global Water System Project.

INBO. (2011). Adapting to the effects of climate change in basins: Tools for action. INBO World General Assembly, Dakar, 20–23 January 2010. *INBO Newsletter*, No. 19 (May 2011).

IWMI. (2011). *Water: The unifying element in our system* International Water Resources Management Institute. Retrieved from http://www.iwmi.cgiar.org/Topics/Climate_Change/

Kemp-Benedict, E., Cook, S., Allen, S. L., Vosti, S., Lemoalle, J., ... Giordano, M. (2011). Connections between poverty, water and agriculture: Evidence from 10 river basins. *Water International, 36*, 125–140.

Lannerstad, M. (2009). *Water realities and development trajectories: Global and local agricultural production dynamics*. Doctoral thesis, Department of Water and Environmental Studies, Linköping University, Sweden.

Lannerstad, M., & Molden, D. (2009). *Adaptive water resource management in the South Indian Lower Bhavani Project command area* (Research Report No. 129). Colombo: IWMI.

Lundqvist, J. (2010). Producing more or wasting less? Bracing the food security challenge of unpredictable rainfall. In L. Martinez-Cortina et al. (Eds.), *Rethinking water and food security (Fourth Botín Foundation Workshop)*. Leiden: CRC Press.

Lundqvist, J., & Falkenmark, M. (2010). Adaptation to rainfall variability and unpredictability: New dimensions of old challenges and opportunities. *International Journal of Water Resourcs Development*, *26*(4), 595–612.

Molden, D., Frenken, K., Barker, R., de Fraiture, C., Mati, B., & … Svendsen, M. (2007). Trends in water and agricultural development. In D. Molden (Ed.), *Water for food, water for life: Comprehensive assessment of water management in agriculture* (pp. 57–89). London: Earthscan; Colombo: IWMI.

Pittock, J., & Connell, D. (2010). Australia demonstrates the planet's future: Water and climate in the Murray-Darling Basin. *International Journal of Water Resources Development*, *26*(4), 561–578.

Rockström, J. (1997). *On-farm agrohydrological analysis of the Sahelian yield crisis*. PhD-disstertation, Natural Resources Managament, Dept of Systems Ecology, Stockholm University, Stockholm, Sweden.

Rockström, J., & Karlberg, L. (2010). The quadruple squeeze: Defining the safe operating space for freshwater use to achieve a triply green revolution in the Anthropocene. *Ambio*, *39*(3), 257–265.

Rockström, J., Karlberg, L., & Falkenmark, M. (2011). Global food production in a water-constrained world: Exploring 'green' and 'blue' challenges and solutions. In R. Q. Grafton & K. Hussey (Eds.), *Water resources planning and management* (pp. 131–152). New York: Cambridge University Press.

Turall, H., Burke, J., & Faurès, J.-M. (2011). *Climate change, water and food security*. Rome: Food and Agricultural Organization.

Vörösmarty, C. J., Green, P., Salisbury, J., & Lammers, R. (2000). Global water resources: Vulnerability from climate change and population growth. *Science*, *289*, 284–288.

Vörösmarty, C. J., McIntyre, P. B., Gessner, M. O., Dudgeon, D., Prusevich, A., … Green, P. (2010). Rivers in global crisis: Water insecurity for humans and biodiversity. *Nature*, *467*, 555–561.

Australian water policy in a climate change context: some reflections

James Horne

James Horne and Associates, Deakin, ACT, Australia

This paper focuses on Australian water reform in a climate change context over the period between mid-2006 and end 2011, with a particular focus on the Murray Darling Basin (MDB). In Australia, during this period, the potential impacts from climate change became more central to the policy debate, and the implementation of what can be said to be a large-scale climate change adaptation programme commenced. The paper outlines the policy framework adopted by the government of the day and then draws out some of the key issues for water management against this background, and the attendant increased uncertainty.

Background to current water reforms

The current thrust of Australian water reform began in earnest in the mid-1990s, well before climate change became an important policy driver. In the face of economic development over the preceding decade, there was recognition that the environment in some key catchments was being adversely affected. These problems could be mainly linked to over-allocation of water resources that had occurred over many years, but also included problems related to salinity, siltation and nutrients. In the context of a broad national microeconomic reform debate, it was also apparent that a more efficient water management system could generate additional economic activity using the same volume of water. Action in the decade from 1995 sought to implement a process for addressing these issues (COAG Working Group on Water Resource Policy, 1994; COAG, 1994).

Progress with reform was slower than desired by the Commonwealth (or national) government, leading to some fundamental re-examination of the existing water management paradigm. This resulted in a new high level policy commitment, the 2004 National Water Initiative (NWI), agreed by the Commonwealth and most states and territories after lengthy negotiations. The NWI was a 'best endeavours' agreement, with governments agreeing that an increased effort should be made to improve water management across the board. The Commonwealth played an important leadership role in establishing this new consensus but the states remained primarily responsible for water management in both rural and urban areas.

The thrust of the NWI was to "deliver(ing) a nationally compatible market, regulatory and planning based system of managing surface and groundwater resources for rural and urban use that optimizes economic, social and environmental outcomes" (COAG, 2004).

The notions of unchanging climate and the adequacy of existing water management practices and institutions to address the emerging challenges were clearly questioned in the context of developing the NWI. The NWI sets out in some detail an agreed assignment of risk should there be "future reductions in the availability of water for consumptive use" (COAG, 2004, paragraphs 46–51). These had been agreed with key interest groups (particularly the National Farmers Federation) in 2004 before being signed off by the then Prime Minister and State Premiers and Chief Minister. The relevant climate change NWI provision is that "Water access entitlement holders are to bear the risks of any reduction or less reliable water allocation . . . as a result of . . . seasonal or long-term changes in climate" (COAG, 2004, paragraph 48).

Already, it was clear in Western Australia that past inflows did not seem to be a good predictor of future inflows into the water storages of its main urban area, Perth. This led to a decision in 2004 by the Western Australian Government to build a large water desalination plant, which added about 20% capacity to the urban water supply. This was the first major supply augmentation from non-rainfall dependent sources (water-technology.net, 2011).

Increasingly but not universally, the concept of water entitlements being seen as a share of the consumptive pool was becoming the norm – this concept was one of the key features of the NWI. This approach explicitly acknowledges Australia's highly variable stream flows and of course is highly relevant to developing a water planning methodology that incorporates climate change. The potential impacts of climate change or increased climate variability were explicitly recognized in the NWI in 2003–04, but policy makers did not have a good handle on the relative size of problems because of the lack of consistent and transparent data, and the fact that little scientific work had been undertaken on a basin-wide basis.

Elements of a sustainable approach to water planning

In early November 2006, after some five years of severe drought in southeast Australia, the Prime Minister held an emergency meeting of MDB state Premiers, seeking to focus attention on the deteriorating water availability outlook in parts of the MDB. This meeting resulted in close cooperative work being undertaken by the states and the Commonwealth in a short-term crisis management framework through late 2006 and 2007, but most importantly it signalled the commencement of CSIRO's first water availability study (then called a 'sustainable yields study') (CSIRO, 2011). This will be discussed further below.

Three key issues came together in late 2006 in the MDB:

- Implementation of the NWI all around Australia was very slow, reflecting the fact that most jurisdictions really did not put in the effort and funding that was needed to secure real change. The slowness in reaching good outcomes in water trading in the MDB was a case in point. By late 2006, water quantity and quality issues continued to mount, with adverse impacts on agriculture and the environment and urban communities dependent on water resources for their future (COAG, 2006, Howard, 2006a, 2006b).
- Second, existing institutional arrangements (based on consensual decision making, giving any jurisdiction (state government or national government) an effective veto potentially resulting in lowest common denominator outcomes on key issues) had reached their use by date. Governance arrangements in the MDB were not delivering desired outcomes. Key institutional concerns surrounded the then Murray

Darling Basin Commission (MDBC). This is not a criticism at all of the staff of those institutions but rather the governance/institutional structure itself. This was recognized by the Australian Government, which had just commissioned a study on how to reform it.

● Third, an unprecedented drought in the southern MDB, seen by some as the tipping point on evidence that we were dealing with climate change rather than climate variability, was beginning to unfold. At the very least, the drought highlighted that water security was lower than had hitherto been widely accepted.

In summary, the MDB had become a group of catchments where water demand exceeded supply, and the existing planning and management framework was acknowledged by most to be inadequate to put the it (the Basin as a whole) back onto a sustainable long-term path. The evidence was mounting that while the irrigation sector had benefited significantly from the roll out of secure water entitlements and water trading, the sector and state governments had not embraced so readily the implementation of other critical elements of the NWI such as cost recovery, statutory water planning and rural water metering.

Together, these issues provided a genuine and very strong basis to ask whether the water world as we knew it, covering water information, institutions and rules, and markets and regulatory framework, was satisfactory or whether new arrangements were required to produce optimal outcomes. The Commonwealth sought to stand back from specific state interests, and ask what change was required, regardless of 'accepted practice'.

In his January 2007 Australia Day speech, the then Prime Minister John Howard announced a new Commonwealth vision, called *A National Plan for Water Security*.

> Despite this [recent effort], the current trajectory of water use and management in Australia is not sustainable. In a protracted drought, and with the prospect of long-term climate change, we need radical and permanent change. ....

> There does appear to have been a contraction to the south in the weather systems which traditionally brought southern Australia its winter, and spring rains. Our rainfall has always been highly variable. The deviation around average rainfall is enormous. And it seems to be getting bigger. We need, so to speak, to make every drop count, on our farms, in our factories and in our homes. Our water management systems must be geared not to a world of steady averages that rarely materialise, but to the variability that has been part of Australia's climate since time immemorial. (Howard, 2007)

There were six key objectives:

● First, to provide governance arrangements that would allow strategic planning and management of the MDB at a basin-wide level.
  – This would be achieved through a Basin wide plan, which could set out requirements of catchment level plans.
  – The aim was to manage risks to Basin water resources that government could do something about – the aim as far as possible would be to eliminate 'leakage' from the system which is undermining the value of assets all water entitlement holders (e.g. plantation forestry, farm dams, ground water bores, (particularly those linked into river systems)).
  – It proposed an independent Murray Darling Basin Authority would put the plan in place. State level management in the Basin was not achieving the required results, nor were the consensual governance arrangements operating in the MDBC.
● Second, to ensure sustainable environmental and agricultural sectors (and associated communities) by establishing an integrated and enforceable Basin

wide limit (or 'cap') on water diversions, incorporating forward-looking science. This was a key outcome that the existing governance structures had not delivered, and seemed unlikely to deliver.

  – This would allow long-term aggregate water diversions to be managed and adjusted as necessary, allowing climate change impact on aggregate available resources to managed, and a path adopted to reduce over-allocation and overuse back to a sustainable level if studies indicated systemic overuse.

• Third, to ensure decisions by policy makers, businesses and the public would be well grounded, provide a better, more transparent information base facilitating improved understanding of water availability in the Basin. Giving the Bureau of Meteorology (BOM) a new broader water information mandate, and strengthening the science base, would achieve this.

• Fourth, to enable the best use of available water resources by all water users, whether they are irrigators, urban users or the environment, create a strong fully functioning water market and framework for efficient water trading and charging by service providers.

  – The approach would be to implement the NWI principles more vigorously than had been possible under existing state based arrangements. Under the proposed arrangements, the competition regulator, the Australian Competition and Consumer Commission, would have a considerably strengthened legislated role.

• Fifth, to promote sustainable environmental outcomes into the future by establishing a Basin wide environmental watering plan in the MDB, built on close cooperation with the MDB Basin states.

• Sixth, to ensure that the irrigation sector and their dependent communities were well prepared to meet the challenges they would face if the best available science indicated large reductions in diversions were required, arising either from past over-allocation and overuse or from projections of significant future reductions in water availability reflecting climate change impacts.

It was proposed that the delivery of these objectives would be through legislation and an expenditure programme involving new institutions, new rules and sufficient funding to 'reset the system' (for example, through Commonwealth purchasing water in the market for the environment). This approach would address the over-allocation of water resources through development-focused water management from the 1970s to the early 1990s, and allow effective management of reduced water availability through the impact of climate change. While the rationale for action was often characterized as a response to climate change, the prospect of climate change in reality became the driver to address past inaction or inappropriate action.

'Water for the Future' and climate change

From a climate change perspective the then 2007 *National Plan for Water Security* (a policy of the national Coalition government) (Government of Australia, 2007) and its successor, the April 2008 *Water for the Future* (a policy of the current national Labor government) shared most elements in common, and these will be outlined below, drawing on the *Water for the Future* policy framework as at end 2010.

As noted above, the policy framework *Water for the Future* was essentially built around the NWI, but backed up by resourcing and actions to ensure sustainable policy outcomes in both urban and rural Australia, albeit with a strong focus on the MDB. It is an

AU$12 billion programme (or around US$12 billion at early April 2012 exchange rates) to be implemented over 10 years, buttressed by ambitious regulatory, legal and institutional reform. *Water for the Future* was built on four key priorities of taking action on climate change; using water wisely; securing water supplies; and supporting healthy rivers. The national Water Minister's April 2008 speech setting out the framework went on to underscore the importance of climate change:

> The rapidly emerging threat of climate change, with its inherent uncertainties and risks, is something that we must plan for and manage. (Wong, 2008)

The reform was designed to substantially improve environmental outcomes, but in the context of optimizing environmental, economic and social outcomes it was equally important to make sure farming communities were well prepared for the realities of the coming decades. Given ongoing uncertainty around terms such as 'sustainability', and what climate change might mean at the catchment level, selling the large-scale reform was never going to be straightforward. However, the thinking was that a well-constructed package of measures could go a long way in managing risk and uncertainty, through making much more explicit the value of water.

Importance of information and science

An important starting point was the state of Australia's knowledge on water information. As noted above, even before the major policy announcements had been made, the Australian Government commissioned its premier science body, the CSIRO, to commence a water availability study of the MDB in late 2006. This study was anchored in a climate change paradigm and established a methodology for a number of subsequent studies in key catchments to assess water availability scenarios out to 2030 (CSIRO, 2011).

Climate change modelling suggested we can expect an increase in temperatures, reduced rainfall and runoff across eastern and the southwest of Australia over coming decades, and an increase in rainfall variability and evaporation. Some largely uninhabited areas in the northwest of Australia may also become considerably wetter.

The challenge posed by climate change in the MDB is stark. In 2006, policy makers had a sense of what the scientific study might show, but lacked access to solid quantitative information, as no detailed investigation had been done. No one had ever integrated the various state based models that underpinned water planning and management in the MDB. Moreover, the existing models were not transparent, and data and modelling assumptions were not freely available. Redressing these issues was a key purpose of the CSIRO study.

As the original *National Plan for Water Security* noted:

- It has not been possible to conduct timely, rigorous and independent assessments of water resources, seriously impeding the ability to forecast future water availability and make wise water allocation decisions.
- The lack of accurate measurement has made it impossible to estimate how much water is being diverted to irrigation and being used on farms, and how much is being lost or wasted.
- The lack of transparency, independence and rigour in managing water information has eroded community and business confidence in water management across Australia. (Government of Australia, 2007)

To reiterate, Australian rainfall is typically highly variable, and runoff even more so. In looking at the impact of climate change on water availability, there are obviously a range of factors that need examining, including the amount of rainfall, the timing of rainfall events, temperature and associated evaporation. Understanding the interaction of these factors on water availability, on the environment and on agricultural production will be critical over the coming decade.

The impact of changes in key variables affecting water availability will, over time, need to be absorbed into water planning, as traditional water planning methodologies become less reliable. A key endeavour in this regard is the collaborative South Eastern Australia Climate Initiative, which commenced in 2006. Findings from Phase 1, published in 2010, showed how the recent drought was quite different from previous droughts. It was confined to southern Australia, included no wet years, saw declines in rainfall concentrated in autumn rather than winter and spring, and rising average temperatures in all seasons. Taken together, these factors produced a larger than expected decline in streamflow. A 13% decline in rainfall observed in the southern MDB from 1997–2006 resulted in a 44% decline in streamflow. Improving streamflow forecasts will be critical to agriculture in the years ahead, and the role of new finer scale models will have much to contribute (South Eastern Australian Climate Initiative, 2010). The BOM already has an active programme in this area, and collaborative work with CSIRO can be expected to produce new policy and business relevant tools over coming years (Bureau of Meteorology, 2011a, 2011b).

Clearly in any world, let alone in a world in which the climate is expected to become drier, it is important to have a clear understanding of key aspects of the water resource. From a policy perspective, effective risk management required that this issue be accorded a very high priority. Hence an important strand of the policy framework was to provide BOM with substantial new resources ($460 million over a 10-year period) to remedy the extant shortcoming in capacity. Much of this work needed to be done in conjunction with the states, but it was critical to have an independent national body able to provide transparent, reliable information. In a world with a more variable and uncertain water outlook, more timely access to more accurate information will help participants manage heightened risks and uncertainty. Of course none of this is costless, but it is clear there are significant net benefits from the upgrading that is currently in progress.

Water Act 2007 recognizes climate change

Getting the MDB back onto a sustainable footing and keeping it there is at the heart of the *Water Act 2007*. It seeks to facilitate this outcome, *inter alia*, by providing for water planning at a basin level in the MDB, to be undertaken by an independent, expert-based body with a whole-of-Basin focus.

- The activities of the former Murray Darling Basin Commission (MDBC) are now undertaken by the Murray Darling Basin Authority (MDBA) on the basis of a corporate plan, not via the convoluted decision making of the past. This provides the states and the Commonwealth with an initial decision-making role, but then allows the MDBA to get on with implementation.
- The MDBA is also responsible for preparing the Basin Plan. This basin-wide planning document will for the first time set sustainable diversion limits for every catchment and aquifer in the Basin. The Basin Plan will also include an Environmental Watering Plan, designed to put the environment back on a sustainable footing.

In simple terms, there are two steps in arriving at sustainable diversion limits. First, there is a need to ascertain what the current sustainable diversion limit is and then to understand how future climate might affect this limit. These limits are to be based on 'best available science'. The legislation requires that the MDBA manage the resource at a basin level, "optimising environmental, economic and social outcomes" (Commonwealth of Australia, 2008, 2009; Burke, 2010; see also Turnbull, 2010).

These sustainable diversion limits have yet to be determined, but from the proposed Basin Plan released in late 2011 it is clear that the major step in the short to medium term is to get the MDB back onto a sustainable footing, on the basis of the climate we already have (MDBA, 2011). That is a large step in its own right in some catchments, probably involving reductions in use of at least one-quarter. The water availability studies have underscored the need for an adaptive management framework in water planning to adjust the rights of all users (irrigators and farmers, urban users and the environment) in a transparent way. Models need to be open, transparent and verifiable, entitlement frameworks clearly defined and the market well functioning important to make best use of the resource in the Australian context.

By April 2012, the MDBA had completed extensive consultation with governments, research agencies and affected communities on the proposed plan, which was released for consultation in late 2011. The process has been delayed several times, and is now nearly two years behind the original schedule. It is likely that the Basin Plan will be 'made' by the responsible Minister sometime in 2012.

Addressing over-allocation through direct water purchasing

Water for the Future has commenced addressing the over-allocation issue while discussions on new sustainable diversion limits continue under the Basin Plan framework. The 'Restoring the Balance' expenditure programme has made a significant start to the process of achieving a sustainable equilibrium by direct water purchases in the market, to be held by a new statutory position the Commonwealth Environmental Water Holder (CEWH), to undertake environmental watering using water accruing to purchased entitlements. As at end April 2012, over 8% MDB surface water entitlements (on a long-term average basis) previously diverted for use in irrigation have been purchased through this programme, considerably more than the total adjustment that was previously undertaken (Department of Sustainability, Environment, Water, Population and Communities, 2011a).

A key concern driving the MDB reform was and remains the fact that the water resource is over-allocated and being overused, before any consideration is given to the impact of climate change. An over-allocated system is one where more entitlements to use water have been allocated to entitlements holders than can be sustained. Overuse is where more water is allocated to irrigators for consumption within a given period, or extracted by other means, than can be sustained. One central concern is that water availability to irrigators is being undermined by unregulated extraction of water through an expansion in the number and size of bores, farm dams and plantation forests.

By addressing these issues now, all water users will be in a significantly better position to face the impact of a drying climate, and diminished and more variable water supply, in a way that treats all water users equitably. A key finding of the CSIRO MDB water availability study was that in dry periods, water plans had a hitherto not well-known, systemic bias against the environment (CSIRO, 2008). That is, during drought periods water would often be preferentially allocated to agriculture over environmental flows, even when provision for environmental flows had previously been made. If environmental outcomes are to improve, not only does the impact of climate change need to be addressed but also existing over-allocation and overuse needs to be addressed fundamentally.

Modernizing irrigation infrastructure

A fourth strand of action involves modernizing Australia's irrigation infrastructure. This involves a range of initiatives designed to improve the operational effectiveness of key irrigation districts in the MDB.

Modernization planning

One of the first programmes put in place involved irrigation modernization planning. It sought to assist irrigators and irrigation service providers in the MDB to develop modernization plans for their districts, encouraging irrigators to consider their future a decade or two into the future. These plans now cover districts using over 80% of water entitlements in the Basin. The central task was to have irrigators assess their district's viability well into the future, and assess options to adapt to a future with less water. These plans are pivotal in having irrigation communities identify for themselves the actions needed to secure a viable, sustainable future. They are undertaken in the context of the CSIRO water availability studies incorporating climate change scenarios mentioned above, at a catchment level. A government cash co-contribution of 80% of the cost of the planning study was provided to eligible groups, with irrigators being required to fund the remaining 20%. Undertaking these plans was made a necessary first step for service providers to apply for funding under other government irrigation infrastructure programmes (Department of Sustainability, Environment, Water, Population and Communities, 2011b).

This programme was designed to encourage a conversation at a district level about the future of irrigation:

- Was existing infrastructure in the right place?
- Should some districts close or be reduced in size?
- What additional investments, if any, made sense?

This planning process helped take the prospect of climate change down to the farm gate, although equally importantly it provided an opportunity to reassess what adjustment was necessary reflecting past inappropriate planning decisions, even if climate change did not affect aggregate water availability. It is clear that the lure of funding was an important enticement, but there is also little doubt that the process saw the beginning of discussions on the future of irrigation at the regional level in Australia, and on sub-regional closure of irrigation districts for the first time, as irrigation communities came to take a hard look at their future. The overhang of a deep and long lasting drought helped to achieve a greater focus on future climate than might have otherwise been the case. It remains unclear how the extremely wet 2010–11 water year will affect longer-term irrigator behaviour.

On and off farm irrigation infrastructure modernization

Water for the Future involves the government rolling out an extensive on and off farm investment programme, designed to put irrigation assets onto a sustainable long-term footing. It originally set aside $5.8 billion over 10 years to help state governments, irrigation communities and irrigators upgrade their irrigation infrastructure, with the key desired outcomes of more being done with a given amount of water, and the return some of water gained from the efficiency improvements to MDB rivers, to provide enhanced ecosystem services. Project proponents were required to develop assessable business cases and much effort has been put into testing the viability of projects. A number of projects are already underway, but the 2010–11 floods have further delayed delivery.

There is a question whether some elements of *Water for the Future* involving irrigation infrastructure, pursued under the Rudd Labor government, will be continued under the Gillard Labor government: the contribution of infrastructure investments to the adjustment process will reflect critically the quality and cost of projects selected. Some forms of infrastructure expenditure will tend to make water management more flexible while other elements will make it less so. Some will make it more sustainable and others less so. It will be critical to invest in areas that deliver results rather than provide funding to 'wish list' projects of dubious quality. There is a once-in-a-generation opportunity to make the MDB more sustainable, and careful use of committed resources will be required to ensure this happens. Interest groups and the states will continue to make claims for 'their' share of these reforms, as is always the case. This will not always coincide with optimizing national outcomes for the basin as a whole.

Community adjustment

In a very direct sense much of the *Water for the Future* programme is about adjustment, particularly in the MDB. Many specific groups are and will be assisted in adjusting to the impact of reduced water availability (BDA Group, 2010). For example, irrigators (as individuals and irrigation communities) are being assisted significantly to adjust to new circumstances. Groups that are dependent on tourism or the environment will benefit from a healthier environment. Funds have also been made available to small and medium sized urban areas to assist them adjust to reduced 'water availability'. In the short to medium term, it is clear that funds from programme expenditure (both direct water purchase and from infrastructure investment) will have a positive economic impact on regional economies, notwithstanding some leakage as to other regions as retirees move elsewhere or farmers and irrigators diversity their asset base outside of the region. Moreover, in 2010 the Labor government committed to buying back all the water needed to meet reduction targets under MDB Basin Plan when it is made. This effectively means the government has taken over the obligations of farmers in relation to climate change, meaning that the government had agreed in a very substantial way to take on the adjustment that this group had previously agreed to take responsibility for.

The issue of the role of government in economic adjustment is a complex one. Many parts of the MDB (and the rest of rural and regional Australia) have been adversely affected by the massive appreciation in the Australian dollar over the past decade (from around AU$1 equals US$ 50c in 2002 to above parity in 2011–12), oversupply in some industries (such as wine) and the lengthy drought. Against this background it is hardly surprising that when government offers some elements of a community direct assistance, others who are indirectly affected (such as much of the retail/industry support sector) say 'what about us?' In some areas water has become a lightning rod for a raft of other issues, and government needs to ensure that whatever assistance is offered does not dilute the adjustment that needs to take place. The shape of regional Australia, and the investment programme required to achieve this, is a quite separate issue for society and government to consider, and about which there is likely to be an ongoing vigorous debate.

While the *Water for the Future* programme is not a regional assistance programme per se, government has made it clear it will consider assisting communities in the MDB that are likely to face significant adverse circumstances from contracting irrigation. Communities and a range of commentators have offered views on how and to what extent assistance should be provided (MDBA, 2012). Much should depend on the recommendations of the draft MDB Basin Plan, and what the responsible Minister does in 'making' the Basin Plan. If recent experience is anything to go by, further adjustment programmes over coming years seem likely to be introduced to help manage this issue in the most vulnerable communities. Care will need to be exercised to ensure programmes allow adaptation to occur while managing negative consequences. Regional assistance is dogged by a plethora of overlapping programmes which lack clarity and purpose.

Water policy reform

During 2009 and 2010, COAG agreed an ambitious work programme to strengthen the policy/regulatory framework, including several key economic policy initiatives to improve the operation of water markets and trading. These initiatives should assist in managing uncertainty from climate change and better prepare market participants to make soundly based decisions. Failure to implement them fully will reduce significantly the benefits from reform processes to date.

All governments have been working together to develop a National Water Market System (National Water Market, 2011). If fully implemented, the system will efficiently manage water registry, transaction and market information functions. It will include a common registry system, a national portal and inter-operability. The initial phase will provide: a comprehensive overview of water trading nationally and the specific arrangements in place within jurisdictions/regions; up-to-date project information; and indirect access via links to the relevant state or territory website or system. The significance of this system in increasing the transparency around the economic aspects of water management, and therefore increasing understanding around the value of water, cannot be underestimated.

The Australian Government in conjunction with the states and other stakeholders has developed new water market, charge and trading rules under the *Water Act* to improve the operation of the water market.

- The market rules on the transformation and termination fees allow irrigators to transform their water right into a title that can be freely traded, without needing the approval of an irrigation infrastructure operator, and ensure termination fees do not create barriers to trade.
- Charge rules relate to fees levied by infrastructure operators for water storage and delivery services and state agencies for the provision of water planning and management services.
- The trading rules will address remaining artificial trade barriers. Here the Australian Competition and Consumer Commission (ACCC) have issued draft advice that the MDBA will consider in preparing the Basin Plan.

Getting these rules in place for the long term will do much to promote efficiently operating water markets, which will also assist in understanding and extracting value from the scarce resource in all circumstances.

Good compliance and enforcement is an important feature of an effective water market. Water theft is not a new phenomenon in Australia but a history of overuse and low water availability has brought the problem and consequences of 'unauthorized' extraction and use of water to the forefront. A stronger, more consistent compliance and enforcement regime recognizes that when people take water that is not theirs, it hurts other water users and the environment. Again, this assists in establishing a culture that water has value and needs to be treated as a scarce resource (COAG, 2009; Australian Institute of Criminology, 2010).

A final area that deserves mention, although it is very much work in progress at this point, relates to a national water research strategy and a national hydrological modelling strategy. Should this be put in place, it would help raise understanding, and allow new approaches to river management to be trialled, and would result in greater cohesion in management strategies throughout the basin as a whole. The former will help to use scarce science resources effectively to answer high priority questions around the quantities and quality of water needed to achieve a specified suite of environmental outcomes. The intent of the still nascent National Hydrological Modelling Strategy is to ensure that governments collaborate on the development and maintenance of a single, integrated hydrologic modelling capability. Whether the level of co-operation required can be achieved will provide an indicator of overall progress being made in managing basin resources as an integrated whole.

Urban water policy and climate change

A key impact of a climate change in Australia is on water availability in urban areas. Urban water shortages in Australia over the past decade demonstrated the challenges Australia must meet in the face of a drying climate, a growing urban population and a rising demand for water. Recent floods in Queensland, NSW and Victoria, and in many other countries, suggest that the changing intensity of storm events also needs much more consideration than given hitherto, particularly in relation to water management and land use planning.

Historically, state and local governments have been responsible for securing urban water supplies. State governments and their urban water authorities have strongly embraced desalination, in a way seen in few other countries, with large-scale desalination plants being operational or under construction in five major cities. While there are good reasons to debate the appropriate size of some of these plants and perhaps their timing, they provide important insurance policies as part of a risk management framework to reduce the risk of water supply failure. Their construction certainly provides an effective way of addressing severe declines in water availability and greater variability of inflows into storages. Whether it is an efficient and cost effective way is much more problematic.

The water supply crises seen in Australia's urban areas in the middle of the last decade can be attributed to 'backward looking' water planning, and reducing incentives to supply augmentation by inappropriately low pricing. In a short space of time, the crisis seen in most major capital cities resulted in significant demand and supply side policy responses, and a greater appreciation of the importance of pricing water properly, as well as 'forward looking' planning incorporating climate change projections. Governments around Australia have agreed principles covering recovery of capital expenditure, urban water tariffs, water planning and management, recycled water and stormwater reuse. These principles, if fully implemented, would support the proper functioning of water markets and pricing arrangements that reflect the real costs of water supply. Much progress has been made in putting them into place, particularly in larger urban areas, but there is still plenty of opportunity for improvement. There has been a plethora of reports and studies on metropolitan and regional urban centres over the past six or seven years, and considerable but largely unacknowledged action by many service providers. The Productivity Commission's 2011 report provides some pointers on unfinished business (Productivity Commission, 2011). One can only hope that its report is not shelved in the same way as the other dozen or so studies. Concerted action is still needed in some areas.

Water supply for remote and indigenous communities is a concern because in some areas responsibility resides with small, poorly resourced local government authorities with limited capacity to ensure safe and reliable water supplies. A key part of unfinished business is to improve the quality of governance around smaller urban delivery systems. This has little to do with a reaction to climate change but reflects a systemic weakness in governance. More action is required in this area.

Demand management policies have a role to play, particularly for developing a water conscious culture. Water use restrictions are a crude method of managing demand. In an Australian climate, water restrictions may be an appropriate management tool in severe infrequent drought (say, a one in 25-year 'drought'), but they have no place as everyday demand management instruments. For the most part, they simply reflect poor water management and planning. Raising public awareness through information programmes can be a very cost effective method of developing a culture of valuing water properly, particularly in urban areas. Different levels of government have introduced a suite of these programmes, with the national government focussing on water efficiency labelling (Australian Government, 2011).

IPCC conclusions on climate change and water

Published in 2008, the Intergovernmental Panel on Climate Change (IPCC) technical paper lists key water issues in a climate change context. The IPCC's broad conclusion that "observational records and climate projections provide abundant evidence that freshwater resources are vulnerable and have the potential to be strongly impacted by climate change, with wide ranging consequences" is hard to dispute (Intergovernmental Panel on Climate Change, 2008). Table 1 provides some brief comments on its main conclusions in the context of the Australian policy framework.

There will be a brief look at each.

Impact on operation of infrastructure

The need for upgrading or recalibrating the infrastructure base, and examining how the existing base should be used, has been an active part of water management in both rural

Table 1.   IPPC conclusions in an Australian context.

IPCC conclusions	Australian approach
"Climate change affects the function and operation of existing infrastructure" (p. 5)	Very little initial consideration was given to flood events (reflecting the drought 'crisis'). However, the BOM has been developing underlying information and to address *both* drought and flood impacts and, at a management level, governments have explored new approaches to river management
"Current management practices may not be robust enough to cope with impacts of climate change" (p. 5)	Recognized in NWI, and currently being reinforced
"Adaptation options designed to ensure water supply during average and drought conditions require integrated demand-side as a well as supply side strategies" (p. 6)	Being developed through MDB Basin Plan, which should become an exemplar; considerable progress in urban areas
"Water resource management clearly impacts on many other policy areas" (p. 6)	Well recognized; question of setting priorities. Policy practitioners need to be particularly mindful of adverse impacts
"Several gaps in knowledge exist in terms of observations and research needs related to climate change and water" (p. 6)	Large projects have been commenced, but much remains to be done

and urban Australia. There is a question about whether these activities should in part or as a whole be undertaken in a decentralized corporate way, as is currently the case, or whether there is a role for a more centralized approach. Both issues will need to be further addressed over the coming five to 10 years, but it is clear that the increased rainfall variability seen in recent years has made this a headline issue.

Robustness of management practices

It is clear that existing management practices will need to continue to improve, be it in the area of irrigation service provision, urban water management or environmental water management. Upgrading information and science, increased transparency in markets, and impact of hydrological 'events' such as increased intensity or variability of rainfall events will all suggest new ways of management. Closer interaction between river managers and environmental water managers will also offer scope to enhance outcomes. It is already very clear that some institutions, such as small urban water service providers, have outlived their usefulness. Others, such as environmental water managers, have much to learn and incorporate into management practices, and scientific studies will need to contribute to answer questions around sustainability. The dominant model of urban water service providers of a decade ago is also likely to change significantly, as users look to alternative approaches to enhance water security and calibre service provision to their needs. This includes a gradual shift from supply management to more intensive demand management. Technology and infrastructure will play a role in this transformation. Changing the culture of existing management is likely to be a major ongoing issue.

Adaptation requires both demand and supply strategies, and an integrated approach

Private sector bodies, as well as governments, have a role in improving integration. Governance frameworks are critical. Markets have a larger role to play where there is an institutional framework that will support them. Where that framework is not present, consideration should be given to ensuring both demand and supply side options are carefully examined. Innovation has a central role to play. Strategies should be focused on managing risks, and increasing system flexibility and efficiency.

Water resource management and other policy areas

It is a truism that everything impacts everything else. Carefully enumerating key interactions and priorities will continue to be important (Allen Consulting Group, 2005). Adaptation strategies involve identifying systems, sectors and regions vulnerable to change. Here, this paper has touched on key elements of the policy framework and the implications for the environment, agriculture and communities. The emphasis on the MDB reflects its level of vulnerability and importance. The paper has not discussed measures taken by the agricultural sector in relation to, for example, the need for new varieties or cultivars. These responses will emerge over time. There is a range of other key interactions not discussed above. For example, a major ongoing problem in Australia is the approach of local government to building in flood prone areas. Understanding the risks of flooding (for example, providing assessments, based on latest models, of the 100-year flood line of rivers) and sheeting home responsibility for land use planning decisions is an important place to start. Some of impacts of climate change will be to heighten these risks. Transparent information and adequate compliance to rules would be a useful start in some key areas.

Gaps in knowledge and research

Australia has made considerable progress in this space over the past four years. More concerted work is required, even as signs of reform fatigue again start to appear. A national knowledge and information strategy is an important next step for Australia, to ensure that scare resources in this space are used effectively, and that this area, while not politically as high profile as some, receives an appropriate share of available government resources. Dissemination of results and ensuring findings are considered thoroughly will be critical

Conclusions

Already Australia has accepted that it needs to husband water resources better in the MDB and more generally. There is also significant acceptance of the notion that climate change is affecting water availability; water management and planning, and developing the role of water markets, is addressing this front on, although considerable debate remains around some details. These impacts will be small in some areas and very large in others, and a similar situation can be found in many regions around the world. The implications of this are profound, but in most countries there is insufficient information to allow sensible policy to be put in place.

The starting point needs to be the baseline: what is a sustainable path before we take into account climate change? Then the impact of climate change can be incorporated. In practice, the two stages often merge; in some cases the threat of climate change can be used to good effect to secure reforms that might otherwise have been elusive.

Australian water policy reforms over the past decade, but particularly over the past four years, have made significant progress. That said, and this is recognized by governments, much remains to be done in both rural and urban Australia. It will be critical to continue to progress the reforms commenced in 2004, with the NWI, and accelerated in the period since 2006. Much remains to be done.

Acknowledgements

Until early 2011 the author was Deputy Secretary, Water, Australian Department of Sustainability, Environment, Water, Population and Communities. The author would like to thank former colleagues for comments on an earlier draft of this paper, and conference organizers for persistently encouraging policy makers to consider key issues in water management.

References

Allen Consulting Group. (2005). *Climate change – risk and vulnerability: Promoting an efficient adaptation response in Australia*. Report to the Australian Greenhouse Office. March 2005.

Australian Government. (2011). *Water Efficiency Labelling and Standards (WELS) scheme*. Retrieved from http://www.waterrating.gov.au.

Australian Institute of Criminology. (2010). *Water theft: Scope and definitions*. Retrieved May 9, 2012, from http://www.aic.gov.au/publications/current%20series/rpp/100-120/rpp109/11.aspx.

BDA Group. (2010). *Review of social and economic studies in the Murray Darling Basin*. Report to the Murray Darling Basin Authority. Retrieved from http://www.mdba.gov.au/draft-basin-plan/s ocioeconomic-analysis/social-and-economic-analysis-key-reports.

Bureau of Meteorology. (2011a). *Improving water information*. Retrieved from http://www.bom. gov.au/water/.

Bureau of Meteorology. (2011b). *National water account 2010*. http://www.bom.gov.au/water/nwa/ 2010.

Burke, T. (2010). Ministerial statement: *Murray Darling Basin reform – interpretation of the Water Act 2007*. Speech transcript, 25 October 2010.

Commonwealth of Australia. (2008). *Water Amendment Bill 2008*. Explanatory memorandum, p. 2.

Commonwealth of Australia. (2009). Water Act 2007 reprint 1. Canberra. Retrieved from http://www.environment.gov.au/minister/burke/2010/sp20101025.html.

COAG Working Group on Water Resource Policy. (1994). *Report of the Working Group on Water Resource Policy to the Council of Australian Government*. Mimeo, 1994.

COAG. (1994). *Council of Australian Governments' communiqué 25 February 1994. Attachment A – Water resource policy*. Retrieved from http://archive.coag.gov.au/coag_meeting_outcomes/1994-02-25/index.cfm#water.

COAG. (2004). *Intergovernmental Agreement on the National Water Initiative*. Retrieved from http://archive.coag.gov.au/coag_meeting_outcomes/2004-06-25/index.cfm#nwi.

COAG. (2006). *COAG meeting outcomes. Council of Australian Governments' meeting, 14 July 2006*. National Water Reform. Retrieved from http://archive.coag.gov.au/coag_meeting_outcomes/2006-07-14/index.cfm.

COAG. (2009). *Council of Australian Governments' meeting, 7 December 2009. 7. WATER REFORM*. Retrieved from http://www.coag.gov.au/node/90#7.%20Water%20Reform.

CSIRO. (2008). *Water availability in the Murray Darling Basin*. Retrieved from http://www.clw.csiro.au/publications/waterforahealthycountry/mdbsy/pdf/WaterAvailabilityInTheMDB-FinalReport.pdf.

CSIRO. (2011). *Sustainable yields projects*. Retrieved from http://www.csiro.au/partnerships/SYP.html.

Department of Sustainability, Environment, Water, Population and Communities. (2011a). *Restoring the balance in the Murray-Darling Basin*. Retrieved from http://www.environment.gov.au/water/policy-programs/entitlement-purchasing/progress.html.

Department of Sustainability, Environment, Water, Population and Communities. (2011b). Irrigation modernisation planning ssistance. Retrieved from http://www.environment.gov.au/water/publications/action/impa-factsheet.html.

Government of Australia. (2007). *A national plan for water security*. Canberra.

Howard, J. (2006a). *Transcript of the Prime Minister the Hon John Howard MP joint press conference*. 7 November 2006. Retrieved from http://pandora.nla.gov.au/pan/10052/20061221-0000/www.pm.gov.au/news/interviews/Interview2235.html.

Howard, J. (2006b). *New Office of Water Resources*. Press release 26 September 2006. Retrieved from http://pandora.nla.gov.au/pan/10052/20061221-0000/www.pm.gov.au/news/media_releases/media_Release2153.html.

Howard, J. (2007). *Address to the National Press Club*. Great Hall, Parliament House, 25 January 2007. Retrieved from http://pandora.nla.gov.au/pan/10052/20070321-0000/www.pm.gov.au/media/Speech/2007/speech2341.html.

Intergovernmental Panel on Climate Change. (2008). *Technical paper on climate change and water*. June 2008, p.4. Retrieved from http://www.ipcc.ch/pdf/technical-papers/climate-change-water-en.pdf.

MDBA. (2011). *The proposed Basin Plan for consultation*. Retrieved from http://www.mdba.gov.au/draft-basin-plan/draft-basin-plan-for-consultation/.

MDBA. (2012). *View submissions*. Retrieved from http://www.mdba.gov.au/have-your-say/view-submission.

National Water Market. (2011). *National Water Market*. Retrieved May 17, 2012 from http://www.nationalwatermarket.gov.au.

Productivity Commission. (2011). *Australia's urban water sector*. Report No. 55, Final Inquiry Report, Canberra, volume 1 and 2. Retrieved from http://www.pc.gov.au/__data/assets/pdf_file/0017/113192/urban-water-volume1.pdf; http://www.pc.gov.au/__data/assets/pdf_file/0018/113193/urban-water-volume2.pdf.

South Eastern Australian Climate Initiative. (2010). *The South Eastern Australian climate initiative synthesis findings from Phase 1*. Retrieved from http://www.seaci.org/publications/summary.html.

Turnbull, M. (2010). *The Water Act and the Basin Plan*. Retrieved May 17, 2012 from http://www.malcolmturnbull.com.au/blogs/the-water-act-and-the-basin-plan/.

water-technology.net. (2011). Perth Seawater Desalination Plant, Kwinana, Australia. Retrieved May 17, 2012 from http://www.water-technology.net/projects/perth/.

Wong, P. (2008). *Water for the future*. Speech to the 4th Annual Australian Water Summit, Sydney Convention and Exhibition Centre, 29–30 April 2008. Retrieved from http://www.climatechange.gov.au/~/media/Files/minister/previous minister/wong/2008/major-speeches/April/sp20080429.pdf.

Characterizing the water extremes of the new century in the US South-west: a comprehensive assessment from state-of-the-art climate model projections

Aleix Serrat-Capdevila[a], Juan B.Valdes[a], Francina Dominguez[b] and Seshadri Rajagopal[c]

[a]*International Center for Integrated Water Resources Management (UNESCO) and Department of Hydrology and Water Resources, University of Arizona, Tucson, Arizona, USA;* [b]*Department of Atmospheric Sciences, University of Arizona, USA;* [c]*Desert Research Institute, Reno, Nevada, USA*

The impact of climate change scenarios in the hydrology of the Verde River basin (Arizona) is analyzed using an ensemble of downscaled climate model results, SPI analysis, and two hydrologic models of different complexity. To assess model uncertainty, 47 ensemble members combining simulations from 16 global climate models and 3 emission scenarios were used to provide an uncertainty envelope in the hydrologic variables. The analysis shows that simple lumped models and more complex distributed runoff models can yield similar results. Results show that under all scenarios, the distribution functions of hydrologic states will shift towards lower values and droughts will progressively become more frequent, longer and more intense.

Introduction and background

The qualitative cause-and-effect relationships between human activities since the industrial revolution (greenhouse gas emissions and land use changes) and warming trends in climate are well established (Intergovernmental Panel on Climate Change, 2001). The effects of anthropogenic influences on climate are superimposed on its natural variability and long-term cycles. While stochastic hydrology provides powerful tools to characterize climatic uncertainty, global climate models (GCMs) have emerged in the last decades as the only physically based tool to project future climate. GCMs allow simulations with and without greenhouse gas emissions to assess the impact of human activities on climate (Intergovernmental Panel on Climate Change, 2007).

These models are generally in agreement regarding global general trends, but their complexity, their structure, the need to discretize the continuous medium, the uncertainty in future socio-economic projections and greenhouse emissions, and the inherent structural uncertainty of climate itself cause GCM results to spread over a large range and in some cases to disagree. Uncertainty is even larger at the regional scale, where small-scale physical processes are parameterized in the models and less well captured than large-scale processes. For these reasons, the quantification of climate change impacts over a specific region and the rates at which they will take place contains significant amounts of uncertainty. The use of multi-model projections is superior to the use of a single 'best' projection, and is an appropriate way of handling model uncertainty through hydrologic simulations, providing highest-likelihood estimates as well as a measure of their uncertainty (Hagedorn, Doblas-Reyes, & Palmer, 2005; Serrat-Capdevila et al., 2007).

The current paper presents and compares three methodologies for characterizing droughts and wet spells during the current century using an all-encompassing multi-scenario array of climate model predictions and combining traditional drought analysis with two hydrologic modelling approaches to quantify the uncertainty of climate change impacts for different variables of the hydrologic cycle. The work presented in this paper is based on simulations from 16 different climate models for 3 different IPCC greenhouse gas emissions scenarios. The goals of this work are: (1) to extract and present information from ensemble climate projections and hydrologic simulations in different ways; (2) to quantify climate impacts and their uncertainty through different variables of the hydrologic cycle; (3) to assess changes in frequency of dry periods (droughts) and wet periods; (4) to assess changes in the probability distribution functions of hydrologic states; and (5) to compare lumped and distributed hydrologic model simulations driven by climate change predictions. The combination presented here of simple but wide-ranging techniques for extracting information from climate models is a unique and integrative approach to the assessment of climate change impacts in hydrology and their associated uncertainty.

Pros and cons of climate model predictions

Traditional stochastic methods can help us quantify future climate uncertainty through the use of statistics, but are unable to predict future climate because they are not concerned with physical processes. Climate model simulations are currently the only available tool to project future climate, though they too have limitations and assumptions. A few studies have analyzed the influence of solar activity on the earth's climate (Camp & Tung, 2007) as well as the dynamics of the complex natural factors affecting climate (Stott, Timmermann, & Thunell, 2007; Tsonis, Swanson, & Kravtsov, 2007; Zhen-Shan & Xian, 2007), none of which are usually included in GCM simulations. Koutsoyiannis, Montanari, Lins, and Cohn (2009) presented a critique of Kundzewicz et al. (2008), describing how GCM projections and consequent water resources impact assessments underestimate uncertainty. It is argued that, since uncertainty is a structural component of climate and hydrologic systems, it cannot be addressed through increased model complexity. Anagnostopoulos, Koutsoyian-nis, Christofides, Efstratiadis, and Mamassis (2010) found that large uncertainties and poor skill were shown by GCM predictions without bias correction, even when averaged over time and large regional scales. Uncertainty becomes even larger when trying to project changes in the nature of individual extreme events. Stating that the term 'stationarity' should be used following its strict significance to avoid misleading announcements (as in "stationarity is dead" – Milly et al. [2010]), Koutsoyiannis (2011) showed that an ensemble of climate model projections is fully contained within the uncertainty envelope of traditional stochastic methods using historical data, including the Hurst phenomenon. First used as a mathematical tool for the study of turbulence by Kolmogorov (1940), the Hurst phenomenon (Hurst, 1951) describes the large and long excursions of natural events above and below their mean, as opposed to random processes, which do not exhibit such behaviour. The uncertainty range in time-averaged natural Hurst-Kolmogorov processes is much greater than that shown in GCM projections and classical statistics. While statistics enables the broadest envelope of future uncertainty, GCMs are today the only physically based tools to predict the average trends of the next decades, whatever they may be worth.

They have been and continue to be an essential tool in understanding climate dynamics and anthropogenic influences. Barnett et al. (2008) used GCMs and detection and attribution techniques to argue that some hydrologic changes observed in the US South-west are exclusively attributable to human-induced climate change effects. Notwithstanding the evidence that human activities are influencing climate, a better integration of understanding regarding the combined effects of human and non-human drivers of climate over longer time-scales will allow improved projections and forecasts in the future.

Climate change impacts on hydrology and the US South-west

Numerous studies have recently attempted to quantify climate change impacts in hydrology (Christensen, Wood, Voisin, Lettenmeier, & Palmer, 2004; Hamlet & Lettenmaier, 1999; Jiang, Chen, Xu, Chen, & Singh, 2007; Loaiciga, Maidment, & Valdes, 2000; Nijssen, O'Donnell, Hamlet, & Lettenmaier, 2001; Scibek & Allen, 2006; and numerous others). Hay, Markstrom, and Ward-Garrison (2011) presented a comprehensive study of impacts on water resources across basins in the United States, albeit none in Arizona where the present study is focused.

The south-west US is expected to get dryer and hotter due to climate change: Seager et al. (2007) predict an overall decrease of P–E (precipitation minus evaporation), and thus less water available for environmental and societal needs. Projections in the Colorado River basin indicate reductions in streamflows due to a future increase in temperature and a slight decrease in mean precipitation (Gao, Vano, Zhe, & Lettenmaier, 2011; Milly, Dunne, & Vecchia, 2005). Serrat-Capdevila et al. (2007) used an ensemble of climate model predictions to simulate climate change impacts on the aquifer and riparian system of the San Pedro Basin in Arizona, obtaining decreasing trends and an envelope of uncertainty for variables of interest (recharge, riparian evapotranspiration and streamflow gains). Serrat-Capdevila, Scott, Shuttleworth, and Valdés (2011) explored the impacts of a warmer climate on the evapotranspiration of a riparian ecosystem and changes to its growing season, quantifying increases of riparian groundwater use in a south-western basin. Wi et al. (submitted) found significant decreases of snowfall and percentage of precipitation that falls as snow in the Colorado River basin using dynamical downscaling. Barnett et al. (2008) reported the detection of hydrological changes in the western US exclusively attributable to human-induced climate change effects. Namely, they observed a decrease in ratios of snow water equivalent versus liquid precipitation, an increase in the average of daily minimum temperatures from January through March, and an earlier date by which half of the annual flow has occurred. Population growth in the West has been and continues to be the greatest stressor on water resources management, for which long-term planning decisions are made. Water resources in most western US basins are currently over-allocated, many aquifers are being mined and management happens to be unsustainable in many areas. Climate change impacts in the region could exacerbate scarcity problems. McCabe and Wolock (2007) combined hydrologic projections in the Colorado Basin with long tree-ring reconstructions of historical streamflow in the basin and concluded that future water shortages will be more severe than those observed in the paleoclimatic records, seriously undermining the water allocations of the Colorado River Compact. Barnett and Pierce (2008) estimate that under current operating policies (i.e. water use), water storage in Lake Mead and Lake Powell has a 10% chance of disappearing by 2013, and a 50% chance by 2021, under the impacts of climate change.

The Verde River basin in Arizona (Figure 1) is used here as case study because of its relevance to potential impacts on a region that is already water stressed. The Verde River

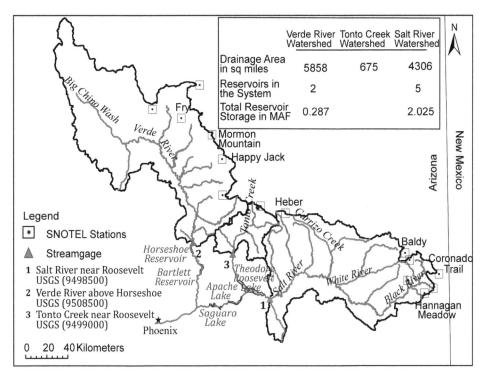

Figure 1. The Verde River, Tonto Creek and Salt River watersheds in Arizona (from Rajagopal, 2011).

is located in Central Arizona, draining an area of 17,133 km² in the elevation gradient leading to the Mogollon Plateau. With an approximate length of 170 miles, an annual mean streamflow of 16.6 m³/s (USGS, 2012), and certain reaches designated as Wild and Scenic River (see http://www.rivers.gov), the Verde crosses three dams and becomes a tributary to the Salt River before merging with the Gila River in the vicinity of Phoenix, the capital and largest city of Arizona. Precipitation is bimodal, with frontal systems in winter, a moderate influence of snow in the upper basin, and monsoon-type storms in the late summer months. The Salt River Project is the company that manages the reservoirs in the Salt-Verde watershed, distributing electricity and water to agricultural users in the Lower Basin and municipalities in the greater Phoenix area. Pumping for agriculture and municipalities in the Upper Verde Basin, as well as irrigation diversions in the Middle Basin, are conflicting with hydropower production and population demands from the lower basin and the growing Phoenix area.

Methods

Data

Precipitation and temperature data from downscaled climate model simulation results was obtained from the publicly available Bias Corrected and Downscaled WCRP CMIP3 Climate Projections archive at http://gdo-dcp.ucllnl.org/downscaled_cmip3_projections/ (Maurer, Brekke, Pruitt, & Duffy, 2007). Data is available at 1/8-degree resolution from 1950 to 2100. Monthly data from 16 climate models driven by conditions from 3 IPCC emission scenarios (A1B, A2 and B1) were used in this work. For scenario B1, data from

15 climate models (not 16) were used because one of the models lacked a simulation for that specific scenario.

Observed historical records of streamflow for the Verde River above Horseshoe Dam in Arizona (USGS station 09508500) for 1951 to 2010 were obtained from the USGS's publicly available Surface-Water Data for the Nation (http://waterdata.usgs.gov/usa/nwis/sw). Available at a daily time scale, streamflow data has been aggregated monthly.

SPI analysis

Precipitation series from each of the downscaled climate model simulations have been used to calculate series of the Standardized Precipitation Index (SPI) with different aggregation periods from 1950 to 2100 for each model run and IPCC scenario. The SPI was developed by McKee, Doesken, and Kleist (1993) to characterize drought solely on the basis of precipitation anomalies. Precipitation is characterized by a gamma distribution, which is skewed to the right with a lower bound of zero. The cumulative probability of this gamma distribution (slightly transformed to account for zeroes) is then transformed to a standard normal random variable (with mean zero and variance one), which is the value of the SPI. The SPI was calculated for three different levels of aggregation – 3, 12 and 24 months – reflecting different consecutive periods of anomalous precipitation. Using the 47-member ensemble of downscaled climate model precipitation projections, the number of droughts and wet periods in the resulting SPI series of each ensemble member was calculated for the three consecutive 50-year periods from 1950 to 2100. Anomalous SPI values less than −2 were defined as 'extremely dry' conditions and values greater than 2 as 'extremely wet' conditions (Guttman, 1999). The average duration (average number of consecutive periods below or above the threshold) and intensity (average SPI value during dry or wet events) of the dry or wet events for each ensemble member and 50-year period were also calculated. In brief, for each 50-year period the number of dry and wet events were obtained and their average intensity and duration.

Hydrologic simulations

Two hydrologic models were used in this study: a simple lumped model and a more complex distributed model. Simple lumped models provide a baseline against which more complex models can be compared. The comparison of hydrologic models of different natures can show what is gained with more complex and computationally demanding models and to what extent they are required for different decision-making purposes, especially when forcing data may contain large sources of error (as in GCM projections). In the context of the current work, the uncertainty envelope from the ensembles of climate projections will also be compared. The *abcd* model was used as a simple four-parameter lumped model (Martinez & Gupta, 2010, 2011; Thomas, 1981). The four parameters control (a) the runoff occurrence before soil saturation, (b) the sum of evapotransporation (ET) and soil moisture storage, (c) the distribution between groundwater recharge and direct runoff, and (d) the groundwater residence time. The *abcd* model was calibrated with historical rain-gauge data for the basin using the shuffled complex evolution (SCE-UA) algorithm (Duan, Gupta, & Sorooshian, 1992; Sorooshian, Duan, & Gupta, 1993). A total of 47 simulations were performed, each one using the downscaled precipitation and temperature projections from a specific climate model and scenario.

As a more complex distributed model, the variable infiltration capacity (VIC) model was used. The VIC model represents surface and subsurface hydrologic processes on spatially distributed grid cells. The model has the ability to represent sub-grid-scale variability in vegetation coverage, topography, precipitation and soil moisture storage capacity. The subsurface is represented by three soil layers. Evapotranspiration can occur from soil moisture stored in any of the three layers, while slow response runoff or baseflow is only generated from the third layer. To represent the sub-grid spatial variability in soil moisture storage, the model assumes that infiltration capacity is a non-linear function of the soil moisture storage within the grid cell (Liang, Lettenmaier, Wood, & Burges, 1994; Liang, Wood, & Lettenmaier, 1996). The VIC model can operate in either an energy-balance or a water-balance mode; the latter was used in the current work. Simulations were performed at a resolution of 1/8 degree and daily time step and then aggregated at a monthly time step. The VIC model was calibrated using the SCE-UA optimization algorithm with historical rain gauge observed meteorological gridded data (Maurer, Wood, Adam, Lennenmaier, & Nijssen, B., 2002) to match streamflow observations at the USGS stream gauge above Horseshoe Dam. In view of the computational demands, a total of 11 simulations were performed using precipitation and temperature forcings from the following climate models: MPI, HAD, CCSM3 (each under A1B, A2 and B1 scenario conditions), MIRO, and PCM (under A2 scenario conditions). The VIC model was used because it accounts for spatial variability of physical processes that generate runoff, such as soil moisture and snow. In addition, the VIC model has been used in multiple studies of climate impacts on watersheds.

In addition to the hydrologic models used, estimates of Hargreaves reference crop evapotranspiration (Hargreaves, 1994) were used as analogous for potential ET in the basin, to allow comparison with actual ET. Hargreaves ET was calculated using minimum and maximum daily temperature projections from the global climate models and the equivalent solar radiation at the surface in water evaporation for the latitude of the basin, as described by Hargreaves (1994).

Results

SPI analysis

The ensembles of the calculated SPI series from all 47 climate model projections and the multi-model means of each IPCC scenario are shown in Figure 2, as well as the SPI mean of all ensemble members (all models, all scenarios) for three levels of aggregation (3, 12 and 24 months). It can be seen that all SPI means show decreasing trends. A seasonal Mann-Kendall test was performed on the multi-model mean SPI for the three levels of aggregation, and decreasing trends were detected in all three cases at a 95% confidence level. The SPI ensemble spread becomes wider towards the future. It can be observed that the period from 2000 to 2100 has a wider SPI spread than the previous 50 years. SPI projections seem to indicate that wet months will become wetter and dry months will become dryer, with a bias towards negative values (i.e. the increase in 'dryness' is greater than the increase in 'wetness').

The numbers of dry and wet events in each 50-year period are shown in Figures 3 and 4 respectively, as projected by each climate model ensemble, with their average intensity and duration. The number of events contained in the ensemble member is plotted against their average intensity and duration for each 50-year period and SPI aggregation period of 3, 12 and 24 months. The projected number of drought events, as simulated by the climate model ensembles, is likely to increase through the three 50-year periods (Figure 3). The intensity of the events is also expected to increase as SPI values become more negative. An increase in the duration (in months) of droughts can be observed for the 3-month

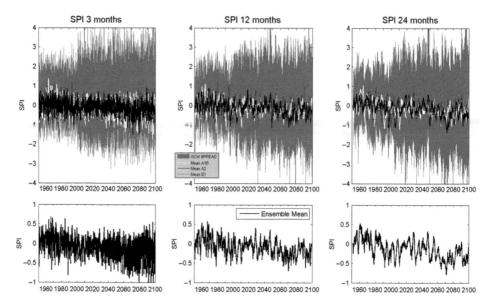

Figure 2. First row: Ensembles of SPI series calculated from the 47 climate model rainfall projections, shown for three levels of aggregation (3, 12 and 24 months) in grey, and the SPI means for each IPCC Scenario. Second row: Mean of ensemble members from all models and all scenarios for the same three levels of aggregation.

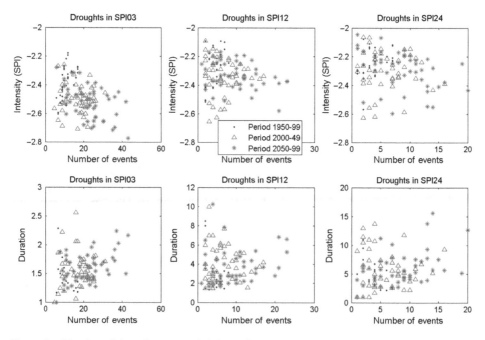

Figure 3. Number of droughts versus their intensity (1st row) and versus duration (in months, 2nd row) for three aggregation periods, as predicted by the climate model ensembles. The dots correspond to the period 1950–1999, the triangles to 2000–2049 and the crosses to 2050–2099.

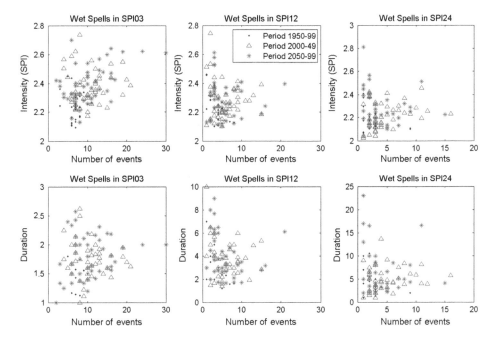

Figure 4. Number of wet periods versus their intensity (1st row) and versus duration (2nd row) for three aggregation periods, as predicted by the climate model ensembles.

aggregation of the SPI analysis, but the change appears less significant before and after 2050, for aggregations of 12 and 24 months. In Figure 4 it can be seen that the number of wet periods may also increase, but an increase in the value of their SPI and the duration of the events through the current century (first and second half) is less clear in most SPI aggregation periods.

Hydrologic simulations

The results of hydrologic simulations using the lumped *abcd* model provide projections of the following state variables: actual model evapotranspiration; soil moisture; groundwater recharge; groundwater outflow or baseflow; and streamflow. The use of ensembles of precipitation and temperature in hydrologic simulations yields an ensemble series of the state hydrology variables simulated, with the mean showing the overall trend. All variables are presented in terms of mm per month or mm per year, depending on the plots. The Hargreaves ET ensembles and their mean are also plotted in the plots of actual ET. Simulations were performed for three IPCC scenarios; however, for reasons of space, and because the results are not significantly different, only results from scenario A2 will be shown in the figures that follow.

Annual precipitation projections are not expected to change significantly, even if a slight decreasing trend in the multi-model average can be observed (Figure 5). While potential evapotranspiration (PET) is expected to increase through the century because of higher temperatures, actual evapotranspiration is in fact limited by water availability, and the *abcd* model does not show any significant changes. Actual ET is plotted here with potential ET, but even it is when plotted by itself (not shown), closer analysis reveals a hint of a decrease through the century, logically related to the decrease in rainfall. The small decrease in precipitation does seem to significantly affect the other hydrologic variables.

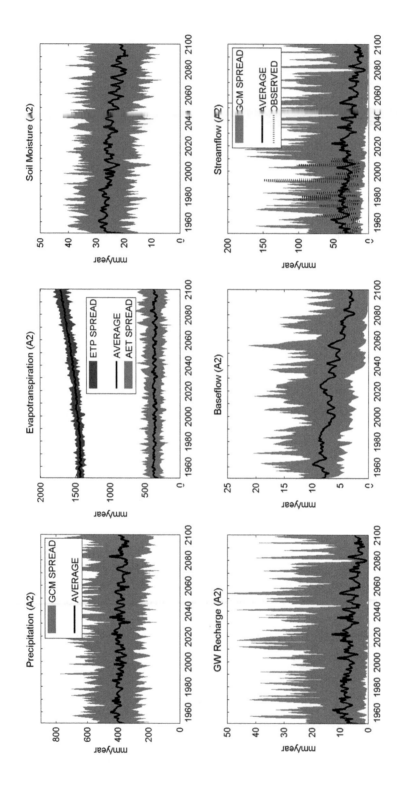

Figure 5. Ensemble and average projections of precipitation, actual and potential evapotranspiration, soil moisture, recharge, baseflow and streamflow in the Verde Basin for scenario A2.

Soil moisture, groundwater recharge, baseflow and streamflow clearly show decreasing trends. It is important to note the difference in the orders of magnitude of the latter variables with respect to those of precipitation and ET. A change of a few mm/y in precipitation may easily go unnoticed or be deemed of little significance. However, an increase in temperature and PET, and the fact that ET is sometimes more than 90% of the water budget in Arizona, implies that small changes in precipitation may translate directly to changes in soil moisture, recharge and baseflow. A decrease can also be seen in the streamflow results. Historical annual streamflow has also been plotted in red for 1950–2010, and it can be observed that all of the values in the historical record are effectively contained within the multi-model spread representing uncertainty. The large peaks of the observations are of the same order as the large peaks simulated using climate model forcings. This shows that the current approach is valid for characterizing uncertainty at the annual level in the Verde Basin for the period of record.

The evolution of mean monthly values for the same variables as simulated by the climate models and the *abcd* hydrologic model simulations are shown in Figure 6 for the periods 1950–1999, 2000–2049 and 2050–2099, for scenario A2. Precipitation is projected to decrease in all months, except during the monsoon season (July and August), when it is expected to slightly increase. Mimicking water availability and temperature increase, ET is likely to increase during winter and the monsoons, and decrease during the spring months leading to the monsoon. Soil moisture values are projected to decrease in all months of the year, as are recharge, baseflow and streamflow. The most dramatic decreases in groundwater recharge are projected to occur from October to April, as a result of the decrease in precipitation and increase in ET. Being mostly energy limited during winter (and not so much water limited), ET increases as the result of the increase in temperatures during the cold season. It is interesting to see that mean soil moisture, recharge and baseflow also decrease during the summer season, despite an increase in precipitation – these variables are directly compensated by an increase in summer ET, which is water limited (and not energy limited). The streamflow results show that the simple lumped *abcd* model does an acceptable job of capturing the observed average inter-annual seasonality of streamflow and that it is a valuable tool for the analysis of multiple climate model simulations under different scenarios.

A different way to assess changes in the variables of the hydrologic cycle is to look at the distribution of their probability density functions. Given that significant changes were not observed between results from the three IPCC scenarios, all 47 ensemble members from all model runs at monthly time scale were used to derive empirical cumulative distribution functions. The ensemble series for each hydrologic variable was divided into five consecutive periods of 30 years from 1950 to 2100. The changes in the cumulative distributions can be observed in Figure 7. What is often termed "intensification of the hydrologic cycle" can be observed in the precipitation plot, where values in the upper quartile are projected to increase, while values in the lower three quartiles are projected to decrease. This behaviour is closely followed by evapotranspiration: months with high ET rates will evapotranspirate more in the future, and months with medium-to-low ET rates will evapotranspirate less. Given this, it is not surprising that soil moisture will uniformly decrease, as will recharge, baseflow and streamflow, except for extreme wet months above the 99% percentile, which may see an increase. Groundwater recharge, baseflow and streamflow are likely to be strongly impacted, showing the most dramatic decreases. Recharge currently has its 90th percentile at 2 mm per month, and in the last decade of the century the 90th percentile is expected to be the threshold between zero (90%) and non-zero (10%) values. Baseflow, whose 90th percentile is at about 1 mm per month, is likely

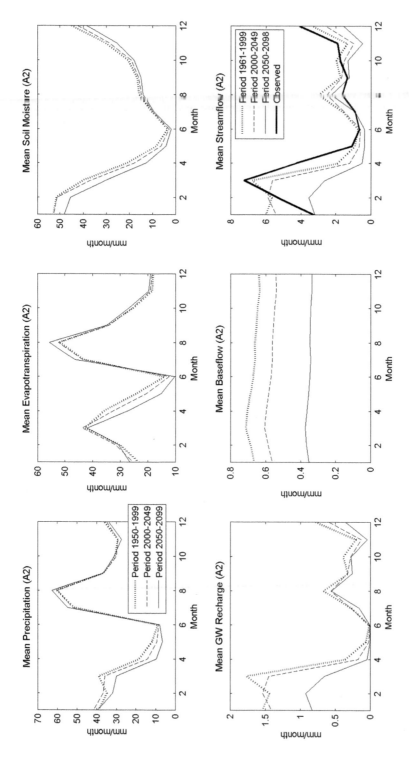

Figure 6. Evolution of the monthly means of the hydrologic variables through each 50-year period, as projected by the abcd model ensemble runs driven by climate model forcings.

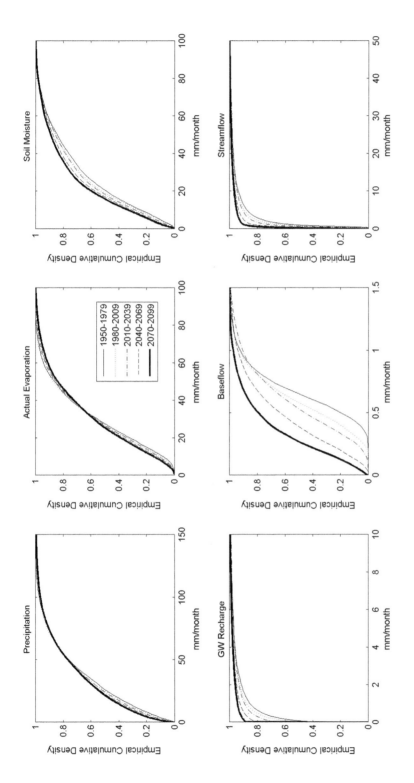

Figure 7.   Evolution of the empirical cumulative density functions of monthly values of hydrologic variables through five 30-year periods from 1950 to 2100, as predicted by climate models and the abcd model.

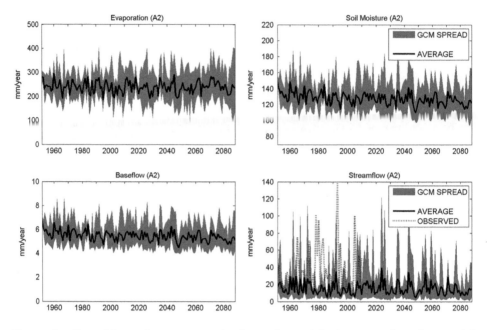

Figure 8. Ensemble and average projections of precipitation, actual and potential evapotranspiration, soil moisture, recharge, baseflow and streamflow in the Verde Basin for scenario A2.

to see most of its values halved by the end of the century. Streamflow values in the upper two quantiles will also decrease significantly by the end of the century, with the 90th percentile value going from 10 mm per month to around 1 mm per month. It can be observed that increases in actual ET (above the 60th percentile) largely offset the slight increases in monthly precipitation (above the 80th percentile).This is because increases in monthly precipitation are projected to take place in the summer during the hot monsoon season, when actual ET is water limited and not energy limited (Figure 6).

The results of the VIC model simulations are shown in Figure 8 for the variables of evapotranspiration, soil moisture, baseflow and streamflow. Five climate models were used; thus the uncertainty spread is slightly greater than in the other VIC model runs for scenarios A1B and B1 (not shown), where results from only three climate models were used. Compared to the results from the *abcd* model, where 16 climate model forcings were used for scenario A2, the multi-model spread of the VIC model results is much smaller than that of the *abcd* model results, as expected. The historical streamflow values spanning 1950–2010 are not contained within the multi-model envelope from climate model projections, because only 5 models were used instead of 16. This illustrates the utility of multi-model ensembles for characterizing the future uncertainty.

Because the VIC model considers both snow precipitation and snow cover, there are some significant differences in ET and soil moisture results compared to the *abcd* model. Because snow coverage reduces ET during the winter and increases partitioning of precipitation towards soil moisture, recharge and baseflow, the consideration of snow can explain the significant difference in the annual values of evapotranspiration (about 100 mm lower for the VIC model). In the same way, it also explains the significantly higher values of soil moisture, compared to those simulated by the *abcd* model. With its accounting for snow, and its more detailed three-layer description of the soil, the VIC model is likely to better represent soil moisture in the upper parts of the basin where snow is present during the winter. This rain/snow structural difference in the models accounts for differences in the timing of ET peaks, soil moisture content and baseflow in the spring, as can be clearly seen in Figure 9.

The evolution of monthly streamflow values is shown in Figure 10 for both models and all IPCC scenarios. The *abcd* model realistically captures the spring streamflow peak because it coincides with the precipitation peak and the influence of snow in the Verde Basin is not uniformly dominant. However, streamflows during the months of December, January and February are significantly higher in the *abcd* model compared to the VIC model, where snow precipitation is significant and does not create streamflow.

The results obtained in the current study show that a complex model with data-intensive inputs is not necessarily the best tool for all purposes, particularly when considering processes of long duration, such as drought. A simple lumped 4-parameter model has easily allowed for 47 ensemble simulations, providing a good uncertainty envelope that is more comprehensive than the one obtained by a few VIC runs. In the same way, the orders of magnitude of the final results are the same, with similar values even in most of the state variables. In the current study the differences in values in the model results can easily be explained by differences in the conceptual representation of the hydrologic cycle and its processes. The *abcd* model without representation of snow was chosen as the most elementary baseline to which a complex model could be compared.

Management implications: what impacts on what resources?

What planning and management decisions are studies like the current one trying to inform, beyond a research exercise? What is the take-home message for decision makers? Putting aside the debate on the accuracy (or appropriateness) of climate change impact studies using GCMs, there are two potential sides to the applicability of studies like the present one: (1) planning and design aspects that relate to coping with extreme events on the upper end of the spectrum (flood return periods); and (2) management aspects that relate to average and long-term annual water availability.

Simulations using GCM results have been deemed inadequate for planning and design purposes, and not suitable for forecasts and reservoir operations (Kundzewicz & Stakhiv, 2010; Stakhiv, 2010). They contain a lot of uncertainty at the monthly and annual levels, even when aggregated over spatial scales (Anagnostopoulos et al., 2010). However, the debate on the accuracy of GCMs misleadingly confuses their ability to project future changes in climate with their accuracy in predicting the weather, a task for which they are not intended. Thus, the question is whether to try to use GCM results to derive new flood frequencies at the hourly scale for specific basins. While climate change projections do best in predicting trends of averages over the long term, it is the changes in the nature of individual events (timing, duration and frequency) that control some of the important impacts of the relationship with water resources. Computationally expensive tools, such as dynamical downscaling at the resolution of a few kilometres (*regional* climate models, RCM), are being developed to provide information for water infrastructure design purposes (see e.g. Dominguez, Rivera, Lettenmaier, & Castro, 2012). However, no tools currently exist to reliably quantify future extreme events with enough certainty to support engineering design and financial investments. Many scientists are of the opinion that with respect to the impacts of climate change on hydrology it will be a few decades before trends can be detected and distinguished from the natural climatic variability (Kundzewicz & Stakhiv, 2010; Wilby, 2010). Lins and Cohn (2003) investigated the sensitivity of

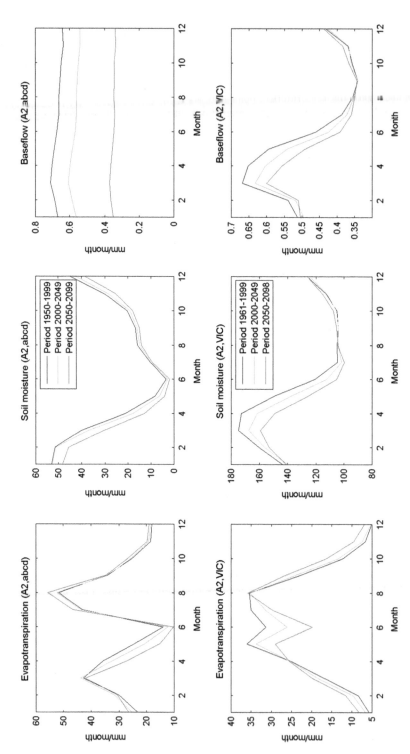

Figure 9.   Comparison of the projected monthly means of evapotranspiration, soil moisture and baseflow as simulated by the abcd model (upper row) and by the VIC model (lower row), for IPCC scenario A2.

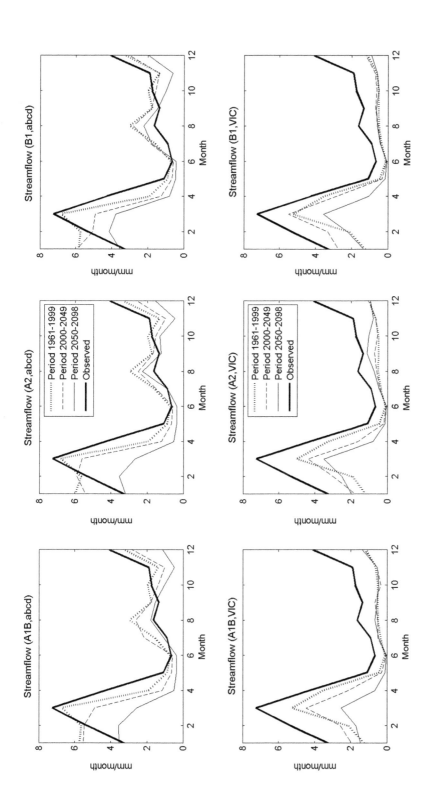

Figure 10. Comparison of the projected monthly means of streamflow as simulated by the abcd model (upper row) and by the VIC model (lower row), for IPCC scenarios A1B, A2 and B1.

various return-period floods to annual precipitation. They found that higher return periods are less sensitive to total annual precipitation, and that average streamflows are more sensitive to annual precipitation than flood flows. They concluded that future changes will mostly affect the mean state of hydrologic regimes and not so much the extremes. However, the results of their study arise from the fact that average precipitation and the intensity of extreme events are governed by different forcings: large-scale circulation controls averages and thermodynamic and dynamic forcing at the local scale control the nature of extreme events (Dominguez et al., 2012). Indeed, several studies have found that in the US South-west, while average precipitation will decrease, precipitation extremes will increase (Dominguez et al., 2012; Emori & Brown, 2005; Meehl, Tebaldi, Teng, & Peterson, 2007). While GCM and RCM projections of change in the frequency and magnitude of extreme events provide good insights into the future, the uncertainty may be too large to inform design investments. In addition, Villarini et al. (2009) showed that land use cover changes can significantly influence the hydrologic response of a basin. During the urbanization of their study basin, the 1000-year flood became the 10-year flood in a period of 50 years. This illustrates that non-climatic anthropogenic changes can often represent a more important stressor to water management in the short term when it comes to flood design parameters.

On the other hand, supported by findings from Lins and Cohn (2003), the benefit of climate impact studies to management and planning aspects related to changes in average and long-term water availability seems very possible and straightforward. While traditional stochastic statistics and the Hurst phenomenon are better at using historical records to characterize future uncertainty, climate models are the only physically based tools that project the climate in the next few decades. Thus, if changes in annual precipitation affect the mean states of hydrologic variables, efforts should be directed at quantifying these average changes (using GCMs) and the envelope of uncertainty that contains them (using whichever combination of methods) so that water managers and decision makers in the South-west can adapt to less water availability. This study aims precisely at that goal because, given the current state of the art, the most productive efforts will focus on adapting to "potential decreases in mean discharge" and water availability (Koutsoyiannis et al., 2009).

The present paper has quantified climate change impacts in the Verde River basin in Arizona by applying a range of different analyses to a 47-member ensemble of climate model predictions of precipitation and temperature, combining 16 climate models and 3 emission scenarios. For this particular region, the projections of IPCC scenarios are not significantly different from each other. An SPI analysis was performed on the ensemble projections, with a simple frequency analysis of dry and wet spells. Simulations from two different hydrologic models driven by the ensemble projections were compared, using a complex distributed model (VIC) and a simple lumped model (*abcd*). The evolution in the mean states of hydrologic variables was quantified, as well as the changes in the average distribution functions of each state variable. Because of uncertainties in climate models, and the fact that their individual results should not be taken at face value (Kundzewicz & Stakhiv, 2010), the uncertainty envelopes, the average changes in the distribution functions of hydrologic states, and the decreasing trends exhibited by hydrologic means provide the most valuable information in the current study. It is also evident that droughts in the Verde Basin may become longer and more intense, as shown by future climate projections. These findings complement and are in agreement with the extensive work of Hay et al. (2011), and can be extended to the neighbouring Salt River basin (of which the Verde is a tributary), as projections are very similar to those in the Verde (Rajagopal, 2011).

The authors' recommendation to decision makers in the Verde Basin is two-fold. (1) Prepare for a progressive decrease in average annual water availability, with more frequent and intense dry periods. (2) Regarding extremes, accept that the risk cannot be predicted accurately: follow the no-regrets approach, as documented in Brown, Werick, Leger, and Fay (2011) or Brown and Lall (2006). Stakeholders such as the City of Phoenix and the Salt River Project, among others, will have to face the burden of such changes and implement water-conservation policies. As in most places, climate change is likely to be a small stressor of water systems in the short term, compared to population growth and other factors in already water-stressed Southern Arizona.

Acknowledgements

The lead author gratefully acknowledges the International Center for Integrated Water Resources Management (ICIWaRM-UNESCO) for his funding support. Some of the *abcd* model codes were adapted from Guillermo Martinez and Hoshin V. Gupta and we thank them for their support. We acknowledge the World Climate Research Programme's (WCRP's) Coupled Model Intercomparison Project Phase 3 (CMIP3) multi-model dataset, the Program for Climate Model Diagnosis and Intercomparison (PCMDI) and the WCRP's Working Group on Coupled Modelling (WGCM) for their roles in making available the WCRP CMIP3 multi-model dataset, as well as the Bias Corrected and Downscaled WCRP CMIP3 Climate Projections archive.

References

Anagnostopoulos, G. G., Koutsoyiannis, D., Christofides, A., Efstratiadis, A., & Mamassis, N. (2010). A comparison of local and aggregated climate model outputs with observed data. *Hydrological Sciences Journal, 55*, 1094–1110.

Barnett, T. P., Pierce, D. W., Hidalgo, H. G., Bonfils, C., Santer, B. D., ... Das, T. (2008). Human-induced changes in the hydrology of the Western United States. *Science, 319*, 1080–1083. doi:10.1126/science.1152538.

Barnett, T. P., Pierce, D. W. (2008). When will Lake Mead go dry? *Water Resources Research, 44*, W03201. doi:10.1029/2007WR006704.

Brown, C., & Lall, U. (2006). Water and economic development: The role of variability and a framework for resilience. *Natural Resources Forum, 30*(4), 306–317. doi:10.1111/j.1477-8947.2006.00118.x.

Brown, C., Werick, W., Leger, W., & Fay, D. (2011). A decision-analytic approach to managing climate risks: Application to the Upper Great Lakes. *Journal of the American Water Resources Association, 47*(3), 524–534. doi:10.1111/j.1752-1688.2011.00552.x.

Camp, C. D., & Tung, K. K. (2007). Surface warming by the solar cycle as revealed by the composite mean difference projection. *Geophysical Research Letters, 34*, L14703. doi:10.1029/2007GL030207.

Christensen, N. C., Wood, A., Voisin, A. N., Lettenmeier, D. P., & Palmer, R. (2004). The effects of climate change on the hydrology and water resources of the Colorado River Basin. *Climatic Change, 62*, 337–363.

Duan, Q., Gupta, V., & Sorooshian, S. (1992). Effective and efficient global optimization for conceptual rainfall-runoff models. *Water Resources Research, 28*, 1015–1031.

Dominguez, F., Rivera, E., Lettenmaier, D. P., & Castro, C. (2012). Changes in winter precipitation extremes for the Western United States under a warmer climate as simulated by regional climate models. *Geophysical Research Letters, 39*, L05803. doi:10.1029/2011GL050762.

Emori, S., & Brown, S. (2005). Dynamic and thermodynamic changes in mean and extreme precipitation under changed climate. *Geophysical Research Letters, 32*(17), L17706.

Gao, Y., Vano, J. A, Zhe, C., & Lettenmaier, D. P. (2011). Evaluating climate change over the Colorado River basin using regional climate models. *Journal of Geophysical Research, 116*, D13104. doi:10.1029/2010JD015278.

Guttman, N. B. (1999). Accepting the Standardized Precipitation Index: A calculation algorithm. *Journal of the American Water Resources Association, 35*(2), 311–322.

Hagedorn, R., Doblas-Reyes, F. J., & Palmer, T. N. (2005). The rationale behind the success of multi-model ensembles in seasonal forecasting. I. Basic concept. *Tellus, 57A*, 219–233.

Hamlet, A. F., & Lettenmaier, D. P. (1999). Effects of climate change on hydrology and water resources in the Columbia River basin. *Journal of the American Water Resources Association*, 36, 1597–1623.

Hargreaves, G. H. (1994). Defining and using reference evapotranspiration. *Journal of Irrigation and Drainage Engineering*, 120(6), 1132–1139.

Hay, L. E., Markstrom, S. L., & Ward-Garrison, C. (2011). Watershed-scale response to climate change through the twenty-first century for selected basins across the United States. *Earth Interactions*, 15, 1–37. doi:10.1175/2010EI370.1.

Hurst, H. E. (1951). Long-term storage capacities of reservoirs. *Transactions of the American Society of Civil Engineering*, 116, 776–808.

Intergovernmental Panel on Climate Change (2001). *Third assessment report: The scientific basis*. Cambridge: Cambridge University Press.

Intergovernmental Panel on Climate Change (2007). *Climate change 2007: The physical science basis*. Cambridge: Cambridge University Press.

Jiang, T., Chen, Y. D., Xu, C. -Y., Chen, X., & Singh, V. P. (2007). Comparison of hydrological impacts of climate change simulated by six hydrological models in the Dongjiang Basin, South China. *Journal of Hydrology*, 336, 316–333.

Kolmogorov, A. N. (1940). Wienersche Spiralen und einige andere interessante Kurven in Hilbertschen Raum. *Doklady Akademii Nauk URSS*, 26, 115–118.

Koutsoyiannis, D., Montanari, A., Lins, H. F., & Cohn, T. A. (2009). Discussion of "The implications of projected climate change for freshwater resources and their management". Climate, hydrology and freshwater: towards an interactive incorporation of hydrological experience into climate research. *Hydrological Sciences Journal*, 54(2), 394–405.

Koutsoyiannis, D. (2011). Hurst-Kolmogorov dynamics and uncertainty. *Journal of the American Water Resources Association*, 47(3), 481–495. doi: 10.1111/j.1752-1688.2011. 00543.x.

Kundzewicz, Z. W., Mata, L. J., Arnell, N. W., Döll, P., Jimenez, B., ... Miller, K. (2008). The implications of projected climate change for freshwater resources and their management. *Hydrological Sciences Journal*, 53, 3–10.

Kundzewicz, Z. W., & Stakhiv, E. Z. (2010). Are climate models "ready for prime time" in water resources management applications, or is more research needed? *Hydrological Sciences Journal*, 55, 1085–1089.

Liang, X., Lettenmaier, D. P., Wood, E. F., & Burges, S. J. (1994). A simple hydrologically based model of land surface water and energy fluxes for general circulation models. *Journal of Geophysical Research*, 99, 14415–14428.

Liang, X., Wood, E. F., & Lettenmaier, D. P. (1996). Surface soil moisture parameterization of the VIC-2L model: Evaluation and modifications. *Global and Planetary Change*, 13, 195–206.

Lins, H. F., & Cohn, T. A. (2003). Floods in the greenhouse: Spinning the right tale. In V. R. Thorndycraft, G. Benito, M. Barriendos, M. C. Llasat (Eds.), *Palaeofloods, historical floods and climatic variability: Applications in flood risk assessment* (pp. 263–268). Madrid: Centro de Ciencias Medioambientales.

Loaiciga, H. A., Maidment, D. R., & Valdes, J. B. (2000). Climate change impacts in a regional karst aquifer, Texas, USA. *Journal of Hydrology*, 227, 173–194.

Martinez, G. F., & Gupta, H. V. (2010). Toward improved identification of hydrological models: A diagnostic evaluation of the "abcd" monthly water balance model for the conterminous United States. *Water Resources Research*, 46, W08507. doi:10.1029/2009WR008294.

Maurer, E. P., Wood, A. W., Adam, J. C., Lennenmaier, D. P., & Nijssen, B. (2002). A long-term hydrologically-based data set of land surface fluxes and states for the conterminous United States. *Journal of Climate*, 15, 3237–3251. doi: 2.0.CO;2"10.1175/1520-0442(2002) 015<3237:ALTHBD>2.0.CO;2.

Maurer, E. P., Brekke, L., Pruitt, T., & Duffy, P. B. (2007). Fine-resolution climate projections enhance regional climate change impact studies. *Eos, Transactions American Geophysical Union*, 88(47), 504.

McCabe, G. J., & Wolock, D. M. (2007). Warming may create substantial water supply shortages in the Colorado River basin. *Geophysical Research Letters*, 34, L22708. doi:10.1029/2007GL031764.

McKee, T. B., Doesken, N. J., & Kleist, J. (1993). The relationship of drought frequency and duration to time scales. *8th Conference on Applied Climatology* (pp. 179–184), 17–22 January 1993, Anaheim, California.

Meehl, G. A., Tebaldi, C., Teng, H., & Peterson, T. C. (2007). Current and future US weather extremes and el Niño. *Geophysical Research Letters, 34*(20), L20704.

Milly, P. C. D., Betancourt, J., Falkenmark, M., Hirsch, R. M., Kundzewicz, Z. W., ... Lettenmaier, D. P. (2008). Stationarity is dead: Whither water management? *Science, 319*, 573–574.

Milly, P. C. D., Dunne, K. A., & Vecchia, A. V. (2005). Global pattern of trends in streamflow and water availability on a changing climate. *Nature, 438*, 347–350, doi:10.1038/nature04312.

Nijssen, B., O'Donnell, G., Hamlet, A. F., & Lettenmaier, D. P. (2001). Hydrologic sensitivity of global rivers to climate change. *Climatic Change, 50*, 143–175.

Rajagopal, S. (2011). Assessing impacts of climate change in a semi-arid watershed using statistically downscaled IPCC climate output. Dissertation defense, Department of Hydrology and Water Resources, University of Arizona, Tucson.

Scibek, J., & Allen, D. M. (2006). Modeled impacts of predicted climate change on recharge and ground water levels. *Water Resources Research, 42*, W11405. doi:10.1029/2005WR004742.

Seager, R., et al., (2007). Model projections of an imminent transition to a more arid climate in southwestern North America. *Science, 316*, 1181–1184.

Serrat-Capdevila, A., Scott, R. L., Shuttleworth, W. J., & Valdés, J. B. (2011). Estimating ET under warmer climates: Insights from a semi-arid watershed. *Journal of Hydrology, 399*, 1–11.

Serrat-Capdevila, A., Valdés, J. B., González Pérez, J., Baird, K., Mata, L. J., & Maddock, T. III (2007). Modeling climate change impacts – and uncertainty – on the hydrology of a riparian system: The San Pedro Basin (Arizona/Sonora). *Journal of Hydrology, 347*, 48–66. doi:10.1016/j.jhydrol.2007.08.028.

Sorooshian, S., Duan, Q., & Gupta, V. K. (1993). Calibration of rainfall-runoff models: Application of global optimization to the Sacramento soil moisture accounting model. *Water Resources Research, 29*, 1185–1194.

Stakhiv, E. Z. (2010). Practical approaches to water management under climate change uncertainty. In H. H. G. Savinje, S. Demuth, P. Hubert (Eds.), *Hydrocomplexity: New tools for solving wicked water problems*, 62–69. (IAHS Pub. 338) Wallingford: IAHS Press.

Thomas, H. A. (1981). *Improved methods for national water assessment: Final report* (Water Resources Contract No. R15 249270). Harvard Water Resources Group.

Tsonis, A. A., Swanson, K., & Kravtsov, S. (2007). Surface warming by the solar cycle as revealed by the composite mean difference projection. *Geophysical Research Letters, 34*, L14703. doi:10.1029/2007GL030207.

Stott, L., Timmermann, A., & Thunell, R. (2007). Southern Hemisphere and deep-sea warming led deglacial atmospheric CO_2 rise and tropical warming. *Science, 318*, 435–438. doi:10.1126/science.1143791.

USGS (2012). *National water information system*, web inteface. Retrieved from: http://waterdata.us gs.gov/usa/nwis/sw.

Villarini, G., Smith, J. A., Serinaldi, F., Bales, J., Bates, P. D., & Krajewski, W. F. (2009). Flood frequency analysis for nonstationary annual peak records in an urban drainage basin. *Advances in Water Resources, 32*, 1255–1266.

Wi, S., Dominguez, F., Durcik, M., Valdes, J., Diaz, H. F., & Castro, C. L. (Submitted). Climate change projections of snowfall in the Colorado River basin using dynamical downscaling. *Water Resources Research*.

Wilby, R. L. (2010). Evaluating climate model outputs for hydrological applications. Opinion paper. *Hydrological Sciences Journal, 55*, 1090–1093.

Zhen-Shan, L., & Xian, S. (2007). Multi-scale analysis of global temperature changes and trend of a drop in temperature in the next 20 years. *Meteorology and Atmospheric Physics, 95*, 115–121. doi:10.1007/s00703-006-0199-2.

Impacts of climate change on the hydrological cycle in Mexico

Felipe I. Arreguín-Cortés and Mario López-Pérez

Felipe I. Arreguín-Cortés and Mario López-Pérez

National Water Commission (CONAGUA), Mexico City, Mexico

Mexico is implementing policies and actions aimed at mitigating and adapting to the impacts of climate change without compromising the country's development process. The plan is to reduce vulnerability through the implementation of the Special Programme on Climate Change 2009–2012, which includes 105 objectives and 294 goals shared among a number of national institutions. The National Water Commission (CONAGUA) is responsible for measuring the most important variables of the hydrological cycle and addressing the impact of climate change. As such, CONAGUA is in charge of attaining 41 of the 294 goals stated in the Special Programme on Climate Change, which include 37 of the goals set in the National Water Programme 2007–2012 (PNH). It is expected that since a great number of goals are shared by both schemes this can help assure their fulfilment and prove useful in working towards the sustainable use of water, mindful of climate change considerations.

Introduction

Climate change (CC) refers to the earth's global climate change that occurs at different periods of time triggered by climatic parameters forming part of the hydrologic cycle: temperature, precipitation, evaporation, humidity, etc. This change takes place due to natural causes and also, in recent decades, to human action through the use of fuels that emit greenhouse gases (GHG) to the atmosphere. The effects such emissions have on global temperatures and on the melting of glaciers, contributing to rising sea levels, have been well documented.

The United Nations Framework Convention on Climate Change (UNFCCC) uses the term 'climate change' only to refer to GHG-induced changes in atmospheric composition that are directly or indirectly attributed to human activity (United Nations, 1992). Burning oil, coal and natural gas, coupled with deforestation and forest fires, have led to increased emissions of carbon dioxide, methane, nitrous oxide and chlorofluorocarbons in the atmosphere, and correspondingly to increased temperatures. In response to this, it is estimated that global precipitation patterns and the hydrological cycle have been in general altered, including evaporation, precipitation, runoff and infiltration. This effect also leads to general changes in water availability, hurricane incidence and pathways, storm intensity, rainfall distribution, heat waves and droughts, with impacts on watersheds, aquifers, coastlines and wetlands. Although there is overall general agreement on these findings, there is also great uncertainty about the magnitudes and rates of these changes at the regional and local level.

In response to the challenges posed by CC, Mexico has developed the Special Programme on Climate Change (*Programa Especial de Cambio Climático*, PECC) a long-term sustainable vision to build a resilient economy, society and environment (SEMARNAT, 2008–2012).

Impacts of climate change on the water cycle

Climate and water variability significantly impact all aspects of our daily lives and socio-economic development. Any modification can bring about important consequences with respect to water availability, health, food, tourism, forestry, transportation, and habitat of living species, also affecting societies and their ability to develop in a sustainable way.

Approximately 90% of all natural disasters worldwide are due to meteorological, weather or hydrological conditions. Life and material losses caused by natural disasters are a major obstacle to sustainable development and security. Therefore, it is essential to compile accurate data, observations and forecasts and ensure the timely and reliable exchange of information on weather, climate and water.

Since 1850, when different national agencies first started to record temperatures, the earth has warmed about 0.6 °C, a rise that has occurred mainly in the last three decades. The Intergovernmental Panel on Climate Change (IPCC) estimates temperature increases of between 1.8 and 5.8 °C and sea-level rises between 9 and 88 cm over the next century. Sea levels have already risen between 10 and 25 cm (IPCC, 2007).

The residence time of CO_2 in the atmosphere is over 100 years; thus, human actions now will affect the plans of future generations. Mexico is located in an area particularly exposed to the impacts of climate change, with damages of different kind, intensity and extension with respect to: (1) health, threatened by invasive species and vectors; (2) agriculture, threatened by reductions in agricultural potential and increasing incidence of forest fires; (3) tourism; (4) water supply; (5) coastal plains, threatened by floods; and (6) biodiversity and natural areas.

The impact of climate change on water resources depends on the changes in volume and quality of surface and groundwater, wastewater discharges, riverbeds, and the size of human settlements as well as water demands for human uses. Therefore, measuring the hydrological cycle provides essential information to be used in early-warning systems to reduce negative impacts or to restore watersheds, aquifers and ecosystems. Measurements of hydrological variables through radar, meteorological observatories, weather and gauge stations and groundwater wells are helpful in assessing the quantity and quality of surface and groundwater, which is essential to protect life, property and the environment.

Impacts on the hydrological cycle are reflected in an increase in temperature and changes in precipitation, as these affect evaporation from seas and oceans and transpiration from plants, runoff of watersheds, and the infiltration that recharges aquifers. At present, evidence and data regarding the magnitude and extent of these variations have proven hard to gather. However, it is certain that climate change will affect water availability and increase water demand for most uses, for instance in ecosystems and agriculture. Demand may exceed supply, creating major disasters in vulnerable areas. Also, there will be differentiated changes in water quality in rivers, lakes, wetlands and coastal ecosystems. It is thus important that countries monitor these changes, a step Mexico is already working towards. Moreover, a strategic element of the concept of integrated water resources management highlights the need to have adequate policies and adaptation actions to climate change based on sound and regularly collected data and information.

Vulnerability to climate change

It is important to emphasize what is now widely recognized, that climate change will have more acute impacts and effects on those countries and social groups that are less able to cope with them. In this sense, vulnerability to extreme weather phenomena is directly related to levels of development, institutional capacities and more particularly to poverty and marginality. Vulnerability to climate change is the extent to which a system is capable or incapable of addressing its negative effects. It depends on the nature, extent and climate variation to which a system is exposed, and on the sensitivity and adaptive capacity or resilience of a system.

The IPCC Fourth Assessment Report (AR4) by Working Groups I and II indicates that Mexico is one of the countries particularly vulnerable to climate change. Some studies on climate change vulnerability show that entire regions located in deserts, coastal areas and zones close to the formation of cyclones are most sensitive to extreme events such as droughts, heat waves, winds, and hurricane rains and flooding. Also, the frequency and impact of the El Niño and La Niña meteorological phenomena will be even greater. As such, Mexico faces heightened risks due to its climatic and topographic diversity, long coastline of 11,122 km, the combination of tropical and semi-arid areas, and the concentration of population and economic activity in areas that are already experiencing water problems (IPCC, 2007).

On average, four destructive cyclones hit Mexico each year, producing heavy rains that are often followed by floods and landslides. Heavy rainfall causes strong sediment flows in rivers and streams on the mountainsides, destroying economic and social infrastructure such as housing units, hospitals, schools and transport routes in states like Puebla, Veracruz and Hidalgo. Hailstorms have caused obstructions and damages to drainage structures in urban areas in the states of Tlaxcala, Michoacán and Puebla. The greatest soil loss in Mexico is caused by rain and the most affected states are Mexico, Tlaxcala and Oaxaca. The states of Michoacán, Chiapas and Guerrero suffered the greatest losses due to natural disasters in 2010. Also, it is well known that the states of Veracruz, Chiapas and Tamaulipas have frequently required economic support to cope with the impacts of natural phenomena and have thus appealed to the Mexican Natural Disasters Fund (FONDEN).

An analysis of maximum temperatures in Mexico shows a trend above the normal value of 31.8 °C during the period 1971–2010, and over 33 °C in the last 4 years (Figure 1). Similarly, Mexico's annual average rainfall is 770 mm per year for the period 1941–2010 and has a decreasing trend (Figure 2). Yet, national and annual analyses do not consider precipitation distribution even when 70% of total rainfall occurs mainly during the months of June, July, August and September. Besides, there is great variation in precipitation across the country: the state of Baja California receives 200 mm of rain per year whilst Chiapas receives above 2000 mm. Other studies indicate changes in rainfall patterns and an increase in the intensity and frequency of severe storms and cyclones. On the other hand, droughts cause heavy economic losses to livestock and agriculture since two-thirds of the Mexican territory is arid or semi-arid with low rainfall and is thus highly vulnerable to severe droughts. The most affected are the Baja California Peninsula in the north-western region, the Central Basins and the Río Bravo basin.

In Mexico, water availability per capita varies widely across the country. The average is 4312 m³ per person per year, which is low according to international standards. For the northern, central and north-eastern regions (where more than 77% of Mexico's population lives and which contribute 87% of the total GDP), the value is 1734 m³ per person per year.

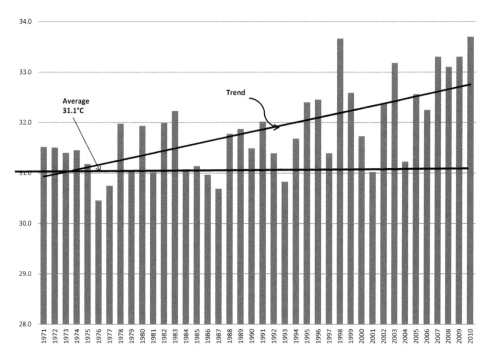

Figure 1.   Mexico's maximum annual temperature (°C).

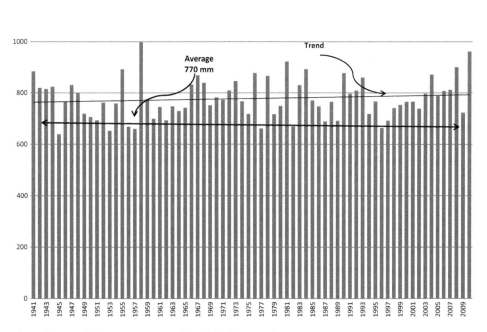

Figure 2.   Mexico's average annual precipitation (mm).

In contrast, the south-east (with 23% of the total population and only 13% of total GDP) has an average water availability of 13,097 m^3 per person per year. This uneven distribution exemplifies Mexico's vulnerability, because the most water-scarce regions are also the most populated. Both the peninsulas of Baja California and Yucatán are also considered highly vulnerable due to low water availability, karst features and hurricane prevalence (which carry heavy rains in a short timespan).

Water scarcity, uneven distribution, the discharge of untreated wastewater and pollution mean that in some areas in Mexico surface water and overexploited aquifers cannot meet demands. In fact, 58% of extracted groundwater (equivalent to an annual average extraction of 28 km^3) comes from 101 overexploited aquifers out of the 653 that have been recorded. Another problem exacerbating vulnerability is low water use efficiency, especially in irrigation. This activity receives 77% of the national water resources but consumes 33% to 55% of this extraction. Water supplied for cities accounts for 14% of the total average annual extraction and has efficiencies in water distribution that range between 50% and 70%. The losses are due to deficiencies in infrastructure maintenance and operation (Arreguin, 2005).

The shores of the Gulf of Mexico and the Caribbean Sea are particularly vulnerable to sea-level rise and coastal erosion. The zones most vulnerable to coastal erosion are those found between the tide level and an altitude of 2 metres. Cities and towns located in deltas and plains are vulnerable to flooding up to 40 km or even 50 km inland, with salt water degrading freshwater reservoirs and aquifers as well as backwater flooding. Contradictory water management and unregulated land use leading to irregular settlements on riverbanks, floodplains and lagoon coastal systems, among other high-risk human behaviours, are also increasing vulnerability to climate change.

Among other solutions, land use restrictions and restoration could be helpful in reducing this risk profile for both human settlements and ecosystems. It is advisable to take actions to promote the conservation and protection of wetlands, coastal dunes and unconsolidated material surfaces in the Gulf of Mexico, since these areas are considered buffers against weather phenomena and rises in sea level.

Seeking to assess its vulnerability to climate change and devise scenarios based on different temperatures and precipitation and their forecasted impacts at the regional, state or watershed level, Mexico has developed the Maya Version 1 database to analyze variations and trends. Daily information for the period between 1961 and 2000 has been put together from existing weather stations covering the entire country (4542 nodes). Average values were inferred by interpolating data from the 24 nearest stations and distances no greater than 32 km with a resolution of 0.2 degrees latitude and longitude. This tool has permitted the analysis of projections for 2030, 2050 and 2100 (Rosengaus, 2007).

This database has also helped identify exposed areas by comparing rises in temperature and drops in rainfall also associated with aquifer boundaries (Figure 3). Yet, this preliminary identification of highly vulnerable inland and coastal overexploited aquifers needs to consider their socio-political, institutional, economic, technological, and cultural situation to categorize them (Arreguin et al., 2008a).

Public policies in Mexico for adaptation to climate change

Mexico's National Development Plan 2007–2012 (*Plan Nacional de Desarrollo*, PND) (Gobierno de México, 2007) establishes a clear and viable strategy and pathway for the country to realize the many objectives it has set to transform the country. It is divided along five action lines, one of which is an environmental sustainability axis where it points

Figure 3.   Increase in vulnerability of aquifers due to rise in temperatures and drop in rainfall.

out that the use of fossil fuels and old industrial technologies, changes in land use and the destruction of millions of hectares of forest are increasing the concentration of GHG in the atmosphere, leading to rising temperatures in the world. Acknowledging the importance of promoting sustainable human development whereby the needs of future generations are not compromised, the plan has as its 10th objective to reduce GHG emissions and as the 11th to foster adaptation to the impacts of climate change.

Similarly, the National Water Programme (*Programa Nacional Hídrico*, PNH) (CONAGUA, 2010c) gives authority to the National Water Commission (CONAGUA) to develop public water policies without compromising Mexico's sustainability and development. As such, the National Water Resources Strategy on Climate Change Adaptation is part of the Mexican comprehensive vision on how to manage a strategic resource, important to national security, which faces the possible negative effects of climate change (Aguilar & Mestre, 2010). This strategy reflects the specific efforts that the country should undertake on adaptation coupled with water resources management. The strategy draws its strength, importance and concrete planned results from the National Planning System (established in the 1983 Planning Law), the National Climate Change Strategy, the National Water Programme, and *Water Agenda 2030* (CONAGUA, 2010a), a long-term vision. It supports ongoing efforts, and transforms major institutional, social, economic, technological and environmental adaptation obstacles into opportunities.

What is more, and in response to the challenges posed by CC, Mexico has produced a climate change hydro-vulnerability atlas, which presents the projected climate scenarios on precipitation and maximum and minimum temperatures for the twenty-first century, the possible impacts of CC on the rainy season and on tropical cyclones, and the vulnerability of irrigated agriculture and water quality. This atlas is oriented towards helping to find measures to reduce the country's vulnerability (IMTA, 2010).

Mexico has also developed a long-term sustainable vision on how it will look to build a resilient economy, society and environment: the Special Programme on Climate Change (PECC). This crosscutting policy instrument calls on federal ministries to acquire binding commitments to reach established goals and targets for CC mitigation and adaptation.

It seeks to promote sustainable development, energy security, food security, clean production processes, efficiency and competitiveness, and the conservation of natural resources.

The Special Programme on Climate Change, which is a binding government document, is the guiding document for the Interministerial Climate Change Commission (CICC, 2008) and was published in Mexico's official gazette on 28 August 2009. Integrated by 10 federal ministries, the commission is responsible for coordinating the formulation of policies on climate change and for providing institutional supports for its implementation. This body also interacts with different sectors and at the federal, state and municipal levels, outlines a long-term vision on climate actions and defines quantified mitigation targets. As a federal special programme, specific resources have been allocated and the Information System on the Crosscutting Agenda for the Special Programme on Climate Change (SIAT-PECC) has been established as a compulsory tracking system to increase transparency and account for progress towards defined targets (SEMARNAT, 2008–2012).

Given its conception as a comprehensive policy to address climate change, the PECC considers four key components: the need for a long-term vision, mitigation actions, adaptation activities, and ensuring that policies are crosscutting. It thus aims at (1) carrying out activities on adaptation focused on reducing Mexico's vulnerability to CC; (2) developing a scheme for comprehensive risk management, particularly regarding risks related to extreme hydro-meteorological phenomena; (3) promoting crosscutting policy efforts in economics, education, training, research, information and communication; and (4) joining multilateral, equitable and large-scale international efforts where individual countries make their best efforts to tackle CC according to the principle of 'common but differentiated responsibilities'.

With this special programme on climate change Mexico is committed, among other things, to:

- develop the first National Atlas of Climate Change Vulnerability
- develop a proposal of public policy instruments to decrease vulnerability
- develop an initial inventory of adaptation costs for key economic sectors and continue cross-sectorial and regional evaluation for adaptation and mitigation
- promote financing mechanisms for adaptation
- strengthen the development of the National Civil Protection System, with a comprehensive management of risk
- incorporate provisions for land use in the National Planning System
- reinforce the inclusion of climate change in education
- promote research and technology development related to the carbon cycle, national emission factors, low-carbon or carbon-neutral technologies, meteorology, climate modelling and integrated risk management.

The vision for 2050 regarding the adaptation and development of strategic capacities considers three main stages. The first stage (2008–2012) applies vulnerability and economic assessment to identify priority actions. The second stage (2013–2030) includes plans to strengthen strategic capacity building for adaptation at national, regional and sectoral levels. And the third stage (2031–2050) is intended to consolidate capacities.

Following the recommendations of the IPCC, the special programme has adjusted its findings to the national context, breaking them down into 105 goals and 294 objectives, and identifying the relevant federal agencies responsible for each one of them. The PECC seeks to reduce vulnerability through adaptation and extension of water infrastructure, and to strengthen the strategic capacity for adaptation through institutional tools, improvements in infrastructure and services, and research and technological development.

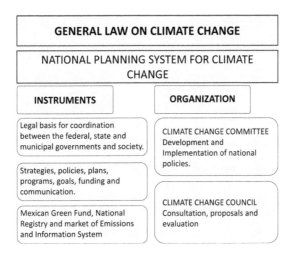

Figure 4.   The General Law on Climate Change.

For instance, given CONAGUA's mandate of administering national waters, managing and controlling the hydrologic system and promoting social development, it is unsurprising that the commission is responsible for the attainment of 37 of the 105 goals stated in the CC scheme – 33 for adaptation and 4 for mitigation. These 37 goals are also in the National Water Programme, which facilitates compliance, and a further 11 goals are to be attained in shared collaboration with other institutions.

Through the implementation of its PECC, Mexico seeks to demonstrate that it is possible to mitigate and adapt to climate change without compromising economic and social development. Even when internationally agreed targets remain controversial, the country has endorsed the indicative objective or aspirational target of reducing GHG emissions by 50% by 2050, with 2000 levels as the baseline. Currently, Mexico contributes 1.6% of global GHG emissions. At the end of the present administration in 2012, PECC compliance will have resulted in an annual reduction of 50 million tons of carbon dioxide equivalent ($MtCO_2eq$).

The country has also put in place the General Law on Climate Change (Cámara de Diputados del H. Congreso de la Unión, 2012) (Figure 4) as another important legal instrument to address CC. A group of senators submitted the proposal for consideration and comments to the Joint Committees on the Environment, Natural Resources and Fisheries and legislative studies, an initiative that was supported by CONAGUA and other federal institutions. The law aims to facilitate adaptation to and mitigation of climate change and contribute to sustainable development by providing the basis for coordination, the creation of a national system of planning and the bases, strategies and mechanisms to create a green fund for mitigation and adaptation.

Achievements in climate change

At the 1992 Earth Summit in Rio, Mexico adopted the United Nations Framework Convention on Climate Change (UNFCCC) and ratified it in 1993. In 1994, the UNFCCC was formalized with the signature of 191 countries. After the Kyoto Conference of the Parties in 1997 (COP 3), Mexico actively participated in the negotiations, and a year later, on 9 June 1998, the country signed the Kyoto Protocol, committing itself to reducing GHG emissions.

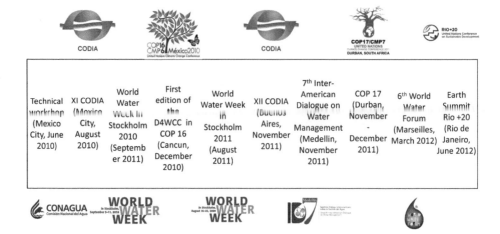

Figure 5.   The Regional Policy Dialogue process.

Based on these international statutes, 2010 was, in water terms, an unusual year with respect to international activities conducted by CONAGUA which included foreign credit operations, bilateral and multilateral cooperation activities, and special projects on climate adaptation and the hydrological cycle. In November of that same year, at the Cancun Climate Change Convention and alongside several water and environmental ministries and agencies from Latin America and the Caribbean, CONAGUA participated in the elaboration of a regional position paper to the 16th session of the Conference of the Parties to the UNFCCC (COP 16) (Figure 5).

In preparation for the Cancun convention, the regional positioning document was presented at a regional seminar to be furnished and enriched with additional feedback (Dialogues for Water & Climate Change, 2010). This version added practical adaptation examples drawn from across the continent. Version 5.0 (September 2011) was updated in preparation for the 12th Meeting of the Conference of Ibero-America Director Generals of Water (CODIA) in Portugal, the Seventh Inter-American Dialogue on Management of Water in Medellin, Colombia (October), and the COP 17 in Durban, South Africa (December). This version served as an input for the Summit and the Americas regional document. Version 6.0 (January, 2012) was presented in its own right in March 2012, during the 6th World Water Forum, in Marseille (Dialogues for Water & Climate Change, 2012).

In September 2010, the Global Water and Adaptation Action Alliance (GWAAA) was created as an informal and voluntary partnership of development banks, aid agencies and environmental organizations dedicated to promoting climate-smart sustainable water resource management, supported by CONAGUA and Conservation International. Some of the members of GWAAA are CONAGUA, Inter-American Development Bank, World Bank, Asian Development Bank, UN-HABITAT, Global Water Partnership, World Wildlife Fund, Cooperative Programme on Water and Climate, Water and Climate Coalition, International Union for Conservation of Nature, International Water Association, Water Advisory Council, European Investment Bank, Stockholm International Water Institute, and International Council for Local Environmental Initiatives.

Also in 2010 but at the regional level, CONAGUA hosted the Regional Policy Dialogue (RPD) on Water and Climate Change in the Americas (CONAGUA, 2010b). Mexico organized a series of informative and capacity-building sessions in preparation for this 'Dialog for Water and Climate Change' (D4WCC) that included technical workshops (June, Mexico City); a session during the Eleventh Meeting of the Conference of Ibero-American Water Directors (CODIA, August, Mexico City); and a Ministerial Panel of Experts held during the Stockholm World Water Week (September). During 2011 and 2012, Mexico continued its commitment to leading the efforts and actions in adaptation to climate change, which has had a positive impact, and called for these initiatives to be internationally recognized by many multilateral and country entities.

The D4WCC event aimed at demonstrating to decision makers and the climate change and development community that water is not a sector but a crosscutting issue affected by climate change. It thus affects other economic sectors, such as energy, agriculture, tourism and environment, where adaptation strategies must take water into account. The event sought to: (1) raise awareness among the general public, experts from other disciplines and decision makers about the link between water resources and climate change; (2) structure a platform to share experiences and generate mutual understanding in the water community regarding adaptation to climate change and water; (3) advocate for long-term formal recognition of water as part of the UNFCCC; and (4) show that even without recognition, the water community is already adapting to climate change.

CONAGUA strongly believes that the D4WCC created a precedent for water, development and environmental communities to come together on climate change. Back in December 2010, the D4WCC served its initial purpose well, but it is now time to reflect upon the progress made so far, and to call for a renewed effort to continue building upon these bases and strengthen our capacity to respond to the challenges climate change poses to water resources in the coming months and years.

There have been many water adaptation initiatives that form part of the Regional Adaptation Solutions Database that CONAGUA has helped develop alongside its regional partners since the D4WCC took place. There is one particularly promising initiative salient to Mexico: setting aside water reserves for the environment. In 2010, CONAGUA and the World Wildlife Fund agreed to develop a nationwide programme that, based on the National Water Law, would identify and create water reserves to ensure the conservation of major ecosystems in the country. Establishing this protection framework for water sources is a key action in implementing a long-term, sustainable and adaptive water policy in Mexico. The 'water reserves for the environment' initiative is in progress and its first studies and findings will be ready in 2013.

Further thoughts

It is clear that Mexico has made strong international and national commitments on climate change mitigation and adaptation as well as a complete and sound strategy on how to face climate change. Among other federal institutions, CONAGUA has made a great effort at the local, regional and international levels to position adaptation actions at the same level of importance as those of mitigation, especially for water. Also, CONAGUA is monitoring and addressing the impacts of climate change on Mexico's water resources. However, more needs to be researched, addressed, studied and published about those effects and their further consequences. Greater efforts are needed to identify, develop and communicate adaptation solutions throughout the country as well as at regional and international arenas.

Mexico's water resources are considered a strategic and national heritage resource. Yet, the main challenge remains to protect and to preserve water sources and expand water supply options in a risky scenario of severely adverse climate change and high vulnerability. For example, the overexploitation of aquifers and basins requires immediate actions to stop this practice; legal, technical and political measures ought to be implemented. It is also crucial to convince society that the impacts of climate change on water resources are real and significant and that its involvement with a broad range of local, state and federal institutions for implementing different kinds of adaptation solutions or actions is of the highest priority. Again, the comprehensive and crosscutting concept of water management and the strategy of integrated water resources management need to be communicated to and implemented in other sectors like health, tourism, agriculture, energy and ecosystems. As these initiatives are being discussed in other parts of the world, Mexico's example will prove insightful to other countries implementing or seeking to implement similar approaches worldwide.

References

Aguilar, F., & Mestre, E. (2010). *Orientaciones Generales para la formulación e implementación de la Estrategia Nacional de Recursos Hídricos relativa a la Adaptación al Cambio Climático* [General Guidelines to develop and implement the National Water Resources Strategy on Climate Change Adaptation] (World Bank for CONAGUA). Mexico City: CONAGUA.

Arreguin, F. (2005). Water management in Mexico. In *IWA Yearbook 2005* (pp. 39–40). London: IWA.

Arreguin, F., Chávez, R., & Rosengaus, M. (2008a). Impactos del Cambio Climático en los Acuíferos de México [Impact of climate change on Mexican aquifers]. *Sexto Congreso Nacional de Aguas Subterráneas* [6th National Congress on Groundwater]. Mexico City: Asociación Geohidrológica Mexicana.

Arreguin, F., Chávez, R., & Rosengaus, M. (2008b). *Maya Versión 1. Base de Datos para el análisis de tendencias de temperatura y lluvia* [Maya Version 1. Database for the analysis of future trends in temperature and rainfall]. Mexico City: CONAGUA.

Cámara de Diputados del H. Congreso de la Unión. (2012). *Ley general de cambio climático* [General law on climate change]. Mexico City: National Gazette.

CICC. (2008). *La Comisión Intersecretarial de Cambio Climático desarrolló el Programa Especial de Cambio Climático en el año de 2008* [The Interministerial Commission of climate change developed Special Programme on Climate Change in the year 2008]. National Gazette Mexico City.

CONAGUA (2010a). *Agenda 2030* [Water Agenda 2030]. Mexico City: CONAGUA.

CONAGUA (2010b). *Diálogos por el agua y cambio climático: Llamado a la Acción [Dialogues on water and climate change: Call to action]*. Mexico City: SEMARNAT.

CONAGUA (2010c). *Programa Nacional Hídrico 2007–2012* [National Water Programme 2007–2012]. Mexico City: CONAGUA.

Dialogues for Water & Climate Change (2010). Regional Policy Dialog in Latin America and the Caribbean: Challenges and opportunities for water-based adaptation to climate change. Retrieved from http://www.d4wcc.org.mx/index.php?option=com_content&view=article&id=4&Itemid=10&lang=es

Dialogues for Water & Climate Change (2012). Water and climate change adaptation in the Americas: Solutions from the Regional Policy Dialog (RPD). Retrieved from http://www.d4wcc.org.mx/index.php?option=com_content&view=article&id=4&Itemid=10&lang=es

Gobierno de México. (2007). *Plan Nacional de Desarrollo 2007–2012* [National Development Plan 2007–2012]. Mexico City: National Gazette.

IMTA (Instituto Mexicano de Tecnología del Agua). (2010). Efectos del cambio climático en los recursos hídricos de México. [Climate change effects on Mexico's water resources] In P. F. Martínez Austria & C. Patiño Gómez (Eds.), *Hydric vulnerability atlas*, vol III. Mexico City: SEMARNAT.

IPCC. (2007). Climate change 2007: Synthesis report. Contribution of working groups I, II and III to the fourth assessment report of the intergovernmental panel on climate change, R.K. Pachauri, & A. Reisinger, Geneva: Intergovernmental Panel on Climate Change.

Rosengaus, M. (2007). *Reporte interno de la Coordinación General del Servicio Meteorológico Nacional de CONAGUA. Procedimientos para estimar tendencias en un análisis parcial de datos históricos* [Internal report for the general coordination of the National Weather Service at CONAGUA. Procedures for estimating trends in the partial analysis of historical data]. Mexico City: CONAGUA.

SEMARNAT. (2008–2012). *Programa Especial de Cambio Climático* [Special Programme on Climate Change]. Mexico City: SEMARNAT.

United Nations. (1992). *United Nations framework convention on climate change*. Document no. FCCC/INFORMAL/84. GE.05-62220 (E) 200705. Geneva: United Nations.

Climate change projections of streamflow in the Iberian peninsula

Domingo F. Rasilla, Carolina Garmendia and Juan Carlos García-Codron

Grupo de Investigación GIMENA, Departamento de Geografía, Urbanismo y Ordenación del Territorio, Universidad de Cantabria, Santander, Spain

This contribution analyzes the impact on Iberian water resources of anthropogenic climatic change, using the output from four simulations obtained from two coupled general circulation models (HadCM2 and PCM) under the A2 and B2 emissions scenarios. The results show that the magnitude of those impacts will depend on the level of global warming and the geographical characteristics of each watershed, although a reduction in runoff, principally in spring and summer, and a change in the timing of the maximum discharge, especially in high-altitude basins, will be two the most noteworthy features.

Introduction

It is not an exaggeration to affirm that water availability will become a fundamental challenge to be faced by humankind. Climate is a fundamental input in the hydrological system, and its variability in time and space exerts decisive consequences in the water resources of any hydrological basin. The latest IPCC report (2007) confirms that human activity is causing an increase in global temperatures that will be accompanied by modifications in circulation patterns and, consequently, in new distributions of precipitation and temperatures. An increase and intensification of drought conditions and a larger frequency of hydrological extreme events linked to torrential episodes are expected globally.

Within this context, one of the most important tasks faced by the scientific community is to provide a reliable evaluation of the current status of the water resources at regional and local scales, and to predict their future response to the climate changes due to global warming. This paper carries out an estimate of the impact on the water resources of the Iberian Peninsula caused by the climate changes advanced by two models under two emission scenarios, following two approaches. First, the alterations experienced by the average state of the main components of the hydrological cycle are assessed, comparing the current situation with the projections for the period 2071–2100. Then the interannual variability of the flows is analyzed under the same climatic conditions in a series of selected fluvial basins.

Data and methodology

Essentially, the analysis of the impact of climatic changes on water resources has followed two approaches. The first consists in the development of hypothetical scenarios of future temperature and precipitation, which serve as inputs to a hydrological model. This approach offers a clear and instantaneous picture of the magnitude of the hydrological response to specific climatic disturbances, although it does not offer additional advantages because the underlying hypothesis of an independent evolution of temperature and precipitation is not physically accurate, and the proposed magnitudes of change ignore subtler variations on a monthly scale.

In contrast, general circulation models (GCMs) provide physically consistent outputs with respect to the dynamics of the climate system, and their outcomes can be used directly as input for the hydrological models, although they are unable to resolve important sub-grid-scale features because they are run at a coarse spatial resolution. As a result, GCMs do not provide satisfactory projections at regional and local scales. A first alternative is the use of *regional* climate models (RCMs), whose design includes a finer spatial resolution; a second is based on the development of procedures of scale reduction ('downscaling'), applying statistical techniques which link several large-scale atmospheric forcing variables, like sea-level pressure or geopotential heights, to the evolution of surface parameters, such as temperature or precipitation. Additionally, when dealing with hydrometeorological issues, a more accurate representation of the spatial variability of a given parameter within a basin, such as precipitation or temperature, is obtained when the point values of the projected parameters (grid points or meteorological stations) are converted into areal averages, which requires taking into account geographical parameters such as altitude, topography or exposure, through geostatistical procedures (Chang, Knight, Staneva, & Kostov, 2002; Knight, Chang, Staneva, & Kostov, 2001).

Keeping in mind the general objectives of this research, a direct application of temperature and precipitation fields obtained from a high-resolution database to a hydrological model based on Thornwaithe's water balance was selected (Thornthwaite, 1948; Mather, 1978) (Figure 1).

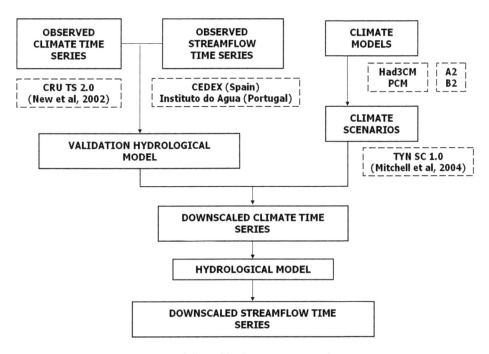

Figure 1. Downscaling procedure followed in the current research.

Table 1. Selected Rivers, watersheds and sources of streamflow data.

N°	River	Watershed	Stream gauge	Source
1	Cares	Norte	Camarmeña	CEDEX
2	Paiva	Costeiras	Castro dÁire	Instituto do Agua
3	Tajo	Tajo	Trillo	CEDEX
4	Degebe	Guadiana	Amieira	Instituto do Agua
5	Turón	Sur	Ardales	Agencia Andaluza del Agua
6	Segre	Ebro	Puigcerdá	CEDEX
7	Ginesta	Costera Catalana	Llemana	Agència Catalana del Agua

Monthly streamflow gauge time series for the period 1961–1990 were obtained from different national (CEDEX, Spain; Instituto do Agua, Portugal) and basin organizations (Confederaciones Hidrográficas del Norte, Duero, Tajo, Sur and Ebro; Agència Catalana de l'Aigua) (Table 1). The final selection of the time series used in this paper was guided by (1) the lack of significant human activities, (2) the relatively small size of the catchment (relatively fast hydrological response to atmospheric variability), and (3) the desire to cover as much as possible of the topographical and climatic diversity of the Iberian Peninsula (Figure 2).

Climate change scenarios due to global warming were based on two databases which provide monthly values of average temperature, daily temperature range, total precipitation, vapour pressure and cloudiness. Their spatial resolution is $10'$, which results in more than 3640 nodes for the whole Iberian Peninsula. The 1961–1990 climate data (control scenario) were retrieved from the CRU TS 1.2 database (New, Lister, Hulme & Makin, 2002), while the perturbed climate fields (2001–2100) were extracted from the TYN SC 1.0 database (Mitchell, Carter, Jones, Hulme, & New, 2004). The latter includes 16 scenarios with different projections of global warming and patterns of change, supplied by several coupled general circulation models (CGCMs), interpolated from the original resolution to the definitive grid based on a Delaunay triangulation procedure. The projections are based on the output of four climate models – GCM2 (Canada), CSIRO (Australia), DOE PCM (USA) and HadCM3 (United Kingdom) – under four special reports on emissions scenarios (SRES) (A1F1, A2, B2 and B1). The SRES report (IPCC, 2000) provides a comprehensive set of 40 socio-economic futures, and details their consequences for anthropogenic emissions of greenhouse gases. The selected scenarios represent 68% of the range of uncertainty in emissions, compared to the full set of 40 SRES scenarios (Mitchell et al., 2004; IPCC, 2000).

One of the shortcomings of the CRU TS 1.2 database is the assumption of the stability of the climate under conditions of global warming – that future climate will be essentially similar to the current conditions, except for a long-term increasing trend of temperatures; in consequence, the natural variability of the future climate will be similar to the current. The new climatic series were obtained in the following way: for any particular variable v, climate model g, and scenario s, the value x at a particular grid point i in any year y and month m is calculated as follows:

$$x_{vgsiym} = c_{vim} + r_{viym} + p_{vgsim}t_{gsy}$$

where c is the average ('normal') value of that variable during the period 1961–1990; r is the resulting residual of normalizing the original values with regard to their 1961–1990

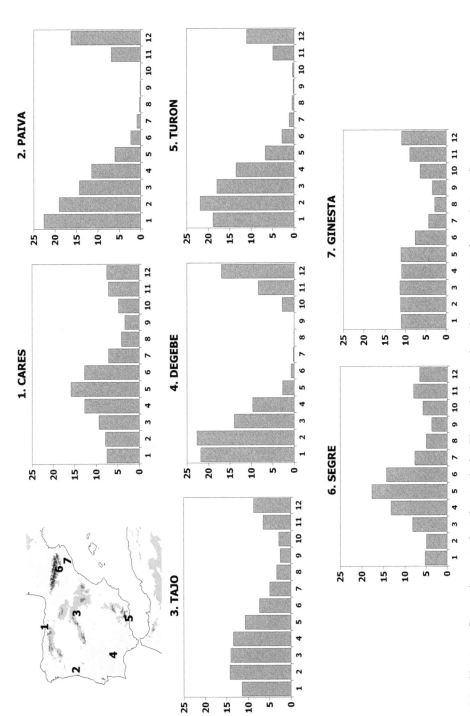

Figure 2.   Monthly streamflow regimes at selected watersheds.   The vertical axes show the percentage of annual streamflow.

average, after eliminating the trend associated with global warming; p is the response pattern to the radiative forcing (expressed in anomalies calculated from the baseline period 1961–1990, for each degree of change in global temperature); and t is the change in this global temperature (relative to the period 1961–1990). Of the four available models, two provided the most extreme scenarios: the warm and relatively humid Had3CM (Hadley Centre Coupled Model v3) and the coolest and driest PCM (National Centre for Atmospheric Research Parallel Climate Model). Regarding the emission scenarios, A2 and B2 were chosen, following the same considerations.

The hydrological model used calculates the different components of the water balance at monthly time scales, taking into account water inputs and outputs. The basic input parameters of the model are the monthly average temperature and total precipitation, along with latitude (for calculation of the length of the day). Since the high altitude of some mountain ranges of the Iberian Peninsula favours the accumulation of a deep and persistent snowpack, the hydrological model includes snowfall and snowpack retention coefficients which are activated when monthly temperature remains below a certain threshold. Such water retention is added to the surplus provided by the difference between precipitation and evapotranspiration when thaw takes place. Equally, a fraction of the precipitation fallen as rain, whose value oscillates around 5–10% (Wolock & McCabe, 1999), becomes runoff directly. The infiltration capability of the terrain was also modelled through specific runoff coefficients for each basin.

The reliability of the model in simulating streamflow values from several Iberian rivers was also assessed (Figure 3). The results, keeping in mind the simple representation of the complex hydrological processes by the model, and the use of reconstructed meteorological fields instead of actual ones, allow validation of the projections obtained, since they reproduce not only the hydrological regime (even snow-dominated rivers) but also their interannual variability. Only a tendency to underestimate the lowest river flows was detected.

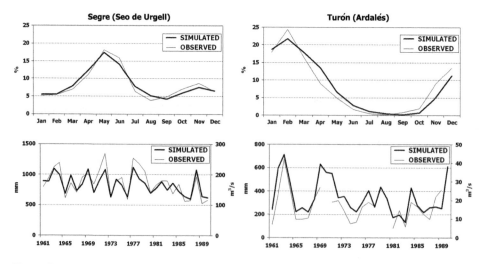

Figure 3. Inter-annual variability of observed and simulated streamflow from current climate conditions (1961–1990) at selected watersheds.

Results

Modifications in the water balance

The future evolution of temperatures on the Iberian Peninsula provided by the warmest and the coolest models under the two scenarios display increasing trends following different rhythms. The projections from the warmest model (Had3CM_A2) result in temperatures 8 °C warmer at the end of the twenty-first century, while 0.6 °C results from the coolest (PCM_B2). Most of this warming will affect the spring and the summer seasons (Figure 4).

Regarding precipitation, an agreement with respect to lower amounts exists among all scenarios and models, although some discrepancies arise for the total amount and its spatial and temporal distribution. As stated in the data section, the Had3CM model predicts the largest overall reduction, which ranges from 12% (B2) to 21% (A2). Such reduction displays a NW-SE spatial gradient, so the most dramatic reductions will affect the already driest areas of the Iberian Peninsula (Ebro Valley and La Mancha), which are isolated by mountains from Atlantic and Mediterranean moisture sources. Changes in spring and fall precipitation will cause the drying, with differences from the current values of 30% to 45% in April and May. On the contrary, winter precipitation will increase, even in the B2 scenario, with values around 10%. The spatial pattern resulting from the PCM model is quite similar, although reduction of the precipitation will remain below 70% in both emissions scenarios. As in the previous model, the southern regions will experience the largest reductions (Figure 5).

Potential evapotranspiration, derived from Hamon's (1961) formulation, clearly shows the effect of the intense warming, increasing in all models, although its magnitude differs with temperature. The values predicted by the PCM model are not very different from the current values, whilst outputs from Had3CM display a spectacular increment. Since the seasonal signal in temperature emphasizes the changes during the warm season, with winters remaining relatively moderate, it is in summer when the contrast between the current conditions and the expected ones will be most shocking (Figure 6). In the same way, dependence on the temperature increase determines a spatial pattern that focuses on

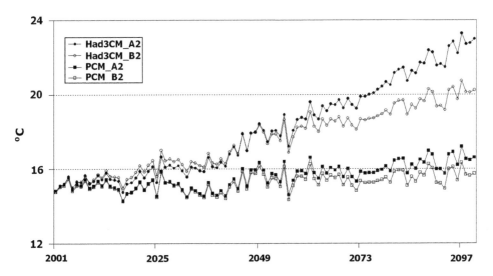

Figure 4.   Temperature evolution under the climate scenarios and models selected.

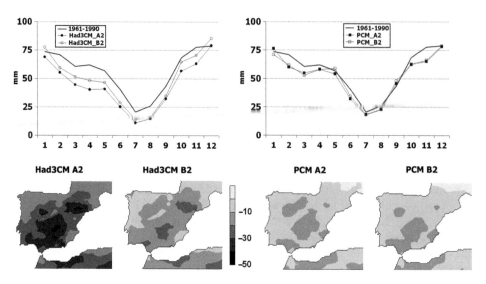

Figure 5. Temporal variability and spatial patterns of precipitation change. From left to right: Had3CM_A2, Had3CM_B2, PCM_A2 and PCM_B2.

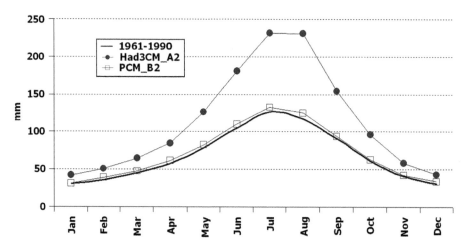

Figure 6. Monthly potential evapotranspiration changes averaged for the Iberian Peninsula.

the interior regions, such as the central Spanish Plateau (La Meseta) and the Guadalquivir and Ebro valleys (not shown).

Finally, reduction of precipitation and increase of potential evapotranspiration result in a significant and widespread reduction of runoff (Figure 7), more noticeable during the warm period and affecting those areas which currently enjoy the largest water surpluses, which are the mountains of the Iberian Peninsula. On this matter, it is worthy to keep in mind two issues. First, although it is possible to modify the water retention threshold in the hydrological model to reproduce different soils and lithologies, for the sake of simplicity a constant value of 150 mm was chosen (McCabe & Wolock, 1999). Secondly, only actual evapotranspiration takes part in the calculation of runoff, instead of potential

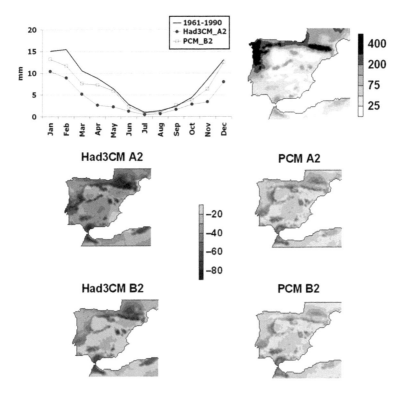

Figure 7. Monthly runoff changes averaged for the Iberian Peninsula (upper panel, left), current runoff on the Iberian Peninsula (upper panel right) and spatial patterns of runoff change: Had3CM_A2 (middle panel, left); Had3CM_B2 (lower panel, left); PCM_A2 (middle panel, right) and PCM_B2 (lower panel, right).

evapotranspiration. Currently, the annually averaged soil-moisture balance in most of the Iberian Peninsula is negative, due to the length of the warm and dry summer season.

In the Thornthwaite (1948) monthly water-balance, actual evapotranspiration is derived from potential evapotranspiration, total precipitation, soil-moisture storage, and soil-moisture storage withdrawal. When total precipitation for a month is less than potential evapotranspiration, then actual evapotranspiration is equal to total precipitation plus the amount of soil moisture that can be withdrawn from storage in the soil. As the soil becomes progressively drier as the dry period advaces, water becomes more difficult to remove from the soil and less is available for actual evapotranspiration.

Impacts on streamflow

The regional picture of the global trends on each model and scenario, combined with the local geographical factors (fundamentally, the altitude of each basin), explains the diversity of hydrological responses to global warming across the Iberian Peninsula (Figure 8). Besides, in general, as is predictable from the general picture offered earlier, projections from Had3CM outputs point towards more radical transformations than those obtained from PCM, although all of them predict a substantial reduction of annual streamflow.

In rain-driven basins, located at low altitudes, the current streamflow regime will hardly be modified, since precipitation will incorporate quickly into the system, as happens today.

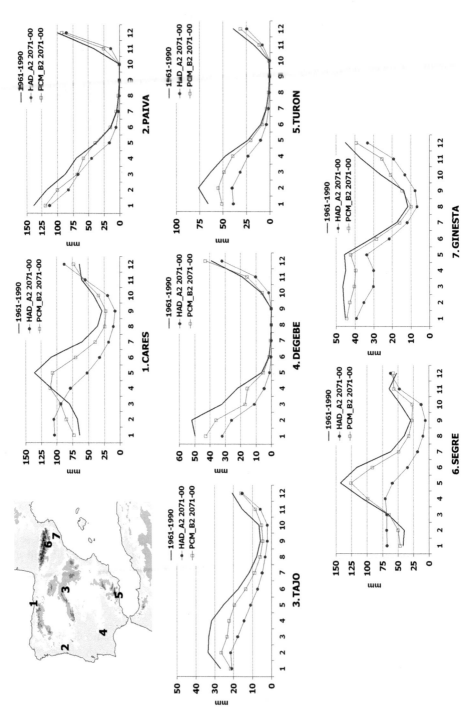

Figure 8.   Monthly streamflow regimes by watershed under current and future climate conditions following the most extreme model outputs.

This pattern is most conspicuous in the Atlantic rivers (e.g. Paiva and Degebe), since they rely only on winter precipitation, whose amounts, as described in the previous section, will remain similar to current ones. Rivers in the Mediterranean Basin, however, will probably suffer a reduction of spring and fall streamflow, mostly due to the decrease of precipitation during those seasons. Nevertheless, in all of them, the temperature increase, and consequently, the greater summer evapotranspiration, will extend the low-water months, which will begin earlier (May) and last longer (up to November). At higher altitudes, global warming will replace snowfall with rain, so the persistence and depth of the snowpack will lessen. For example, some rivers in basins located in mid-altitude mountain ranges, such as the Tajo River at Peralejos de las Truchas, display an annual maximum usually in March or even April, which is a signal of the relevance of snow-driven processes; in the future, this maximum will come earlier. As the altitude of the basins increases, the modification of the seasonal cycle will intensify, as can be detected in the Cares River, whose mixed snow-and-rain annual maximum in May will be replaced by one in late winter. Only in watersheds located deep in the mountains, such as Segre, in the Pyrenees, will the role of the snowpack in shaping the annual streamflow regime persist in the future, although clearly attenuated.

Although we acknowledge that the monthly time scale is not useful for analyzing extreme events (i.e. flooding and droughts), an attempt was made to predict possible changes in their occurrence. For example, the probability of occurrence of monthly streamflows was compared with those resulting from each simulation. In general, a reduction of the intermediate probabilities is the most extended impact on all rivers, due to the reduction of average streamflow levels (lower water surpluses and longer periods of low river flow). However, the persistence of similar rainfall and mild temperatures in winter seems to lead to analogous probability of extreme events in Atlantic basins, especially those located at low altitudes (Figure 9).

A comparison was made between the current probability of monthly very low streamflows (using the 5th percentile as a proxy index of hydrological drought) and their occurrence in the Had3CM B2 model output. Today, as expected in the Mediterranean climate of the region, most periods of very low streamflow occur in summer, the majority between July and September. In the future, even under a relatively benign scenario such as the Had3CM B2 output, it is clear that periods that we will classify today as drought will be more prevalent, with respect to both intensity and length (Figure 10).

Changes in the hydrological system affect the whole envelope of distribution in basins located at higher altitudes. Paradoxically, this striking change will not lead to a reduction of flooding risk in the future; again, the maintenance of winter episodes of precipitation and a new temperature baseline are likely to lead to further destabilization of the mountain snowpack, unexpected and sudden thaws being possible at daily time scales, driving large floods.

Snowpack is a fundamental component of the hydrological cycle in the mountains of northern Spain, where it becomes a natural 'swamp' that in spring progressively liberates the precipitation accumulated during winter. The fraction of solid precipitation increases progressively with the height of the basin (López-Moreno & García-Ruiz, 2004); its immediate hydrological consequence is a delay of maximum river flows to late spring and early summer. Although the analysis of the impact of global warming on the dynamics of the snowpack in the Spanish mountains is beyond the scope of this paper and the capabilities of the hydrological model used (López-Moreno, Goyette, & Beniston, 2008, 2009), it is possible to offer some expected trends in the evolution of the winter snowpack in the Iberian Peninsula in the light of the results of the climate models. However, it is necessary to remark that the outcome of the hydrological model does not provide real

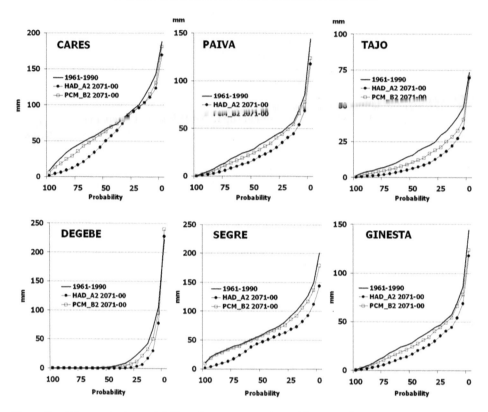

Figure 9. Changes in the probability of occurrence of monthly streamflow amounts by watershed under current and future climate conditions following the most extreme model outputs.

snow thickness; it simply reproduces the fraction of water accumulated as snow, without any additional consideration of increases in snow density or other physical processes associated with snowpack dynamics. However, as global warming progresses, a gradual reduction of the quantity and persistence of the snow cover in the mountains is expected, and this phenomenon will also lead to a progressive advance in the timing of the maximum accumulation (currently March; February in the output from PCM B2; January in Had3CM A2) (Figure 11).

Impacts on urban fresh-water consumption

It is considered that an index of domestic water consumption (measured in litres per capita per day, LCD) is one of best indicators of human well-being, since it accounts for not only the people's requirements but also their level of economic and social development. Diverse reports of the European Environment Agency point out that, currently, conditions of high water stress, which have been recurrent in southern Europe, are beginning to be frequent in northern Europe. Studies carried out in the alpine mountain range show that the increase in temperature during the last century (estimated at 1.4 °C, twice the global average) has caused an important retreat of the glaciers. The upward displacement of the limit of the perpetual snow fields might present a severe threat for the storage and distribution of almost 40% of the fresh water supply in Europe (EEA, 2010). For Spain, a relatively benign scenario (8% reduction in precipitation and temperature increase of 2.5

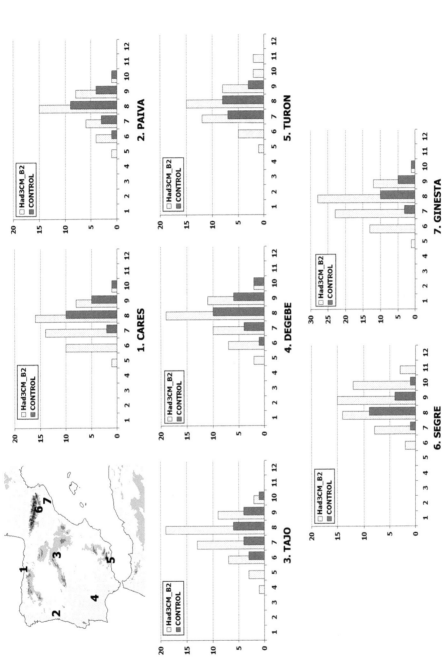

Figure 10. Percentage of occurrence of very low monthly streamflow values (< 5th percentile of the current 1961–1990) under current and future climate conditions under the HadCM B2 scenario. The units on the vertical axes of the graphs represent the percentage of occurrence.

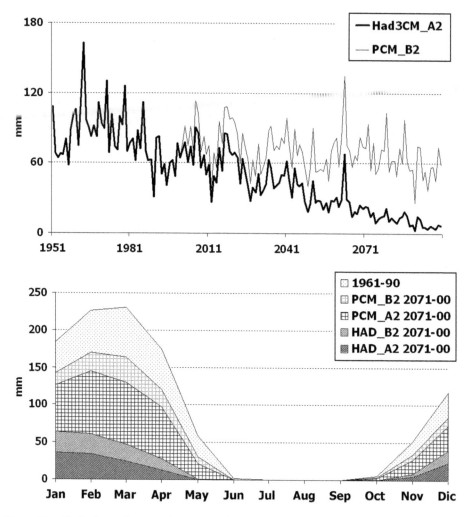

Figure 11. Projections of snow water content for different climate scenarios, corresponding to the Segre watershed.

°C) would reduce water resources by approximately 17% (Ayala-Carcedo & Iglesias, 2001; CEDEX, 1998; MARM, 2005).

The consequences of the decrease in water availability will have unequal effects on human activities and European regions, but in every case it will necessitate an important effort of adaptation to the new conditions. Agrarian activity seems to lead the implementation of relevant changes in their current procedures, as it is the largest water consumer, representing on average 40% of the total water consumption in Europe, although in Mediterranean countries, like Spain, it represents 60–80% (EEA, 2010; INE, 2008). As an example of its relevance, Spain retains water management structures inherited from the Middle Ages: the *Tribunal de las Aguas de Valencia*. Nevertheless, urban water supply also withdraws a significant fraction of the water resources. Average values for Europe are approximately one-third, while urban consumption in Spain is only 12% of the total. Finally, industrial activities account for the rest of the water demands, representing a fifth part in Europe, while in Spain they represent 10% (EEA, 2009, 2010; INE, 2008).

Adapting to the coming water stress conditions will not be an easy task. It will demand economic, social and technical measures beyond the frontiers of each country. In some countries, urban demand might represent an important obstacle, because of complex cultural and perception assumptions with respect to the basis of the progressive increase in water consumption and the simultaneous requirement of investments in infrastructure. In agrarian societies, the urban demands of water remained in the background, restricted to basic personal supply (toileting, feeding) and livestock cleaning and watering.

Nevertheless, the population's gradual concentration in urban nuclei demands a more sophisticated water supply system, growing at the same pace as urban habitation. In Roman times, water supply infrastructure was based on the construction of aqueducts and canals, afterwards reinforced by the opening of wells and public drinking fountains, sometimes reinforced with water carriers. Nevertheless, such systems have become obsolete, and Spanish historical documentation from medieval and modern times offers examples of local authorities' initiatives to improve the water supply, which has been estimated to be between 5 and 10 LCD in those times.

The industrialization of the nineteenth century improved the population's purchasing power, increasing water demands. Besides this, the spread of hygienic proposals amongst the population made between 100 and 120 LCD the indispensable quantity of water for human consumption. Nevertheless, this quantity was reached only at the end of the century in a few cities; for example, in Madrid the average water supply rose from 15 LCD in 1833 to 121 LCD in 1890; in Barcelona this was 80 LCD (1895), and only 70 LCD in San Sebastian (1880) (Matés Barco, 1999).

During the twentieth century, water consumption increased exponentially, developing an unsustainable scenario of strong water stress, but after the beginning of the twenty-first century this situation gradually reversed. A growing sector of the population has become aware of the serious problems that continuing water consumption would generate in the near future, and that new perception supported a new set of educational and adaptive measures for the new scenarios of water supply (MARM, 2006, 2011). As a result of this new paradigm, water consumption in Spain has begun to decrease, starting in 2003–2004, although in some regions the decrease began at the end of the 1990s. For example, in Zaragoza the new policies of water sustainability begun in 1996–1997, being extended through diverse projects (SWITCH, 2011) whose fundamental objective was to achieve efficient water use. Similar plans have been designed for Madrid and for Barcelona, which enjoys one of the lowest water consumptions per capita in Europe in the last two years (107.4 LCD in 2009) (Figure 12). It is worth mentioning that water efficiency is a concept relying on different thresholds. For example, the World Health Organization considers 100 LCD the minimum quantity that satisfies the basic necessities of consumption (food and drink preparation and conservation) and hygiene of a population and supports agricultural and industrial activities as well as the preservation of fresh-water ecosystems. Nevertheless, if only basic needs are considered (drinking consumption and hygiene), the estimated value drops to 50 LCD (Howard & Bartram, 2003), which was the rate of water consumption during the ninteenth century.

Although the water consumption evolution in Spain is decreasing (157 LCD in 2007), such value is far from those recommended values. Excessive water consumption is particularly serious in some regions like Extremadura, Valencia, and even in the northern regions such as Asturias and Cantabria, where it rises to 180 LCD. Cities like Santander maintain high consumption, perhaps because the public perception of the abundance of the

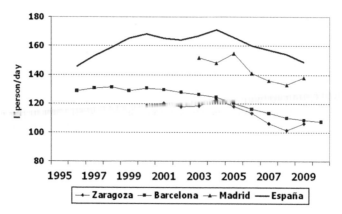

Figure 12.   Evolution of the water consumption in Spain and three cities (in l/person/day).

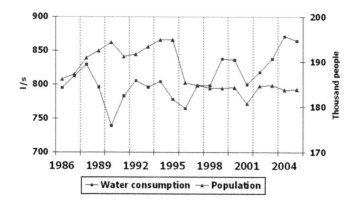

Figure 13.   Water consumption in the city of Santander (l/person/day), 1986–2005 (SEMAS, 2010).

resource ('green Spain') does not consider water shortages real, in spite of the recent occurrence of widespread water supply cut-offs. Such pressure has forced an increase in the exploitation of underground waters, so much so that occasionally the bed of the river which supplies most of the water has dried out, affecting the ecological flows (Figure 13).

Discussion and conclusions

The comparative analysis of the current situation of the water resources against the outputs of two climate models and two emission scenarios enables the prediction of some of the consequences of global warming over the Iberian Peninsula hydrological cycle. The magnitudes of the predicted impacts depend on the climate model and the emissions scenario, but in general, warming will involve a more contrasted hydrological cycle, driven by an increase in potential evapotranspiration, particularly in the warmest months in the year, and a reduction in annual precipitation, with drier springs and summers and slightly wetter winters. Consequently, surface runoff will decrease and be concentrated in the coolest months. Also, a spatial pattern of consequences will arise from those climate changes, because the mountain basins which are today dominated by snow will move to rain-dominated regimes.

Taking into account that most of the river flow data used in this work came from the upper and middle sectors of each watershed (to minimize human influences), the probable hydrological deficits will become worse downstream, where most of the urban, industrial and agricultural demands are located. There, water stress resulting from low water incomes will be boosted by additional water losses from enhanced *in situ* evaporation, thus putting underground water resources under pressure, a phenomenon repeated during recent droughts across Spain.

These tendencies will be exacerbated if the regional response to global warming is also manifested in changes in the frequency and intensity of circulation patterns, responsible in the last term for the interannual variability and occurrence of extreme hydroclimatic phenomena. In this sense, our analyses are limited by the fact that the databases do not contemplate such hypotheses. Finally, the future situation could be further modified by other phenomena linked to the recent socio-economic evolution of Spain and Portugal, such as changes in land use triggered by rural depopulation, which have not been taken into account in this paper (Beguería, López-Moreno, Seeger, & García-Ruiz, 2003). In conclusion, it is clear that the climate scenarios obtained from climate models force us to implement water demand reduction policies at national and international levels, and that such actions should be complemented by the development of efforts to educate the population looking for an increased public awareness about this topic.

References

Ayala-Carcedo, F. J., & Iglesias López, A. (2000). *Impactos del posible cambio climático sobre los recursos hídricos, el diseño y la planificación hidrológica en la España peninsular*. Madrid: El Campo de las Ciencias y las Artes.

Beguería, S., López-Moreno, J. I., Seeger, M., & García-Ruiz, J. M. (2003). Assessing the effects of climate oscillations and land-use changes on streamflow in the Central Spanish Pyrenees. *Ambio*, *32*, 283–286.

CEDEX (1998). *Estudio sobre el impacto potencial del cambio climático en los recursos hídricos y demandas de agua de riego en determinadas regiones de España* [Study of potential impacts of climate change in water resources and irrigation demands in several regions of Spain] (Technical report for the Ministry of Environment). Madrid: Ministerio de Medio Ambiente.

Chang, H., Knight, G., Staneva, M., & Kostov, D. (2002). Water resource impacts of climate change in southwestern Bulgaria. *Geojournal*, *57*(3), 159–168.

EEA (European Environment Agency) (2009). *Water resources across Europe: Confronting water scarcity and drought*, Retrieved from http://www.eea.europa.eu/publications/water-resources -across-europe.

EEA (2010). Los Alpes. Impacto actual del cambio climático en Europa *[The Alps. Current impact of climate change in Europe]*, In *Señales de la AEMA 2010. La biodiversidad, el cambio climático y tú*, (pp. 16–23). Madrid: European Environment Agency.

Hamon, W. R. (1961). Estimating potential evapotranspiration. *Journal of the Hydraulics Division, Proceedings of the American Society of Civil Engineers*, 87, 107–120.

Howard, G., & Bartram, J. (2003). *Domestic water quantity, service level and health* (WHO/SDE/WSH/03.02), OMS, Ginebra. Madrid: Instituto Nacional de Estadística.

INE (2008). *Estadísticas e indicadores del agua* [Statistics and water indices]. Madrid: Instituto Nacional de Estadística.

IPCC (2000). *Special report on emissions scenarios*. Cambridge, UK: Cambridge University Press.

IPCC (2007). *Climate change 2007: The physical science basis. Contribution of Working Group I to the Fourth Assessment Report of the Intergovernmental Panel on Climate Change*. Cambridge: Cambridge University Press.

Knight, G., Chang, H., Staneva, M., & Kostov, D. (2001). A simplified basin model for simulating runoff: The Struma River GIS. *Professional Geographer*, *53*, 533–545.

López-Moreno, J. I., & García-Ruiz, J. M. (2004). Influence of snow accumulation and snowmelt on streamflow in the Central Spanish Pyrenees. *International Journal of Hydrological Sciences, 49,* 787–802.

López-Moreno, J. I., Goyette, S., & Beniston, M. (2008). Climate change prediction over complex areas: Spatial variability of uncertainties and expected changes over the Pyrenees from a set of regional climate models. *International Journal of Climatology, 28,* 1535–1550.

Lopez-Moreno, J. I., Goyette, S., & Beniston, M. (2009). Impact of climate change on snowpack in the Pyrenees: Horizontal spatial variability and vertical gradients. *Journal of Hydrology, 374,* 384–396.

MARM (2005). *Evaluación Preliminar de los Impactos en España por Efecto del Cambio Climático* [Preliminary assesment of the impacts of climate change in Spain]. Madrid: Ministerio de Medio Ambiente y Medio Rural y Marino.

MARM (2006). *Plan Nacional de Adaptación al Cambio Climático* (PNACC) [National Plan for Adaptation to Climate Change]. Madrid: Ministerio de Medio Ambiente y Medio Rural y Marino, Oficina Española de Cambio Climático.

MARM (2011). *Evaluación del Impacto del Cambio Climático en los Recursos Hídricos en Régimen Natural* [Assesment of the impact of climate change on natural water resources]. Madrid: Ministerio de Medio Ambiente y Medio Rural y Marino, Gestión de la Dirección General del Agua – CEDEX.

Matés Barco, J. M. (1999). *La conquista del agua. Historia económica del abastecimiento urbano* [The conquest of water. A story of urban water supply]. Jaén: Universidad de Jaén.

Mather, J. R. (1978). *The climatic water balance in environmental analysis.* Lexington, MA: Heath and Company.

McCabe, G. J., & Wolock, D. M. (1999). Future snowpack conditions in the western United States derived from general circulation model climate simulations. *Journal of the American Water Resources Association, 35,* 1473–1484.

Mitchell, T., Carter, T., Jones, P., Hulme, M., & New, M. (2004). *A comprehensive set of high-resolution grids of monthly climate for Europe and the globe: The observed record (1901–2000) and 16 scenarios (2001–2100)* (Working Paper No. 55), Tyndall Centre for Climate Change Research. Retrieved from http://www.tyndall.ac.uk/sites/default/files/wp55.pdf

New, M. G., Lister, D., Hulme, M., & Makin, I. (2002). A high-resolution data set of surface climate for terrestrial land areas. *Climate Research, 21,* 1–25.

SEMAS (2010). *Captaciones tomadas para Santander (1983–2005).* Santander: Ayuntamiento de Santander, Servicio Municipalizado de Agua y Saneamiento.

SWITCH (2011). Managing water for the city of the future. Retrieved from http://www.switchurbanwater.eu/

Thornthwaite, C. W. (1948). An approach toward a rational classification of climate. *Geographical Review, 38,* 55–94.

Wolock, D. M., & McCabe, G. J. (1999). Effects of potential climatic change on annual runoff in the conterminous United States. *Journal of the American Water Resources Association, 35,* 1341–1350.

Downscaled climate change projections over Spain: application to water resources

P. Ramos[a], E. Petisco[b], J.M. Martín[b] and E. Rodríguez[b]

[a]*Delegación Territorial en Andalucía, Ceuta y Melilla, Agencia Estatal de Meteorología (AEMET), Sevilla, Spain;* [b]*Servicios Centrales, Agencia Estatal de Meteorología (AEMET), Madrid, Spain*

Evaluation of impacts, vulnerability and adaptation to climate change for sectors sensitive to climate conditions requires climate change projections with adequate resolution, both spatial and temporal. These projections are affected by uncertainties coming from a number of sources. The probabilistic approach is the natural framework for integrating uncertainties of diverse origin in the estimation of climate evolution. Two state-of-the-art data-sets are presented, providing downscaled climate change projections over Spain based on ensembles of projections for a variety of emission scenarios, global models and downscaling techniques. Results are applied to the Spanish region of Aragón as an example of the estimation of mean and extreme precipitation changes for the twenty-first century and their uncertainty.

Introduction and framework

Climate change is probably one of the most serious problems – perhaps the most serious – that mankind faces. The United Nations secretary general, Ban Ki-Moon, in his opening remarks to the UN Climate Change Summit Plenary (September 2009), stated that "climate change is the pre-eminent geopolitical and economic issue of the twenty-first century" (United Nations, 2009). It is also an extraordinarily difficult issue, given the complex network of anthropogenic drivers, impacts of and responses to climate change and their linkages. To make the problem even more complicated, political actions addressing climate change have to take into consideration other closely related challenges in the socio-economic domain, such as sustainable development and equity issues.

In 1992, most countries joined an international treaty – the United Nations Framework Convention on Climate Change (UNFCCC, see http://www.unfccc.int) – to begin to consider what can be done to reduce global warming and to cope with whatever temperature increases are inevitable. The Framework Convention on Climate Change sets up an overall framework for intergovernmental efforts to tackle the challenge posed by climate change. It recognizes that the climate system is a shared resource whose stability can be affected by emissions of carbon dioxide and other greenhouse gases (GHG). The convention entered into force on 21 March 1994. In December 1997 a number of nations adopted an addition to the treaty, the Kyoto Protocol, which included more powerful (and legally binding) measures and which entered into force in February 2005 (United Nations, 1998). The major feature of the Kyoto Protocol is that it sets binding targets for 37 industrialized countries and the European community with respect to reducing GHG emissions. These amount to an average of 5% against 1990 levels over the five-year period 2008–2012. The major distinction between the protocol and the convention is that while the convention encouraged industrialized countries to stabilize GHG emissions, the protocol commits them to doing so. Recognizing that developed countries are principally responsible for the current high levels of GHG emissions in the atmosphere, as a result of more than 150 years of industrial activity, the protocol places a heavier burden on developed nations under the principle of "common but differentiated responsibilities".

Once the problem and the consequences of climate change are recognized, different parallel lines of action can be followed in response to it. Firstly, one should act directly on the causes of climate change. Given that the warming of the climate system is very probably caused by the steady increase of atmospheric concentrations of GHG since the beginning of the industrial era, mitigation strategies must be pursued aimed at reducing GHG emissions and expanding and enhancing carbon sinks. Secondly, as there is an already committed warming due to past emissions and to the large inertia of the climate system, one should address the effects of climate change by adapting the different ecosystems and socio-economic sectors that are sensitive to climatic conditions to the new situation. Finally, other instruments, such as development and adoption of new technologies and financial tools, can help to address the problem. The UN Climate Change Conference held in Bali, Indonesia, in December 2007, placed at the same level, for the first time, mitigation and adaptation as the key building blocks of a successful fight against climate change. A good knowledge of the physical basis of climate change, including observations and downscaled scenario projections, is the very first step in studying the impacts it has on different sectors and the subsequent planning of adaptation. This paper describes some examples of downscaled scenario projections for the particular case of Spain, with a focus on their application to water resources management.

Due to the high complexity of the climate change issue, policymakers need an objective source of information about the causes of climate change, its potential environmental and socio-economic consequences, and the adaptation and mitigation options for responding to it. To meet this need, the World Meteorological Organization (WMO) and the United Nations Environment Programme (UNEP) established the Intergovernmental Panel on Climate Change (IPCC) in 1988. The IPCC does not conduct research or monitor climate-related data or parameters. Rather, its role is to assess, on a comprehensive, objective, open and transparent basis, the latest scientific, technical and socio-economic literature produced worldwide that is relevant to the understanding of the risk of human-induced climate change, its observed and projected impacts and the options for adaptation and mitigation. IPCC reports should be neutral with respect to policy, although they need to deal objectively with policy-related scientific, technical and socio-economic factors. They should adhere to high scientific and technical standards, and aim to reflect a range of views, expertise and wide geographical coverage. The IPCC provides its reports at regular intervals, and they immediately become standard works of reference, widely used by policymakers, experts and students (see http://www.ipcc.ch for more detailed information on the IPCC organization and its reports).

At the Spanish national level, one cornerstone of the institutional response to climate change is the National Climate Change Adaptation Plan (PNACC in Spanish) (Ministerio de Medio Ambiente y Medio Rural y Marino, 2008). This programme was adopted in October 2006 after endorsement by the Cabinet of Ministers. The PNACC is the reference framework tool for the coordination of public administrations' efforts dealing with the assessment of impacts of, vulnerability to and adaptation to climate change in the Spanish sectors acknowledged as potentially affected – water management being the sector first cited in the documents due to its paramount role among the Spanish activity sectors. The National Adaptation Plan provides tools for the elaboration of diagnosis analyses and the development of more efficient measures for adaptation. One of the first activities carried out to facilitate the development of the PNACC is to prepare a series of regional climate change scenarios for Spain throughout the twenty-first century. The scenarios estimate the possible features of the climate in the future and they serve as a reference to prepare specific impact and vulnerability assessments for different ecological, economic and social sectors and systems. The said scenarios are built from global climate models that are adapted to the particular features of this country. For this purpose, downscaling techniques are applied so as to incorporate regional physiographic characteristics (topography, vegetation, coastline, etc.). Generation of regional climate change scenarios is one of the fundamental starting points in assessing impacts of, vulnerability to and future needs with respect to adaptation to climate change. Thus, one of the challenges faced by this plan is to have sufficient operational capacity, continuously progressing, to carry out the production of the successive scenarios at a regional level (Ministerio de Medio Ambiente y Medio Rural y Marino, 2008).

The paper is organized as follows. The next section presents the tools for generating downscaled climate change projections. The third section discusses the uncertainties affecting climate projections and the probabilistic approach used to cope with them. The fourth section is the central part of the paper. It provides first a brief overview of the recent evolution of temperature and precipitation over peninsular Spain, with special emphasis on precipitation because it is more relevant for water management purposes. It also presents the projected evolution of both variables, focusing, as an example, on the region of Aragón. The needs of the water management sector with respect to climate change projections and the features of currently available projections are discussed in the fifth section. Some conclusions, perspectives and recommendations are outlined in the final section.

Climate models and downscaling algorithms

Climate models are numerical representations of the climate system based on the physical, chemical and biological properties of its components and their interactions and feedback processes. Different climate models constitute multiple realizations of the climate system based on computer programs. Climate models are differentiated by which approximations and discretizations are used to solve the mathematical equations that represent physics, chemistry and biology. Although climate models (also known as Atmosphere-Ocean Coupled General Circulation Models, AOGCM) are conceived as a simplified image of the climate system, they are expected to account for its more relevant features. There is currently a considerable confidence in the simulations provided by climate models because model principles are based on well-established physical laws, such as conservation of mass, energy and momentum. An additional source of confidence is their ability to simulate important aspects of current and past climates, as well as their changes (Randall et al., 2007). The climate system includes a variety of physical processes, such as cloud, radiative and boundary-layer processes, which interact with each other on many temporal and spatial scales. Due to the limited resolutions of the models, many of these processes are not resolved adequately by the model and must therefore be parameterized.

State-of-the-art climate models have resolutions ranging from 150 to 300 km. To accommodate projections produced by global climate models to regional or even local features, a variety of downscaling techniques can be applied. These techniques can be grouped into two approaches: statistical algorithms and nested regional climate modelling. Each approach has its strengths and weaknesses. Although climate change projections must necessarily be undertaken with global models, such models will never have sufficient spatial detail for all applications, given the limited availability of computing resources.

Statistical (also called empirical) downscaling is based on the idea that regional climate may be thought of as being conditioned by two factors: the large-scale climatic state and regional/local physiographic features (e.g. topography, land-sea distribution and land use). From this point of view, regional or local climate information is derived by first determining a statistical relationship between large-scale climate variables (or predictors) and local variables (or predictands) based on present-day climate. Then the predictors from a future climate simulation produced by a global model and the previously obtained statistical relationship are used to estimate the corresponding future local climate characteristics. A range of statistical downscaling models, from regressions to neural networks and analogues, have been developed for regions where sufficiently good data-sets are available for model calibration. One of the primary advantages of these techniques is that they are computationally inexpensive and thus can be easily applied to the output of different global models. Another advantage is that they can be used to provide local information, which can be most needed in many climate change impact applications. The major theoretical weakness of statistical downscaling methods is that their basic assumption is not verifiable – that is, that the statistical relationships developed for present-day climate also hold under the different forcing conditions of possible future climates. In addition, the data needed for the development of statistical relationships may not be readily available in certain regions. Another caveat is that these empirically based techniques cannot account for possible systematic changes in regional forcing conditions or feedback processes (Wilby et al., 2004).

Dynamical downscaling is based on the use of nested regional climate models (RCM) driven by time-dependent lateral meteorological conditions and surface boundary conditions provided by global models. RCMs account for smaller-scale forcings not resolved by global models (e.g. complex topographical features and land-cover inhomogeneity) in a physically based way. RCMs can currently provide high resolution (up to 10 to 20 km) and multi-decadal simulations and are capable of describing climate feedback mechanisms acting at the regional scale. A number of widely used limited-area modelling systems have been adapted to, or developed for, climate application. More recently, RCMs have begun to couple atmospheric models with other climate process models, such as hydrology, ocean, sea-ice, chemistry/aerosol and land-biosphere models. Two main theoretical limitations of this technique are the effects of systematic errors in the driving fields provided by global models, and the lack of two-way interactions between the regional and the global climate. Depending on the domain size and resolution, RCM simulations can be computationally demanding, which has limited the length of many experiments to date (Mearns et al., 2003).

Both downscaling approaches should be viewed as complementary, each approach having distinctive strengths and weaknesses. The IPCC (2001, 2007) concludes that both methods are comparable for simulating current climate. No single downscaling method is superior to the others for all regions, variables and seasons (Haylock, Cawley, Harpham, Wilby, & Goodess, 2006). Therefore, a variety of downscaling methods should be applied to explore the uncertainties coming from the generation of downscaled projections. In almost all forms of downscaling today, the coarse-scale conditions given by the GCM are taken as fixed. However, this does not reflect the reality of the real climate system, in which there are feedbacks between coarse and fine scales. This is a limitation of statistical downscaling schemes, but of course it applies equally to RCMs (Wilby et al., 2004).

Probabilistic downscaled climate change projections

The process of generating climate change projections is characterized by inherent uncertainty coming from a number of sources. Uncertainty in predictions of anthropogenic climate change arises hierarchically in all steps towards a climate downscaled projection (Mitchell & Hulme, 1999). Given our lack of predictive capacity for changes in solar irradiation (apart from the 11-year cycle) and for volcanic eruptions, this natural forcing is the very first source of uncertainty. The specification of future emissions of GHGs, aerosols and their precursors is also highly uncertain. Different scenarios are alternative and plausible images of how the future might unfold and are an appropriate tool for analyzing how driving forces may influence future emission outcomes and assessing the associated uncertainties.

In addition, for a given emissions scenario, various biogeochemical models are used to calculate concentrations of constituents in the atmosphere and explore this source of uncertainty. Various radiation schemes and parameterizations are required to convert these concentrations to radiative forcing. The response of the different climate system components, such as the atmosphere, ocean, sea ice, land surface, or chemical status of atmosphere and ocean, is calculated in a comprehensive climate model. The formulation of and interaction with the carbon cycle in climate models also introduces important feedbacks, which produce additional uncertainties. Uncertainty in the true signal of climate change is introduced both by errors in the representation of Earth system processes in models and by internal climate variability. The effects of internal variability can be quantified by running models many times from different initial conditions, provided that simulated variability is consistent with observations. The effects of uncertainty in the knowledge of Earth system processes can be partially quantified by constructing ensembles of models that sample different parameterizations of these processes (Meehl et al., 2007). However, some processes may be missing from the set of available models, and alternative parameterizations of other processes may share common systematic biases. Since the ensemble based on a set of available models is strictly an 'ensemble of opportunity', without sampling protocol, the spread of models does not necessarily span the full possible range of uncertainty, and a statistical interpretation of the model spread is therefore problematic.

The IPCC recognizes the existence of uncertainties not contemplated by climate projections based on multi-model simulations (Meehl et al., 2007). This is the case of uncertainties coming from feedbacks in processes, such as e.g. carbon cycle and vegetation, not fully coupled in most AOGCMs, which are responsible for additional sampling of model uncertainties. The use of very large ensembles with multiple options for parameterization schemes and parameter values has shown that the sampling of projections based on the standard multi-model approach applied by the Fourth Assessment Report (AR4) of the IPCC is somehow restrictive and cannot span the full range of plausible model configurations (Murphy et al., 2004; Stainforth et al., 2005). Only large ensembles of AOGCM projections sampling the widest possible range of modelling uncertainties can provide a reliable specification of the spread of possible regional changes. The crucial problem of knowing how well model uncertainties are sampled with the standard multi-model approach still remain. Finally, downscaling methods add another factor of uncertainty in regional climate change which should be explored using different downscaling techniques (Haylock et al., 2006; Huth, 2004).

Integration of all available information on climate change projections coming from different sources into a probabilistic view of climate evolution constitutes a challenge for those groups involved in climate change impact and adaptation studies, and in particular for research on the impact on water management under climate change. Successive IPCC assessment reports have served to provide a set of climate change projections for alternative emission scenarios. Research projects such as PRUDENCE and ENSEMBLES (Dequé et al., 2007; van der Linden & Mitchell, 2009) have produced a valuable set of climate change projections which have also helped to explore uncertainties coming mainly from the selection of emission scenarios, AOGCMs, downscaling algorithms and initial conditions. To optimize the probabilistic approach, all information available coming from a variety of projects should be integrated in a mega-ensemble better able to sample the space of uncertainties in the spirit of projects such as climateprediction.net (see http://climateprediction.net/) for generating climate projections based on perturbed physics or TIGGE (see http://tigge.ecmwf.int/) for weather prediction up to two weeks out. No source of information should be neglected.

The probabilistic estimation of climate change projections at the regional scale combines two essential ingredients: (1) the need to explore the uncertainties coming from a variety of sources in an optimal way, and (2) the need to downscale scenario projections generated by global climate models. Of course, the sample of scenarios, projections and downscaling algorithms must be large enough to guarantee an adequate representation of the entire population by a realistic probability distribution function (PDF). The IPCC in its assessment reports has mainly explored uncertainties of climate change evolution coming from future GHG and aerosol emissions (using a limited set of scenarios) and from AOGCM (using an ensemble of 23 members in AR4).

Observed and projected climate change over Spain

Spain, occupying approximately 85% of the Iberian Peninsula (IP), is located in south-western Europe between parallels 36°N and 44°N (see Figure 1). Its location, complex orography, great extension (491,517 km^2) and long coastline (4865 km) produce a mosaic of climates (Mediterranean, Atlantic, continental Mediterranean, arid, semiarid and mountain, among others), with predominance of the Mediterranean climate, characterized by dry summers and wet winters. A consequence of such climate variety is the high space and time variability of rainfall over Spain. Mean annual precipitation varies from around 300 mm in south-eastern Spain to up to 1800 mm in the north-western part of the country (Agencia Estatal de Meteorología & Instituto de Meteorologia, 2011).

The region of Aragón, located in the north-eastern IP, with an extension of 47,719 km^2, also has strong climatic contrasts mainly due to differences in topography. Although Aragón's climate can be defined as continental moderate, temperatures are determined mainly by altitude, ranging from cold or very cold in winter and cool in summer in the mountains to the north (Pyrenees) and to the south and west (Iberian range), to mild in winter and hot in summer in the central lowlands crossed by the Ebro River. Rainfall is also highly variable, with very low mean values in the Ebro valley and increasingly higher values in mountain areas, especially in the high Pyrenees.

Observed temperature and precipitation over Spain

While observed temperature increased during the twentieth century, the warming trend has been strongest in the most recent period (up to 0.5 °C/decade from 1973 to 2005).

Figure 1.   Location of Spain and the Aragon region.

In contrast, no widespread precipitation decline has been observed in the IP during the twentieth century (Bladé & Castro-Díez, 2010). Seasonal analyses using century-long series show no clear seasonal trends for precipitation. However, since mid-twentieth century the trend is notably negative (– 13.2 mm per decade). Since 1951 there has been a statistically significant negative trend (– 3.3 mm per decade) in the summer season (Luna, Guijarro, & López, 2012). The large natural inter-annual variability and the short length of the instrumental record complicate detection and interpretation of possible trends. Except for the south-eastern Mediterranean coast, the daily precipitation rate has decreased in the last 50 years, the number of days with small rainfall amounts (below the 5th percentile) has increased, and the number of days with large amounts (above the 95th percentile) has decreased (Bladé & Castro-Díez, 2010).

Climate change projections over Spain

With respect to climate change projections, there exists a wealth of information on downscaled projections over Spain coming from the Coupled Model Intercomparison Projects (CMIP) feeding IPCC reports, projects within the European Framework Programmes such as PRUDENCE (Christensen & Christensen, 2007; Déqué et al., 2005, 2007), ENSEMBLES (van der Linden & Mitchell, 2009), STARDEX (Goodess, 2009), etc., and Spanish national projects currently under development such as ESCENA (http://www.meteo.unican.es/en/projects/escena) and ESTCENA (http://www.meteo.unican.es/en/projects/estcena). In addition, the Spanish State Meteorological Agency (AEMET) routinely generates downscaled climate change projections as part of its climate services. As mentioned in the previous section, the challenge is to merge all available information to get a true probabilistic picture of the evolution of variables describing the climate. This evolution should estimate not only average values but also extremes and uncertainties.

Some examples of downscaled climate change projections with estimation of uncertainties computed for Spain and exemplified for the region of Aragón are presented in this section. The projections refer not only to mean values but also to some extremes, which are highly relevant for impact studies.

Data

We present here two different sets of downscaled climate change projections available from AEMET (http://escenarios.aemet.es/), sharing one important feature: in both cases they are based on an ensemble including a number of members sufficient to explore and provide an idea of the uncertainty we have to cope with when applying climate change projections to water resources management.

The first ensemble of climate change projections (STAT_ANALOGUE) makes use of all the global climate models available from the CMIP3 and ENSEMBLES projects. Downscaling of the projections is conducted by an empirical algorithm based on analogues making use of a set of 2324 precipitation and 374 temperature stations covering reasonably well the entire Spanish territory (Petisco de Lara, 2008a, 2008b). Only models with availability of daily data on the predictors needed were used. The main merit of this ensemble of downscaled climate projections is the comprehensiveness of the available data, both on observations and on global model simulations, to provide the best estimation of uncertainties coming both from global models and from emission scenarios. Three IPCC

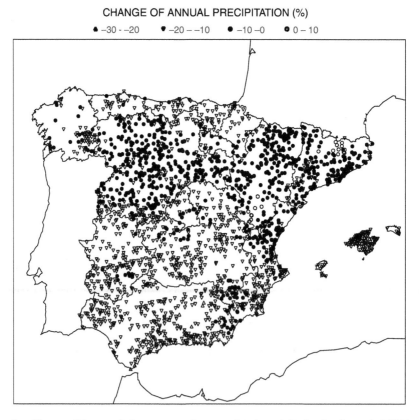

Figure 2.   Change of downscaled mean annual accumulated precipitation for the period 2081–2100 with respect to the reference period 1961–2000 for A1B SRES emission scenario (from STAT_ANALOGUE data-set). Each point in the map corresponds to the average of 19 AOGCMs from CMIP3 and ENSEMBLES projects.

emission scenarios (frequently referred as SRES scenarios (IPCC, 2000) were explored: A2 (high emissions), A1B (intermediate emissions) and B1 (low emissions). Additionally, an aggressive mitigation scenario (E1) consistent with the target of avoiding more than 2°C of global average surface warming relative to pre-industrial levels was also explored (see more details at http://ensembles-eu.metoffice.com/docs/Ensembles_final_report_Nov09.pdf). The four emissions scenarios were sampled with 11, 19, 13 and 4 different global models, respectively.

The second ensemble of climate change projections (DYN_ENSEMBLES) makes use of the already downscaled projections generated in the ENSEMBLES project (van der Linden & Mitchell, 2009). The original fields (from the ENSEMBLES RT3 data archive, http://ensemblesrt3.dmi.dk/) were interpolated to a common grid using a nearest-neighbour method to reduce impact on extreme values (Brunet et al., 2008). These projections, with 25 km horizontal resolution, have been generated for the A1B SRES (intermediate emissions) scenario by 11 different climate regional models forced by several global models.

Projections over Spain and the region of Aragón

Figure 2 represents the change of downscaled mean annual accumulated precipitation over peninsular Spain for the period 2081–2100 with respect to the reference period 1961–

UNCERTAINTY OF ANNUAL PRECIPITATION CHANGE (%)

▼   0 – 10   •   10 – 20   •   20 – 30

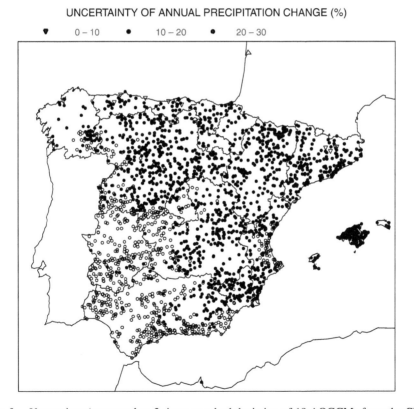

Figure 3.   Uncertainty (expressed as 2 times standard deviation of 19 AOGCMs from the CMIP3 and ENSEMBLES projects) of change of downscaled mean annual accumulated precipitation for the period 2081–2100 with respect to the reference period 1961–2000 for A1B SRES emission scenario (from STAT_ANALOGUE data-set).

2000 corresponding to the intermediate emission scenario A1B computed from the STAT_ANALOGUE data-set. Points on the map correspond to the stations to which global scale data were downscaled based on an empirical algorithm. Each point represents the average of 19 downscaled projections estimated from global climate models from the CMIP3 and ENSEMBLES projects. The northern half of the IP shows a trend of decrease in annual precipitation ranging between zero and 10%, while the southern half tends to a precipitation reduction ranging between 10% and 20%. This reduction is unevenly distributed among the year's seasons. The relatively large number of members of the ensemble of downscaled projections guarantees an acceptable and robust estimation of the average change and of the uncertainty linked to global model simulations. Differences in estimates provided by the 19 downscaled projections here considered allow quantification of the uncertainty coming from global climate models. Figure 3 shows an estimate of the global models' uncertainty expressed as twice the standard deviation of 19 downscaled projections. Most of the points show an uncertainty ranging between 10% and 20%, with higher values (20–30%) in the south-west IP.

Figures 4 and 5 show the evolution of maximum annual mean temperature and annual accumulated precipitation, respectively, for the Spanish region of Aragón, based on information from the same STAT_ANALOGUE data-set. In both figures, the mean value and an estimate of the uncertainty coming from the global models and from the emission scenarios are represented. The uncertainty coming from the global models is expressed as a band of $\pm$ one standard deviation over all global models around the mean value. The uncertainty coming from the emission scenario is represented using different colours for the four alternative emission scenarios. The uncertainty band coming only from global

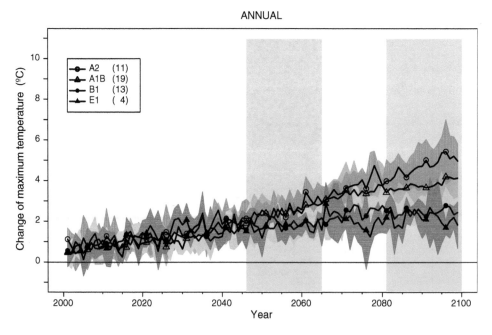

Figure 4. Change of downscaled maximum temperature from STAT_ANALOGUE data-set with respect to the reference period 1961–2000 averaged over all stations in the region of Aragon for four emission scenarios. Thick solid line represents the average over all global models considered for each emission scenario. The shaded band depicts the uncertainty expressed as $\pm$ one standard deviation around the mean value.

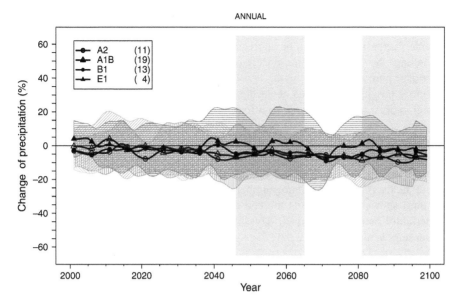

Figure 5.   The same as Figure 3, but for annual accumulated precipitation smoothed with a 10-point Gaussian filter.

models easily reaches 2 °C for maximum temperature at the end of the twenty-first century for a given emission scenario, while for annual accumulated precipitation the uncertainty band easily reaches 20% for the same conditions. This last uncertainty changes greatly along the year. The Figure 6 panel shows that, in percentage terms, the biggest uncertainty

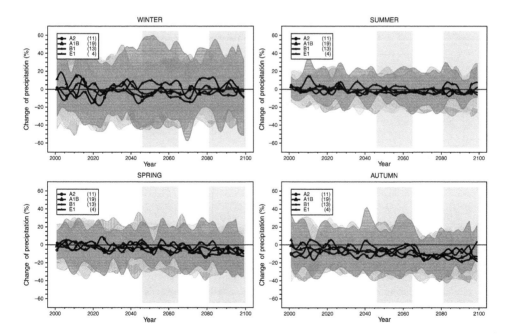

Figure 6.   The same as Figure 4, but for winter (DJF, upper left), spring (MAM, upper right), summer (JJA, lower left) and autumn (SON, lower right).

corresponds to the winter season, reaching values up to 40% with strong decadal variability. While no clear trend appears in precipitation amount for winter and summer, a noticeable decreasing trend can be appreciated for spring and autumn. Both the variable trends along the year and the uncertainty are highly relevant features for water management purposes.

Figure 7 provides some idea about the evolution of extremes of precipitation for the same region of Aragón, based now on information from the DYN_ENSEMBLES data-set. The figures correspond to the intermediate emission scenario A1B SRES. Here also, the width of the uncertainty band is around 20% (as it was for the STAT_ANALOGUE data-set), with decreasing trend for annual accumulated precipitation. However, as we focus on some extreme indices the uncertainty grows significantly. For example, the *consecutive dry days* index (CDD: maximum number of consecutive days with precipitation less than 1 mm) shows an increase at the end of twenty-first century of about 15 days, with an uncertainty band of around 20 days. Although this trend is statistically significant for the ensemble model (0.13 ± 0.02 days per year), some runs (20%) show no clear trend

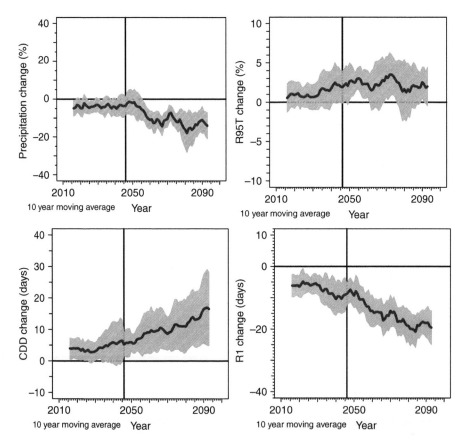

Figure 7. Change of downscaled annual accumulated precipitation (upper left), very heavy precipitation contribution (upper right), consecutive dry days (lower left) and precipitation days (lower right). All are 10-year moving averages. Data were obtained from the DYN_ENSEMBLES data-set. Changes are expressed with respect to the reference period 1961–1990 averaged over all grid points in the region of Aragon for the A1B SRES emission scenario. Thick solid line represents the average over all regionalized projections based on different RCMs and AOGCMs. The shaded band depicts the uncertainty expressed as ± one standard deviation around the mean value.

(p-value > 0.2). The change in the *precipitation days* index (R1: number of days with precipitation ≥ 1 mm) shows a decrease of around 20 days, with an uncertainty band of approximately 10 days. In this case, coherence between runs is greater than for CDD, with 73% of runs showing significant trends (p-value < 0.05). Precipitation extremes related with intense events are especially important for water management. As an example, the change in the *very heavy precipitation contribution* index (R95T: fraction of annual precipitation due to events exceeding the 95th percentile in the reference period) increases about 3%, with an uncertainty band around 5%. This trend is only significant (p-value < 0.05) for approximately 20% of runs (see Tank, Zwiers, & Zhang [2009] for definition of extreme indices).

Both data-sets described here (STAT_ANALOGUE and DYN_ENSEMBLES), with a resolution of approximately 25 km and based on daily data, allow a finer and more detailed description for smaller and more homogeneous regions, including estimation of changes in average values, changes in extremes and the corresponding uncertainties.

User needs for water management under climate change scenarios

The most relevant meteorological variables for hydrological impact studies are precipitation and temperature (Bronstert, Kolokotronis, Schwandt, & Straub, 2007; Xu, 1999b). Precipitation, in particular, is the most important driver for water resources (Kundzewicz et al., 2007). However, it is considerably more difficult to model than temperature, mostly because of its high spatial and temporal variability and its nonlinear nature.

The high spatial and temporal variability of the precipitation field poses the crucial question of what assumptions are appropriate given the nature of the specific problem being addressed. Hydrological impact analyses can have different objectives and hence focus on different components of the hydrological cycle. Furthermore, they employ models of varying complexity and temporal resolution, depending on their purpose and on model availability. For example, empirical models are used on an annual scale, while water-balance models are used for a monthly one, conceptual lumped-parameter models for a daily one and process-based distributed-parameter models on hourly or finer temporal scale assessments (Xu, 1999a). Therefore, study objective, study area characteristics and type of model used will determine the sensitivity of the system to different precipitation data characteristics (spatial and temporal distribution) and the form of the precipitation data required (e.g. continuous time series, seasonal averages, or annual extremes) (Maraun et al., 2010).

Because climate change projections, mainly provided by AOGCMs, lack enough spatial and temporal resolution for their direct usage by hydrological models, downscaling of precipitation is frequently the very first step before their application in water resources studies. Many papers (e.g. Maraun et al., 2010) have addressed the quality of downscaled precipitation coming from either dynamical or statistical methods. In fact, during the last two decades, extensive research on downscaling methods and applications has been carried out (Christensen & Christensen, 2007; Fowler, Blenkinsop, & Tebaldi, 2007 [with a focus on hydrology]; Prudhomme, Reynard, & Crooks, 2002). Several reviews of downscaling methods have been published (e.g. Hanssen-Bauer, Achberger, Benestad, Chen, & Foland, 2005; Hewitson & Crane, 1996; Wilby & Wigley, 1997; Xu, 1999a; Zorita & von Storch, 1997).

When estimating future climate for hydrological applications, it is as important to provide an estimate of the uncertainty of future precipitation projections as it is to provide precipitation fields with the required spatial and temporal resolution. Very frequently the focus is set on downscaling algorithms, aiming to reach enough spatial and temporal detail, and disregarding the predictability issues associated with the existing uncertainties of future projections (Hawkins & Sutton, 2009; Palmer, 1999). In fact, it can be stated that the major gap for water management applications is the lack of enough studies based on probabilistic downscaled climate projections. This is perhaps the actual challenge not only for hydrological and water management applications but for many other sectors sensitive to climate conditions. The range of uncertainty due to model formulation, natural variability and downscaling methods can be assessed by ensemble simulations based on different AOGCMs (multi-model ensembles or perturbed parameterizations), different initial conditions and different downscaling techniques (RCMs or statistical algorithms). Apart from the mentioned international initiatives, such as PRUDENCE, ENSEMBLES, STARDEX, climateprediction.net and CORDEX (see http://wcrp.ipsl.jussieu.fr/ SF_RCD_CORDEX.html), the UKCP09 project (see http://ukclimateprojections.defra. gov.uk) has developed probabilistic national climate change projections for the UK based on the Hadley Centre regional climate model driven by a large AOGCM ensemble with perturbed physics parameterizations (Murphy et al., 2009). The relative role of these different sources of uncertainty depends on the time scales under consideration. On decadal time scales, the climate change signal is small compared to natural variability, so that uncertainty caused by initial conditions and natural forcing dominates, while, on secular time scales, the relevant uncertainty is caused by AOGCMs and emission scenarios (Cox & Stephenson, 2007).

In the case of Spain, as mentioned, some data-sets already exist with enough resolution (daily in time and around 25 km in space) for application to certain hydrological models. The original resolution of this data-set can be further enhanced by the application of interpolation techniques to meet the requirements of many hydrological models. This further increase in spatial resolution was carried out, e.g., in a recent study of climate change impact on water resources over Spain (Centro de Estudios y Experimentación de Obras Públicas, 2010). The hydrological model SIMPA (Álvarez, Sánchez, & Quintas, 2004) applied in this study needed a spatial scale finer than 25 km, and climatic fields were interpolated to the working resolution of 1 km. Because the model makes use of a temporal resolution of one month, many intermediate storages and flow propagation can be obviated. This study aimed to estimate uncertainties in future projections by using a limited number of downscaled projections based on two emission scenarios and a few global models and downscaling techniques. The study can be considered one of the first attempts to estimate a range for the uncertainties affecting climate change projections. Both data-sets here presented for Spain also meet the requirement of supplying information on uncertainties of climate change projections. Ensemble-like approaches with enough members allow estimation of uncertainties affecting climate projections and how these uncertainties are inherited by different climate-dependent sectors, such as water resources over the IP.

Another highly relevant question is whether the current state-of-the-art tools for estimating climate projections meet the expectations of resolution and accuracy demanded by the water resources community. The answer is probably negative, given that most studies face the problem of estimating future water resources using the same tools and approaches applied for real-time or near-real-time evaluation of water resources, based frequently on a very dense network of precipitation observations. We must be aware that estimation of future precipitation is a problem fundamentally affected by many uncertainties and that we are not yet able to estimate precipitation projections with the accuracy required by water resources managers. Downscaling techniques help in adapting climate projections to regional and local features, but there are still major gaps not addressed by downscaling algorithms. Among such gaps, the following ones can be mentioned: (1) many regions have sparse data; (2) performance of downscaling schemes is currently better for synoptic and frontal systems than for convective precipitation; (3) sub-daily precipitation is poorly represented; (4) feedback of small-scale processes on a large scale is not adequately captured in projections of precipitation change; and (5) all downscaling approaches inherit errors in the representation of temporal variability from the driving global models (Maraun et al., 2010).

Conclusions and perspectives

The availability of downscaled climate change projections is a prerequisite for assessing impacts and vulnerability of all ecological and socio-economic sectors sensitive to climate conditions, in particular the water resources sector. The evaluation of impacts and vulnerability will help in planning the corresponding adaptation measures required by each affected sector. Given that the climate change projections generated by global climate models lack the spatial and temporal resolution needed by most impact models, downscaling techniques are needed to downscale and accommodate projections to regional or even local features.

The process of generating climate change projections is characterized by inherent uncertainty coming from a number or sources (e.g. natural forcing; future emissions of GHGs, aerosols and their precursors; representation of physical processes in global climate models; and downscaling techniques). So, it is strongly recommended to use a probabilistic approach to represent climate change projections, integrating all available information on climate change projections coming from different emissions scenarios, different global climate models and different downscaling techniques. To adequately sample the population of climate change projections, a sufficiently large number of emission scenarios, global models and downscaling techniques must be used to represent the probability distribution function of climate change projections.

There are several sources of climate change projections over Spain meeting the mentioned requirements of being downscaled and being able to represent the most relevant uncertainties affecting projections. This paper has presented two data-sets generated and provided by AEMET as part of its routine production of climate services for the community of impacts of climate change. The data-sets presented here allow a reasonable estimation of the evolution of mean and extreme values as well as their uncertainties.

Some results of downscaled climate change projections have been presented here, using the region of Aragón as a illustrative example and putting special emphasis on the precipitation variable. The projections for precipitation show relatively high uncertainty as compared with natural variability and for certain seasons and time horizons it is difficult to see any trend signal which might be useful to the water management community. Furthermore, the uncertainty of some precipitation-extreme indices, e.g. CDD, grows significantly as the time horizon progresses through the twenty-first century. Moreover, not all runs show statistically significant trends. For the precipitation-extreme indices R1D and R95T used here, the coherence between runs is greater than for other indices.

With respect to the water management community, the variety of models simulating a range of temporal and spatial scales and processes have different requirements for climatic data, singularly of precipitation. Unfortunately, precipitation has features of strong variability which frequently are not captured well enough even by observational data in real time. Demands for more accurate precipitation data to use as inputs for hydrological models are frequently heard in the hydrology and water management communities. Climate projections have improved significantly during the last decades through the use of downscaling techniques. Also, the use of ensembles has allowed some estimation of uncertainties. However, a clear gap still exists between the requirements of the hydrological/water management sector and the accuracy of the data provided by the community of climate modellers (Maraun et al., 2010).

References

Agencia Estatal de Meteorología & Instituto de Meteorologia (Ed.). (2011). *Atlas Climático Ibérico – Iberian Climate Atlas*, Retrieved from http://www.aemet.es/documentos/es/divulgacion/publicaciones/Atlas-climatologico/Atlas.pdf.

Álvarez, J., Sánchez, A., & Quintas, L. (2005). SIMPA, a GRASS based tool for hydrological studies. *International Journal of Geoinformatics, 1*, 13–20.

Bladé, I., & Castro-Díez, Y. (2010). Atmospheric trends in the Iberian peninsula during the instrumental period in the context of natural variability. In F. F. Pérez & R. Boscolo (Eds.), *Climate in Spain: Past, present and future. Regional climate change assessment report* (pp. 25–41), Retrieved from http://www.clivar.es/files/doc_completo_clivar_ingles_2010.pdf.

Bronstert, A., Kolokotronis, V., Schwandt, D., & Straub, H. (2007). Comparison and evaluation of regional climate scenarios for hydrological impact analysis: General scheme and application example. *International Journal of Climatology, 27*, 1579–1594. doi:10.1002/joc.1621.

Brunet, M., Casado, M. J., Castro, M., Galán, P., López, J. A., … Martín, J. M. (2008). *Generación de escenarios regionalizados de cambio climático para España*. Madrid: Ministerio de Medio Ambiente y Medio Rural y Marino.

Centro de Estudios y Experimentación de Obras Públicas (2010). *Evaluación del impacto del cambio climático en los recursos hídricos en régimen natural* [Study of climate change impact on water resources and water masses]. Madrid: Ministerio de Medio ambiente y Medio Rural y Marino.

Christensen, J. H., & Christensen, O. B. (2007). A summary of the PRUDENCE model projections of changes in European climate by the end of this century. *Climatic Change, 81*, 7–30. doi:10.1007/s10584-006-9210-7.

Cox, P. M., & Stephenson, D. B. (2007). A changing climate for prediction. *Science, 317*, 207–208. doi:10.1126/science.1145956.

Déqué, M., Jones, R. G., Wild, M., Giorgi, F., Christensen, J. H., … Hassell, D. C. (2005). Global high resolution versus Limited Area Model climate change projections over Europe: Quantifying confidence level from PRUDENCE results. *Climate Dynamics, 25*, 653–670. doi:10.1007/s00382-005-0052-1.

Déqué, M., Rowell, D. P., Lüthi, D., Giorgi, F., Christensen, J. H., … Rockel, B. (2007). An intercomparison of regional climate simulations for Europe: Assessing uncertainties in model projections. *Climatic Change, 81*, 53–70. doi:10.1007/s10584-006-9228-x.

Fowler, H. J., Blenkinsop, S., & Tebaldi, C. (2007). Linking climate change modelling to impact studies: recent advances in downscaling techniques for hydrological modelling. *International Journal of Climatology, 27*, 1547–1578. doi:10.1002/joc.1556.

Goodess, C. (2009). STARDEX: Downscaling climate extremes. Retrieved from http://www.cru.uea.ac.uk/cru/research/stardex/reports/STARDEX_FINAL_REPORT.pdf.

Hanssen-Bauer, I., Achberger, C., Benestad, R., Chen, D,, & Forland, E, (2005). Statistical downscaling of climate scenarios over Scandinavia. *Climate Research, 29*, 255–268.

Hawkins, E., & Sutton, R. (2009). The potential to narrow uncertainty in regional climate predictions. *Bulletin of the American Meteorological Society, 90*, 1095–1107. doi:10.1175/2009BAMS2607.1.

Haylock, M. R., Cawley, G. C., Harpham, C., Wilby, R. L., & Goodess, C. M. (2006). Downscaling heavy precipitation over the United Kingdom: A comparison of dynamical and statistical methods and their future scenarios. *International Journal of Climatology, 26*, 1397–1415. doi:10.1002/joc.1318.

Hewitson, B., & Crane, R. (1996). Climate downscaling: Techniques and application. *Climate Research, 7*, 85–95.

Huth, R. (2004). Sensitivity of local daily temperature change estimates to the selection of downscaling models and predictors. *Journal of Climate*, *17*, 640–652. doi:10.1175/1520-0442 (2004)017<0640:SOLDTC>2.0.CO;2.

Intergovernmental Panel on Climate Change (2000). In: N. Nakicenovic, J. Alcamo, G. Davis, B. de Vries, J. Fenhann, ... Z. Dadi (Eds.) *Emissions Scenarios. A Special Report of Working Group III of the Intergovernmental Panel on Climate Change*. Cambridge: Cambridge University Press.

Intergovernmental Panel on Climate Change (2001). In J. T. Houghton, Y. Ding, D. J. Griggs, M. Noguer, P. J. van der Linden, & D. Xiaosu (Eds.), *Climate change 2001: The scientific basis. Contribution of Working Group I to the Third Assessment Report of the Intergovernmental Panel on Climate Change*. Cambridge: Cambridge University Press.

Intergovernmental Panel on Climate Change (2007). In S. Salomon, D. Qin, M. Manning, Z. Chen, M. Marquis, ... K. B. Averyt (Eds.), *Climate change 2007: The physical science basis. Contribution of Working Group I to the Fourth Assessment Report of the Intergovernmental Panel on Climate Change*. Cambridge: Cambridge University Press.

Kundzewicz, Z. W., Mata, L. J., Arnell, N. W., Döll, P., & ... Jiménez, B. (2007). Freshwater resources and their management. In M. L. Parry, O. F. Canziani, J. P. Palutikof, P. J. van der Linden, & C. E. Hanson (Eds.), *Climate change 2007: Impacts, adaptation and vulnerability. Contribution of Working Group II to the Fourth Assessment Report of the Intergovernmental Panel on Climate Change* (pp. 173–210). Cambridge: Cambridge University Press.

Luna, M. Y., Guijarro, J. A., & López, J. A. (2012). A monthly precipitation database for Spain (1851–2008): Reconstruction, homogeneity and trends. *Advances in Science & Research*, *8*, 1–4. doi:10.5194/asr-8-1-2012.

Maraun, D., Wetterhall, F., Ireson, A. M., Chandler, R. E., Kendon, E. J., ... Widmann, M. (2010). Precipitation downscaling under climate change. Recent developments to bridge the gap between dynamical models and the end user. *Reviews of Geophysics*, *48*. doi:10.1029/2009RG00031.

Mearns, L. O., Giorgi, F., Whetton, P., Pabon, D., Hulme, M., & Lal, M. (2003). *Guidelines for use of climate scenarios developed from regional climate model experiments*. Retrieved from http://www.ipcc-data.org/guidelines/dgm_no1_v1_10-2003.pdf.

Meehl, G. A., Stocker, T. F., Collins, W. D., Friedlingstein, P., Gaye, A. T., ... Gregory, J. M. (2007). Global climate projections. In S. Solomon, D. Qin, M. Manning, Z. Chen, M. Marquis, ... K. B. Averyt (Eds.), *Climate change 2007: The physical science basis. Contribution of Working Group I to the Fourth Assessment Report of the Intergovernmental Panel on Climate Change* (pp. 663–745). Cambridge: Cambridge University Press.

Mitchel, T. D., & Hulme, M. (1999). Predicting regional climate change: living with uncertainty. *Progress in Physical Geography*, *23*, 57–78.

Ministerio de Medio Ambiente y Medio Rural y Marino (2008). *Spanish National Climate Change Adaptation Plan (PNACC)*. Retrieved from http://www.marm.es/en/cambio-climatico/temas/im pactos-vulnerabilidad-y-adaptacion/pnacc_ing_tcm11-12473.pdf.

Murphy, J. M., Sexton, D. M. H., Jenkins, G. J., Booth, B. B. B., Brown, C. C., ... Clark, R. T. (2009). *UK climate projections science report: Climate change projections*. Exeter: Meteorological Office Hadley Centre.

Palmer, T. N. (1999). A nonlinear dynamical perspective on climate prediction. *Journal of Climate*, *12*, 575–591. doi:10.1175/1520-0442(1999)012<0575:ANDPOC>2.0.CO;2.

Petisco de Lara, S. E. (2008a). Método de regionalización de precipitación basado en análogos: Explicación y validación [Downscaling of precipitation based on analogs: Method and validation] (NT AEMCC-3A). Madrid: AEMET. Retrieved from http://www.aemet.es/docum entos/es/idi/clima/escenarios_CC/Metodo_regionalizacion_precipitacion.pdf.

Petisco de Lara, S. E. (2008b). Método de regionalización de temperaturas basado en análogos: Explicación y validación [Downscaling of temperature based on analogs: Method and validation] (NT AEMCC-3B). Madrid: AEMET. Retrieved from http://www.aemet.es/docum entos/es/idi/clima/escenarios_CC/Metodo_regionalizacion_temperatura.pdf.

Prudhomme, C., Reynard, N., & Crooks, S. (2002). Downscaling of global climate models for flood frequency analysis: Where are we now? *Hydrological Processes*, *16*, 1137–1150. doi:10.1002/hyp.1054.

Randall, D. A., Wood, R. A., Bony, S., Coleman, R., Fichefet, T., ... Fyfe, J. (2007). Climate models and their evaluation. In S. Solomon, D. Qin, M. Manning, Z. Chen, M. Marquis, ... K. B.

Averyt (Eds.), *Climate change 2007: The physical science basis. Contribution of Working Group I to the Fourth Assessment Report of the Intergovernmental Panel on Climate Change* (pp. 589–662). Cambridge: Cambridge University Press.

Stainforth, D. A., Aina, T., Christensen, C., Collins, M., Faull, N., ... Frame, D. J. (2005). Uncertainty in predictions of the climate response to rising levels of greenhouse gases. *Nature, 433*, 403–406. doi:10.1038/nature03301.

Tank, K., Zwiers, F. W., & Zhang, X. (2009). Guidelines on analysis of extremes in a changing climate in support of informed decisions for adaptation (WMO-TD No. 1500). Retrieved from http://www.wmo.int/pages/prog/wcp/wcdmp/wcdmp_series/documents/WCDMP_72_TD_1500_en_1.pdf.

United Nations (1998). Kyoto Protocol to the United Nations Framework Convention on Climate Change. Retrieved from http://unfccc.int/resource/docs/convkp/kpeng.pdf.

United Nations (2009). Opening remarks to the United Nations Climate change Summit Plenary, 22 September. Retrieved from http://www.un.org/apps/news/infocus/sgspeeches/search_full.asp?statID=582.

van der Linden, P., & Mitchell, J. F. B. (Eds.). (2009). *ENSEMBLES: Climate change and its impacts. Summary of research and results from the ENSEMBLES project.* Retrieved from http://ensembles-eu.metoffice.com/docs/Ensembles_final_report_Nov09.pdf.

Wilby, R. L., Charles, S. P., Zorita, E., Timbal, B., Whetton, P., & Mearns, L. O. (2004). *Guidelines for use of climate scenarios developed from statistical downscaling method.* Retrieved from http://www.ipcc-data.org/guidelines/dgm_no2_v1_09_2004.pdf.

Wilby, R. L., & Wigley, T. M. L. (1997). Downscaling general circulation model output: A review of methods and limitations. *Progress in Physical Geography, 21*, 530–548. doi:10.1177/030913339702100403.

Xu, C. (1999a). From GCMs to river flow: A review of downscaling methods and hydrologic modelling approaches. *Progress in Physical Geography, 23*, 229–249. doi:10.1177/030913339902300204.

Xu, C. (1999b). Climate change and hydrologic models: A review of existing gaps and recent research developments. *Water Resources Management, 13*, 369–382. doi:10.1023/A:1008190900459.

Zorita, E., & von Storch, H. (1999). The analog method as a simple statistical downscaling technique: Comparison with more complicated methods. *Journal of Climate, 12*, 2474–2489. doi:10.1175/1520-0442(1999)012<2474:TAMAAS>2.0.CO;2.

The application of hydrological planning as a climate change adaptation tool in the Ebro basin

Miguel Ángel García-Vera

Hydrographic Confederation of the Ebro, Zaragoza, Spain

This paper presents an example of how expected climate change effects have been factored into hydrological planning for the Ebro River basin in Spain. Between now and 2030, a 5% reduction in the basin's water resources is foreseen, along with a drop in the hydrographs' snow component and an increase in dry periods. This article explores the several measures to help reduce the basin's vulnerability to climate change as considered in the technical component of the Ebro Basin Hydrological Plan 2010–2015. These adaptation tools include wastewater treatment, control of water intakes, water reuse, agro-environmental measures, modernization of irrigated areas, improvement of urban water supplies, removal of contaminated sediments, improvement of regulation infrastructure to ensure water supply and control inundations, optimization of hydroelectric exploitation, and improvement of drought and flood management.

Introduction

Hydrological decision making requires the diagnosis of the present situation and a prognosis for the future. Preparing future outlooks often requires predicting the effects of climate change, and the water sector is no exception to this. The effects of climate change on the quantity and quality of water resources are not fully known, and forecasts with different conceptual and territorial scopes are being made regarding the possible implications of this global process. Whatever may be said about the cause of climate change, it is proven beyond doubt (IPCC, 2007) that temperatures are increasing across the globe, the effects of which must be taken into account as part of any responsible decision-making process.

Water management requires hydrological planning and the setting up of legislative, economic, financial, administrative and social goals. Moreover, society as a whole can be engaged to make sure that the most appropriate means to achieve such objectives are followed.

Water management in Spain presents a good example of the need to factor expected climate change effects into hydrological planning. According to Article 2 of the Water Act (BOE, 2001a), continental surface and renewable underground waters, river, lake, lagoon and reservoir beds, and aquifers are all property of the Spanish State. These water bodies together constitute what is known as the public water domain.

In Spain, the management of the public water domain is based on the river basin unit principle whereby each basin is managed by its own basin authority. If the hydrographic basins form part of more than one autonomous community, the basin authority has to report to the central government and the autonomous community in which such basin is situated.

The Ebro Hydrographic Demarcation, formed by the Spanish part of the Ebro basin and the headwaters of the Garona River (Figure 1), has a surface area of 85,570 km^2 (CHE, 2011a), a fifth of all Spanish territory. As there are nine autonomous communities in this territory, the Hydrographic Confederation of the Ebro (hereinafter CHE) was established as the managing authority, reporting to the central government's Ministry of the Environment and Rural and Marine Affairs (hereinafter MARM).

The CHE's main functions include: (1) the preparation, monitoring and review of the basin's hydrological plans; (2) management and control of the public water domain; (3) management and control of the exploitations of general interest or those affecting more than one autonomous community; and (4) the design, construction and operation of the works carried out with funding from the authority and those commissioned by the State (BOE, 2001a, Article 23).

The preparation of hydrological basin plans is, therefore, a competency of the basin authorities. This hydrological planning has a clear purpose, set forth in Article 40.1 of the Waters Act (BOE, 2001a), which specifies that the general aims of hydrological planning are to ensure the quality and proper protection of the public water domain and its waters, meet water demands, reach an equilibrium and the harmonization of regional and sectoral development, and increase the availability of water resources, whilst protecting its quality and economizing and rationalizing its usage in harmony with the environment and other natural resources.

In recent years, Spain, like other countries of the European Union, has made a major effort to prepare hydrological plans for the period 2010–2015. The Ebro Basin Hydrological Plan, which is currently in force, was approved in 1998 (BOE, 1998, 1999). The planning process carried out in the decade 2000–2010 integrated the requirements established by European legislation (European Union, 2000) and by Spanish regulations

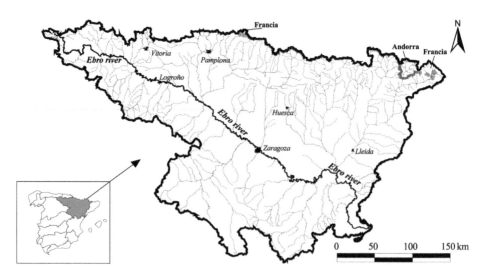

Figure 1.   Geographic location of the Ebro basin in Spain.

(BOE, 2001a, 2007a, 2008). Since February 2010, there has been a draft proposal of the Ebro Basin Hydrological Plan 2010–2015, the summary of which can be consulted (CHE, 2011a) and which is soon to be subject to a public review period.

Expected effects of climate change on the Ebro basin

Characteristics of water resources and water uses

The mean precipitation in the Ebro basin for the period October 1980 to September 2006 was 641 mm/y, of which 448 mm/y was evapotranspired and 170 mm/y (14,554 hm^3/y) was contributed to surface water bodies. Of this amount, 39% came from underground discharges and subsurface throughflow (CHE, 2011a).

Water resources are highly variable, both spatially and over time. Figure 2 depicts the distribution of the total surface runoff data obtained from the gauging stations along the Ebro basin; it clearly shows that the highest annual figures for average total runoff are in the central Pyrenees, reaching a maximum of 44 L·s^{-1}·km^{-2}. The lowest runoff rates are found in the central sector of the basin, where the rate is less than 1 L·s^{-1}·km^{-2}.

The variability of the basin's resources over time is very high. Reduced flows are normal in the summer months due to low precipitation and high temperatures (high evapotranspiration). Overall, annual basin discharge in a natural regime varies between the 8098 hm^3 estimated for the year 1948/49 and the 27,835 hm^3 for the year 1959/60. Monthly differences are also very significant, with the highest flows seen from December to May and very low flows between July and August (Figure 3).

In the current situation, water consumption from the Ebro basin is estimated to be 34% of its total resources (5000 hm^3/y). Once the infrastructure whose construction was scheduled in the 1998 Hydrological Plan begins working, consumption is expected to rise to 49% of annual resources. These new actions are considered to be of great social and economic interest and are characterized by the implementation of projects that are highly efficient in terms of water usage.

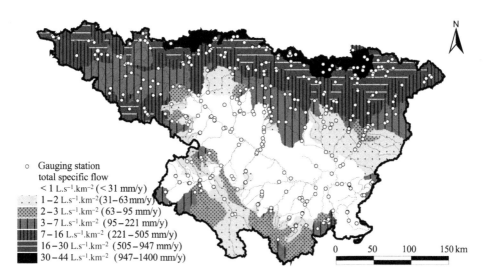

Figure 2. Total estimated flows (surface and underground) for the Ebro basin, based on the data interpretation from gauging stations in the period October 1953 to September 1995. Data taken from CHE (1998).

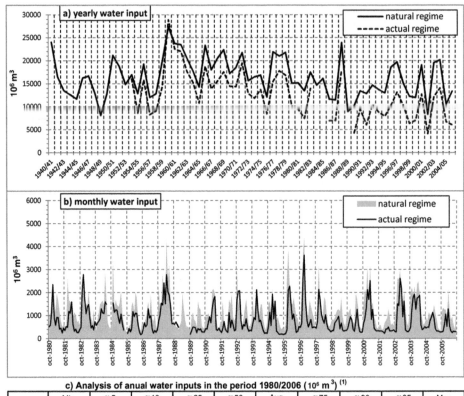

c) Analysis of anual water inputs in the period 1980/2006 (10⁶ m³) (1)

	Min.	%5	%10	%25	%50	Avg.	%75	%90	%95	Max.
natural	8,341	10,172	10,705	12,087	13,475	14,752	18,055	19,662	20,109	23,916
actual	4,121	4,457	6,020	6,811	8,745	9,236	11,297	13,769	14,039	18,115

1. The comparison employs 23 years, excluding 1983/84 and 1988/89 because the real serie is not complete.

d) Statistics of monthly water inputs in the natural and actual regimes.(1980/2006)

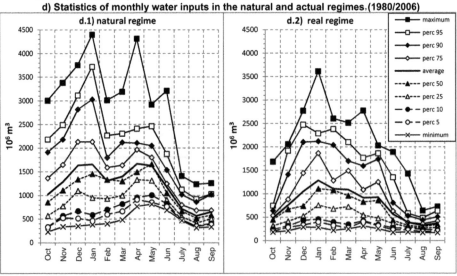

Figure 3. Characterization of the variability of basin water inputs from the river Ebro at Tortosa (station 27; 83,647 km²).

In the hydrological basin plans, mathematical models are used to simulate water development management in major systems known as *juntas de explotación* (water development boards). The Ebro basin has been subdivided into 17 large water development boards overseeing water regulation (dams) and/or transport infrastructure (major canals). The cost and management of each infrastructural development are the joint responsibility of all users under the auspices of the Hydrographic Confederation of the Ebro (Figure 4, Table 1). As things currently stand, there is an acceptable assurance that demands will be met in most of the water development boards. For the basins on the right bank (boards 4, 6, 7, 8, 9 and 10), where the land is more arid, in some cases the water demand satisfaction rate is significantly less than 80%.

Effects on temperatures

An analysis of temperature trends in the Ebro basin in the period 1950–2006 (López-Moreno et al., 2010) found that these had significantly increased across a large area. For instance, 87% of the basin recorded moderate-to-high temperature increases, with an average increase of 0.2 °C per decade.

The warming was more intense in the northern part of the basin (0.3 °C per decade), with the greatest increase (0.4 °C per decade) occurring over the summer. Moreover, in the north-east areas, temperatures increased very markedly in the spring and increased significantly in the Pyrenees and the central area of the basin. Winter temperatures increased in the basin's headwater areas, while in the central sector no increase was detected.

Effects on precipitation

The impact of climate change on precipitation in the Ebro basin was analyzed by the CHE (2001a) and by García Vera, Abaurrea, Asín Lafuente, and Centelles-Nogués (2002), who made a detailed analysis of trends in precipitation series in the Ebro basin using data from 1916 to 2000. The data series were homogenized, aggregated, and completed through a trend analysis that used information from the various observatories. The basin was divided

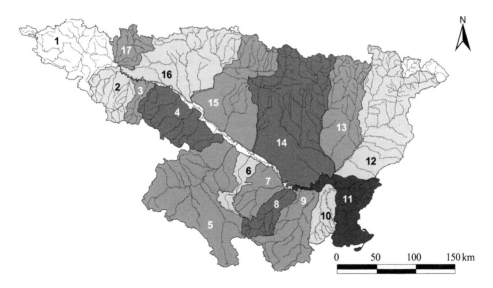

Figure 4.   Locations of the water development boards discussed in Table 1.

Table 1.   Status quo situation of the Ebro basin water development boards and assurance of meeting water demands with forecast to 2027 considering climate change effects.

Water development board	Guaranteed volume (volume provided / volume demanded)	
	Current situation	2027 horizon, factoring in climate change forecasts
1. Headwater of the Ebro to Mequinenza	99.20%	98.32%
2. Najerilla and Tirón basins	92.00%	96.32%
3. Iregua basin	99.90%	94.89%
4. Trib. basins of Ebro: Leza to Huecha	42.60%	49.22%
5. Jalón basin	78.30%	85.42%
6. Huerva basin	88.20%	87.72%
7. Aguasvivas basin	58.60%	50.55%
8. Martín basin	70.90%	70.02%
9. Guadalope basin	79.20%	59.16%
10. Matarraña basin	61.40%	75.81%
11. Lower Ebro	98.60%	76.18%
12. Segre basin	98.30%	95.50%
13 Ésera and N. Ribagorzana basins	91.50%	92.48%
14. Gállego and Cinca basins	94.10%	93.87%
15. Aragón and Arba basins	72.80%	90.06%
16. Irati, Arga and Ega basins	95.10%	83.87%
17. Bayas, Zadorra and Inglares basins	91.40%	90.93%
Ebro basin	**90.10%**	**86.67%**

Source: Data taken from CHE (2011a); author's own compilation.

into regions, for which time series were constructed by describing the rainfall trend in the different territories and then performing a trend analysis on each data-set.

Barrera and Llasat (2004) assessed precipitation in Spain over a 100-year period (1897–1998) and concluded that there were no significant trends. In the Ebro basin, seven areas were identified on the basis of precipitation trends. The authors concluded that when a broad time interval was analyzed, there was no evidence to indicate that climate change had caused a general declining trend in precipitation in the Ebro basin. A downward trend was observed in only one of the seven differentiated regions (Region C in Figure 5), a tendency that has persisted since the late 1930s.

These conclusions were confirmed by other studies conducted by the Hydrographic Confederation of the Ebro itself (CHE, 2002) and by other authors. MIMAM (2000) concluded that it was not possible to identify any significant trend in the Ebro basin. Saladie, Brunet, Aguilar, Sigró, and López (2004) analyzed the lower Ebro area and also deduced that, during the twentieth century, the annual precipitation trend in that area was not statistically significant. The CHE has recently initiated a new study aimed at assessing temperature and precipitation trends in the basin, extending the analysis to include data up to 2010.

Effects on flows

In recent years, a decline in water resources has been detected in many of the basin's rivers and recorded at the gauging stations in Tortosa (Figure 3a). Initially, this decrease was

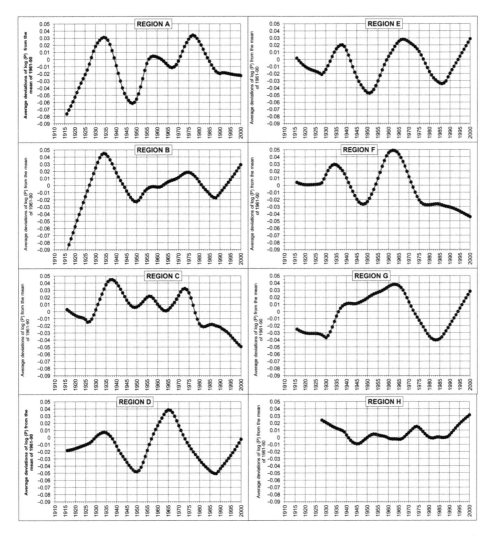

Figure 5.   Regions of precipitation trends over time in the Ebro basin, 1916–2000. Source: García Vera et al. (2002).

explained by the increase in water use that occurred throughout the twentieth century (MIMAM, 2000). In the 1900s, 400,000 ha of the Ebro basin were irrigated, while in recent years the irrigated area is on the order of 700,000 ha (CHE, 2011a).

The CHE (2001b) and García Vera, Coch Flotats, Gallart, Llorens, and Pintor (2003) made an analysis of 31 gauging stations in the Ebro basin, comparing the natural regime to precipitation data and the change in forested area against records in the 1970 and 1991 national forestry inventories. The conclusion reached was that the Ebro basin has seen an increase in forested area of between 4000 and 7600 km^2 (representing 4.7 to 8.9% of the basin's total surface area). New forest areas mean that roughly 20% of the rainfall does not become runoff. This may imply a decline in water resources throughout the entire Ebro basin of about 30 hm^3/y.

Projections of the effects of climate change

Cabezas, Estrada, and Estrela (1999) made a first estimate of the effects of climate change in the Ebro basin for the 2030 horizon. To this end, the authors assumed a hypothetical doubling of CO_2 in Spain and considered two possible scenarios: 1) a 1 °C increase in the mean annual temperature; and 2) a 1 °C increase in the mean annual temperature and a 5% decrease in precipitation. The study used the SIMPA model (Ruiz García, 1999), which makes a monthly simulation on a 1 km^2 grid of precipitation runoff for the whole of Spain. Once the model was calibrated, the results were simulated for both scenarios. A 3% decline in water natural resources was estimated for the Ebro basin under Scenario 1, and an 8% decline under Scenario 2.

These assessments were reviewed in greater detail by Fernández, Mateos, and Estrela (2003) and applied to a 2050 time horizon, where the predictions of the general HADCM2 circulation model were used to make simulations with the regional PROMES circulation model, using the 1xCO_2 and 2xCO_2 hypotheses. The simulated scenarios considered a precipitation reduction of 0–15% and a temperature increase of 0–4 °C. Under these new climate conditions, the results of the SIMPA model show a 5–15% decline in Ebro basin contributions in the region.

Hydrological planning requires likely future water resource behaviour scenarios to be taken into account in forecasts. The technical debate in Spain concerning how to include these predictions concluded with the publication of a Hydrological Planning Instruction, which specified the methodology required for the preparation of hydrological plans in the country (BOE, 2008). With regard to climate change, the document indicated that, in the absence of new estimates, water development management models with a 2027 horizon call for a reduction of water discharges in the natural regime. For the Ebro basin, a reduction of 5% was stated. The balances resulting from discharge cutbacks by the various water development boards are shown in Table 1.

More recently, a review of the assessment of the impact of climate change on resources in the natural regime was carried out (MARM-CEDEX, 2011). SIMPA simulations were analyzed, considering the A2 and B2 emissions scenarios and making projections for the 2011–2040, 2041–2070 and 2071–2100 timeframes, using 1961–1990 as the control period. For the Ebro basin, the average estimated decline was 9% for 2011–2040, 14% for 2041–2070, and 16% (Scenario B2) to 28% (Scenario A2) for 2071–2100.

A spatial breakdown of these forecasts may yield some interesting conclusions. For instance, the CHE (2005a) modelled the hydrological functioning of 15 sub-basins with flow data close to the natural regime and comprising a total surface area of 15,008 km^2. Simulations were run with the daily hydro-meteorological balance model GIS-BALAN (Samper, Huguet, Ares, & García Vera, 1999), which was calibrated with flows from gauging stations and piezometric levels for the 1970–2000 period. Simulations were performed for Scenarios A1B, A2 and B1 of the IPCC's CGCM3 general circulation model and CCCma's Commit scenario for the 2010–2040, 2040–2070, and 2070–2100 periods.

For the 2010–2040 timeframe, a 12% average decline for the Ebro basin was estimated, or what is equivalent to a 17% decrease in surface flows, 9% in throughflow, and 13% in underground runoffs. Impacts will be greater in the summer months and problems aggravated in the dry months. This study also observed that for the 2070–2100 horizon, a significant total runoff drop could occur in the right bank and eastern Pyrenees basins (Figure 6, Table 2): as much as 38% in Guadalope and Jalon, 35% in Segre, and 25% in Esera and Mesa. In the future, expected declines in flows will only aggravate the lower hydrological productivity that already characterizes the Ebro's right bank (Figure 2).

Extreme events: floods and droughts

According to the Ministry of the Environment and Rural and Marine Affairs, climate change may bring about more frequent droughts in the Ebro basin (MARM-CEDEX, 2011). The overall expected effects on flood frequency and intensity were analyzed by Bates, Kundzewicz, Wu, and Palutikof (2008). Looking at the contribution of very wet days to annual rainfall from 1951 to 2003, that study did not observe any significant trends in Spain. In the absence of further studies, and according to the projections made and the degree of uncertainty, it does not appear necessary to anticipate a significant impact of climate change on the management of floodable areas. For this reason, the studies currently being produced regarding the implementation of the 2007 European Union flood directive in the Ebro basin do not consider this effect (CHE, 2011b).

MARM-CEDEX (2011) analyzed the maximum precipitation in Spain and concluded that, during the twentieth century, there was no evidence of a generalized increase in maximum daily precipitation. Only in some areas, such as the Pyrenees (north of the Ebro basin), was an increase observed.

Approach to climate change effects on water quality

The effects of climate change on water quality–related aspects have not yet been quantified. However, it is expected that the decline in water resources will have to be taken into account.

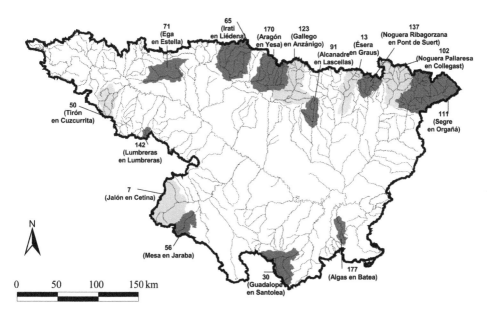

Figure 6.   Locations of the basins discussed in Table 2.

Table 2. Estimated percentage drop in total average runoff for three future periods versus the reference period 1970–2000.

Basin	2010–2040	2040–2070	2070–2100
7 (Jalón at Cetina)	14%	36%	38%
13 (Ésera at Graus)	12%	26%	25%
30 (Guadalope at Santolea)	18%	37%	38%
30 (Thón at Cuzcurrita)	16%	22%	27%
56 (Mesa at Jaraba)	8%	26%	25%
65 (Irati at Liédena)	6%	15%	14%
71 (Ega at Estella)	2%	11%	10%
91 (Alcanadre at Lascellas)	8%	14%	18%
102 (Noguera Pallaresa at Collegast)	7%	19%	21%
111 (Segre at Orgañá)	19%	38%	35%
123 (Gállego at Anzánigo)	2%	15%	15%
137 (Noguera Ribagorzana at Pont de Suert)	6%	16%	16%
142 (Lumbreras at Lumbreras)	1%	11%	12%
170 (Aragón at Yesa)	6%	19%	20%
177 (Algas at Batea)	11%	24%	13%
Ebro basin	**12%**	**21%**	**19%**

Source: Data taken from CHE (2005a); author's own compilation.

The abundant presence of evaporitic materials (gypsums and salts) in the central sector of the Ebro basin shows a clear correlation between element concentrations and flows. The CHE (2005b) worked out a potential $CE = AQ_i^{-b}$ correlation at 31 basin gauging stations, where CE is electrical conductivity, Q_i is the average daily flow, and A and b are adjustment parameters. These regressions proved to be highly significant ($R^2 \geq 0.5$, $P < 0.001$) for the stations in the Ebro's middle section and for end stations where there are a fair number of tributaries. The less abundant the flows, the higher the concentration, because there is a more significant presence of base flows and these are in greater contact with more soluble rock formations.

Figure 7 shows the case of the Q–CE correlation for Ebro gauging stations in Zaragoza, a city that receives water from a 39,981 km^2 catchment basin. Considering that the average flow for the period 1980–2008 was 193 m^3/s, and taking into account the

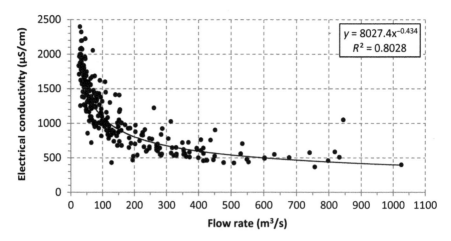

Figure 7. Correlation between flow rate and electrical conductivity at the Zaragoza gauging station, 1980–2002.

exponential fitting curve, we find that a 5% drop in the average flow would mean an average 2% increase in salinity. The impact of discharges on the quality of water in low-water periods may be much higher than what is shown in the analysis, because it considers only average values. For this reason, water quality improvement measures will reduce climate change vulnerability.

In the Ebro basin, water quality changes have been occurring which in some cases may be related to the water's higher temperature. This may be a contributing factor to the detected profusion of macrophytes in stretches downstream of the basin's major reservoirs, whose minimum flows are highly homogeneous. The outbreaks of blue-green algae in the reservoirs may also be related to a rise in water temperature. The quality network stations of the rivers of the Ebro basin, which have been providing information since 1980, have detected a general trend towards rising pH levels in the basin since the year 2000. The possible causal factors of this phenomenon are currently being examined.

Basin Plan 2010–2015 and climate change–related measures

The Ebro Basin Hydrological Plan 2010–2015 (CHE, 2011a) proposes a programme to be implemented by water authorities and users at a cost of €4800 million (€800 million per year). This programme includes measures aimed at achieving environmental targets (good quality of water bodies and no impairment), meeting water demands, and adaptation to extreme events (droughts and floods). Table 3 shows a summary of the proposed measures and the estimated investments involved.

Regarding climate change adaptation, the plan includes the following measures to improve the quality of rivers and their resilience to extreme events.

- *Drainage and treatment*: grouping the latest investments undertaken by the autonomous communities to complete their wastewater treatment plans in compliance with European Union Directive 91/271/EC (1991a). These plans are leading to a substantial improvement in river quality, which will also lessen system vulnerability in periods of low river discharge.
- *River and riverbank restoration projects*, which increase the space where the river can flow and help move it closer to its natural state. This improvement in the basin rivers' environmental quality will help maintain their condition, which in turn will enhance their capacity to respond to droughts and floods.
- *Control of water intakes*. In the Ebro basin, water from the main intakes is controlled. Thus, 516,000 ha of the 800,000 ha of irrigated land are fitted with control devices connected to the Automatic Hydrological Information System of the Ebro's Hydrographic Confederation (more information at http://195.55.247.237/saihebro/index.php?url=/datos/canales).

In 2009, a ministerial order was approved imposing compulsory controls on water originating from, returned to, or discharged into the public water domain (BOE, 2009). This order posed a challenge to control water extractions, whether surface or underground, by small agricultural holdings. Currently, regulatory controls are in place in areas of more intensive water use. Over time, this measure will enable water use to be better managed and more accurately aligned with the conditions established in the concessions and permits with which the Hydrographic Confederation grants users temporary water use rights. This measure will improve the water's environmental quality as well as its management in dry periods. It thus seeks to:

Table 3.   Summary of investment scheduled in the programme of measures outlined in the technical document of the Ebro Basin Hydrological Plan 2010–2015.

	€M	% of 4,800
Measures to meet environmental targets		
Drainage and wastewater treatment	501.4	10.4
River and riverbank restoration actions	44.9	0.9
Control of water intakes	1.5	0.0
Improvement of areas with temporary pollution problems	14.6	0.3
Wastewater reuse plans	9.4	0.2
Agro-environmental measures programmes	40.4	0.8
Protection of underground waters	19.3	0.4
Irrigated areas modernization plans	1,413.7	29.5
Implementation of ecological flow regimes	17.6	0.4
Review of water rights	2.1	0.0
Improvement and development of control networks	22.9	0.5
Improvement of urban water supply quality	335.6	7.0
Ebro Delta improvement plans	95.2	2.0
Action plans for alien species	54.0	1.1
Treatment of contaminated sediments	83.6	1.7
Environmental education plans and volunteer workers	1.9	0.0
River continuity improvement plans	6.5	0.1
Hydrological-forestry projects	5.1	0.1
Climate change	1.9	0.0
R&D + I	13.4	0.3
Other	65.4	1.4
Total environmental target measures	**2,750.4**	**57.3**
Water demand satisfaction		
Agricultural uses	1,267.1	26.4
Regulation infrastructure	230.0	4.8
Energy exploitation	16.1	0.3
Recreational and leisure uses	70.6	1.5
Water heritage enhancement	0.9	0.0
Conservation and safety of hydraulic infrastructure	23.8	0.5
R&D + I	3.6	0.1
Other	15.1	0.3
Total water demand satisfaction measures	**1,627.2**	**33.9**
Extreme events		
Action programme during droughts	36.6	0.8
Maintenance and improvement of the SAIH- SAD system	32.0	0.7
Mapping of floodable areas	10.3	0.2
Action programmes for water streams (cleaning, improvement of defences, emergency works, etc.)	180.4	3.8
Infrastructure for flood control (dams)	144.5	3.0
R&D + I	0.8	0.0
Other	17.7	0.4
Total extreme events	**422.4**	**8.8**
TOTAL SCHEDULED INVESTMENT, HORIZON 2010–2015	**4,800.0**	**100.0**

Source: CHE (2011a).

- *Improve targeted areas with specific pollution problems*, namely those linked to sensitive areas (Ebro Reservoir), areas with urban and industrial water treatment problems (Miranda of Ebro), and areas with industrial problems (Monzon and Pamplona).
- *Reuse wastewater.* The draft National Wastewater Reuse Plan (MARM, 2010), outlined in Royal Decree 1620/2007 (BOE, 2007b), calls for water reuse of 11 hm^3 from five wastewater treatment plants in the Ebro basin by 2015. Reuse implies the elimination of

pollutants from water resources and the consequent improvement in water quality, which will be more effective the lower the rivers' flow.

- *Put in place agro-environmental measures in irrigated areas.* The so-called 'Ebro food-farming complex' includes production, transformation and marketing activities in agriculture, livestock, and the food industry. It is the second-most important industry of the Ebro valley, after metallurgy and transport (excluding service and construction activities), accounting for 10.2% of all employment in the basin and constituting the mainstay of economic activity in small rural territories with low population densities (Domingo Barrado, 2010).

Moreover, European Union Directive 91/676/EC on nitrates (1991b) has resulted in the implementation of a raft of measures, such as the declaration of vulnerable areas; the implementation of specific agricultural practices for each type of crop, region, and water mass (agricultural and livestock farming best practices); and the development of pilot experiments for the treatment of livestock waste. Since 2005, an Ebro basin return water management system has been in operation to control diffuse contamination while enabling the basin's agricultural and livestock practices to be environmentally assessed.

All these measures are aimed at reducing diffuse contamination in rivers and aquifers, thereby enhancing the efficiency of the agricultural and livestock sector. Their implementation improves the quality of water bodies, which receive return irrigation water, thereby improving their response, especially in dry periods.

- *Modernize irrigated areas* (improve irrigation techniques to increase water efficiency), which is a major effort Spain has made during the first decade of the twenty-first century. In the Ebro basin, 30% of all irrigated areas have been modernized, and this number will reach 50% by 2015. From an environmental viewpoint, the increased efficiency of irrigated areas brought about by modernization will reduce the pollutant masses that return to the water system, leading to better-quality surface and underground water (Lecina, Isidoro, Playán, & Aragüés, 2009). This effort includes the development of proposals to reuse irrigation water by re-integrating return water into the irrigation system. These measures will lead to a quality improvement in water ecosystems and less vulnerability to climate change.

- *Improve the quality of high-capacity urban water supply.* The forecasted fall in availability of water has prompted a review of urban water supplies to introduce alternative measures in cases where there is a risk of a lack of reliable water supply in terms of both quality and quantity. The high presence of gypsums in the central sector of the Ebro basin causes the recommended sulphate content of 250 mg/L to be exceeded in low-water periods.

The general strategy has been to displace the water intakes of population centres located along the Ebro's axis, where most of the basin's population lives, towards the irrigation canals transporting high-quality water from the basin's main heads. The 2010–2015 horizon should see the completion of, among others, the water supply to Zaragoza and its surrounding areas, the population centres of the Oja and Tiron Rivers, supply to Montsià and Terra Alta, and urban water supplies drawn from the Navarre Canal. Improvements are also scheduled for surface and underground-intake urban water supplies.

- *Improve plans for the Ebro Delta.* It will face a rise in sea level and a decline in sediment discharges because of climate change. The period of maximum progradation in the delta occurred between the fifteenth and nineteenth centuries as a result of a generalized expansion in the production of cereals and grazing in the basin which coincided with the Little Ice Age. The delta reached its maximum development towards the end of the nineteenth century (García Ruiz & López Bermúdez, 2009).

Law 11/2005 (BOE, 2005) establishes the need to prepare an integrated management plan for the Ebro Delta with the aim of maintaining its specific ecological conditions. As a result, a number of actions were proposed in the Hydrological Plan for 2010–2015, which are now at different phases of execution. Among the most remarkable projects are the removal of contaminated sediments in Flix (an investment of €140 M), improvements to urban water supplies and wastewater treatment, modernization of irrigated areas, and controlled flooding to eliminate macrophytes. Other actions include improvements to the Ebro watercourse, the construction of control networks, studies on environmental flow regimes, proposals to resolve subsidence and regression, and the improvement of the habitat of ecosystems.

- *Establish regulatory infrastructure.* The Ebro basin has 109 operational reservoirs of over 1 hm^3, with a total capacity of 7580 hm^3, of which 40% is for consumption; their capacity is 21% of the average annual resources for the period 1980/81–2005/06. In a climate change scenario, reservoirs have the advantage of mitigating the effects of declining water resources and changing monthly modulation. They also enable floods to be regulated, because every month each reservoir keeps back a volume of water for this purpose.

The Hydrological Plan for 2010–2015 has reviewed the reservoirs proposed in the 1998 Hydrological Plan (BOE, 1999). Of these, 36 reservoirs have been discarded as non-viable, and the rest have been maintained and are now under construction or in their design or advanced study phase.

- *Increase energy production.* There are 360 hydroelectric plants in the Ebro basin, with an installed power of 3594.5 MW and an average annual output of 9383.2 GWh, representing a little over a quarter of the output for all Spain (Omedas Margelí, 2010). The Hydrological Plan contains proposals to increase the number of foot-of-dam power plants at already-built structures and includes projects to increase the power of reversible hydroelectric plants. This will enable properly managing the significant increase in production of renewable energy (especially wind energy) that has occurred in Spain in the last 10 years.

- *Combat drought.* Based on the assessment of droughts in the twentieth century, Law 10/2001 on the National Hydrological Plan (BOE, 2001b) established the need to produce a system of hydrological drought indicators, hydrological basin-specific drought plans, and emergency plans for population centres of over 20,000 inhabitants.

In 2007, the Special Action Plan for Situations of Alert and Temporary Drought in the Ebro Hydrographic Basin (CHE, 2007) was approved. Its purpose is to provide a tool for early drought detection and subsequent decision making. This plan is a suitable tool for drought management given the establishment of action protocols depending on the status of the basin (normal, pre-alert, alert, or emergency).

- *Continue the Automatic Hydrological Information System* (hereinafter SAIH). The SAIH programme started as a consequence of the floods that affected Levante and the Basque Country in 1982. It was then designed as a data-gathering system collecting real time hydrological information (see http://195.55.247.237/saihebro/). The main variables it monitors are river flows and levels, reservoir volumes, flows in irrigation canals and from hydroelectric plants, precipitation, temperatures, piezometric levels, and snow height. It also provides three-day projections by inputting meteorological forecasts into a hydrological simulation model of the basin. As such, the SAIH is a highly efficient tool for managing water resources, controlling floodwaters, and managing dam safety and floods. The potentially greater impact of droughts and the greater frequency of floods call for the continued use of SAIH as a very important management tool for the future of the basin.

- *Manage floods*. In 2007, the European Union approved a directive for the assessment and management of flood risks (European Union, 2007). In 2011, this directive called for the preparation of a preliminary assessment of flood risks (CHE, 2011b), the preparation of flood hazard and risk maps in 2013 and flood risk management plans for 2015. These management plans are to contain specific measures to reduce the negative impact of floods on human health, the environment, cultural heritage and economic activity.

During the first phase (preliminary assessment), new flood maps were drawn up and all the cartographic information on floodable areas for return periods of 10, 50, 100 and 500 years in the National Flood Zone Mapping System was collated (see http://sig.marm.es/s nczi/). This information is being used by the Hydrographic Confederation of the Ebro in granting permits for the use and occupancy of public water. The directive has resulted in improved flood management, which will increase the region's resilience to climate change.

- *Implement actions to improve watercourses and riverbeds*. The Ministry of the Environment, through the Hydrographic Confederation of the Ebro and in some cases through autonomous communities, implements watercourse maintenance and cleaning measures to enhance water evacuation capacity in the event of floods and replaces flood-damaged defence infrastructure (basically channelling structures, breakwaters and earth banks). The actions of this programme are prioritized in such a way that, whenever possible, flow space is increased and urban centres are protected from flood-related problems.

- *Carry out research projects* (research and development). Updating surveys have been commissioned to assess the impacts of climate change on the Ebro basin and propose adaptation and mitigation measures related to water management. These studies are being carried out at the domestic level and within the framework of the Spanish Climate Change and Clean Energy Strategy (UN Framework Convention on Climate Change, 2007). The MARM, in collaboration with the Spanish Public Works Research Centre (CEDEX), is studying the effects of climate change on water resources in the natural regime (MARM-CEDEX, 2011), on water demands and adaptation strategies, on resource availability in development systems, and on the ecological status of water bodies. There are also other university groups and research centres working on other aspects of the effects of climate change on water resources.

Conclusions

This article has presented the Ebro basin as an example of the integration of expected climate change effects into water management policies, which can best be implemented through hydrological planning under the river basin unit principle. For this to hold true, there must be a legislative and institutional regime in place to regulate such plans and to clearly define the targets, institutions and procedures involved in implementing them. Moreover, hydrological plans should be based on, and integrate, all sectoral plans. For the

Ebro basin in particular, it should be ensured that energy and irrigation plans are mutually consistent.

Hydrological planning must also consider the forecasted effects of climate change on water resources and the implications of those effects on all aspects related to water management. Therefore, it is important that scientific and technical bodies exist and that these contribute their research and studies while always making use of the best available techniques. In the case of the Ebro basin, a 5% average reduction in water resources is expected by 2027. Given the basin's characteristics, there may be local differences in this percentage of decline, with higher values in the more arid areas than in the wetter zones. However, the various studies so far conducted have failed to agree on this aspect. For management purposes, the semi-arid basins on the right bank of the Ebro river may be considered the areas most sensitive to the effects of climate change.

Furthermore, measures covered by hydrological plans have to address the effects of climate change. In its technical segment, the Ebro Basin Hydrological Plan 2010–2015 establishes measures to improve regulation infrastructures and ensure water supplies and flood control, and measures to improve drought and flood management. It also outlines a list of provisions to improve water quality, including wastewater treatment, discharge amelioration, control of water intakes, water reuse, agro-environmental measures, modernization of irrigated areas, the improvement of urban water supplies, and the removal of contaminated sediments, amongst others. All these measures reduce the Ebro basin's vulnerability to climate change.

Acknowledgements

The author wishes to express his appreciation to the reviewers of this paper for their constructive comments and also to the language editor for significantly improving its structure and language.

References

Barrera Escoda, A., & Llasat Botija, M. C. (2004). *Evolución regional de la precipitación en España en los últimos 100 años* [Regional precipitation trends in Spain in the last 100 years]. *Ingeniería Civil, 135*, 105–113.

Bates, B. C., Kundzewicz, Z. W., Wu, S., & Palutikof, J. P. (2008). *Climate change and water* (technical document of the Intergovernmental Group of Experts on Climate Change). Geneva: IPCC Secretariat.

BOE (1998). Royal Decree 1664/1998, of 24 July, approving hydrological basin plans. Official State Gazette (BOE), 191, 11 August, 27296–27297.

BOE (1999). Order of 13 August 1999, informing of the publication of the regulatory determinations of the Ebro Basin Hydrological Plan, approved by Royal Decree 1664/1998, of 24 July. Official State Gazette (BOE), 222, 16 September, 33386–33452.

BOE (2001a). Royal Legislative Decree 1/2001, of 20 July, approving the consolidated text of the Water Act. Official State Gazette (BOE), 176, 24 July, 26791–26817.

BOE (2001b). Law 10/2001, of 5 July, on the National Hydrological Plan. Official State Gazette (BOE), 161, 6 July, 24228–24243.

BOE (2005). Law 11/2005, of 22 June, amending Law 10/2001, of 5 July, on the National Hydrological Plan. Official State Gazette (BOE), 149, 23 June, 21846–21856.

BOE (2007a). Royal Decree 907/2007, of 6 July, approving the Hydrological Planning Regulation. Official State Gazette (BOE), 162, 7 July, 29361–29398.

BOE (2007b). Royal Decree 1620/2007, of 7 December, establishing the legal regime for the reuse of treated water. Official State Gazette (BOE), 294, 8 December, 50639–50661.

BOE (2008). Order ARM/2656/2008, of 10 September, approving the Hydrological Planning Instruction. Official State Gazette (BOE), 229, 22 September, 38472–38582.

BOE (2009). Order ARM/1312/2009, of 20 May, regulating the systems for implementing effective control over the volumes of water used by exploitations of water from the public water domain, over returns to the aforementioned public water domain, and over discharges into the same. Official State Gazette (BOE), 128, 27 May, 43940–43966.

Cabezas, F., Estrada, F., & Estrela, T. (1999). *Algunas contribuciones técnicas del Libro Blanco del Agua en España* [Some technical contributions of the White Book on Water in Spain]. *Ingeniería Civil, 115,* 79–96.

CHE (Confederación Hidrográfica del Ebro) (1998). *Estudio de los caudales característicos para la estimación de las ecoregiones en la cuenca del Ebro* [Study of characteristic flows for the estimation of eco-regions in the Ebro basin]. Zaragoza: Hydrographic Confederation of the Ebro. Unpublished report.

CHE (2001a). *Las precipitaciones de la cuenca del Ebro: Caracterización de la evolución espacio-temporal y análisis de tendencias* [Precipitation in the Ebro basin: Characterization of the trend over space and time and trend analysis]. Zaragoza: Hydrographic Confederation of the Ebro. Retrieved from http://www.chebro.es/contenido.visualizar.do?idContenido=14281&id-Menu=3084

CHE (2001b). *La cubierta forestal de la cuenca del Ebro: caracterización espacio-temporal y afección en la disminución de recursos hídricos* [Forest cover of the Ebro basin: Characterization over space and time and effect on the reduction of water resources]. Zaragoza: Hydrographic Confederation of the Ebro. Retrieved from http://www.chebro.es/contenido.visualizar.do?idContenido=14281&idMenu=3084

CHE (2002). *Los recursos en los aprovechamientos de la cuenca del Ebro: tendencia en las precipitaciones estacionales 1920–2000 y análisis previo del periodo 1950–2000* [Resources in the exploitations of the Ebro basin: Trend in seasonal precipitation 1920–2000 and preliminary analysis of the period 1950–2000]. Zaragoza: Hydrographic Confederation of the Ebro. Retrieved from http://www.chebro.es/contenido.visualizar.do?idContenido=14281&id-Menu=3084

CHE (2005a). *Evaluación preliminar de la incidencia del cambio climático en los recursos hídricos de la cuenca del Ebro* [Preliminary assessment of the impact of climate change on the water resources of the Ebro basin]. Zaragoza: Hydrographic Confederation of the Ebro. Retrieved from http://www.chebro.es/contenido.visualizar.do?idContenido=14281&idMenu=3084

CHE (2005b). *Caracterización de la calidad de las aguas superficiales y control de los retornos de riego en la cuenca del Ebro* [Characterization of surface water quality and control of irrigation returns in the Ebro basin]. Zaragoza: Hydrographic Confederation of the Ebro. Retrieved from http://www.chebro.es/contenido.visualizar.do?idContenido=14417&idMenu=3087

CHE (2007). *Plan especial de actuación en situaciones de alerta y eventual sequía en la cuenca hidrográfica del Ebro* [Special action plan for situations of alert and temporary drought in the Ebro hydrographic basin]. Zaragoza: Hydrographic Confederation of the Ebro. Retrieved from http://www.chebro.es/contenido.visualizar.do?idContenido=17383&idMenu=3401

CHE (2011a). *Resumen de la Propuesta de proyecto de Plan Hidrológico de la cuenca del Ebro 2010–2015* [Summary of the Ebro Basin Hydrological Plan 2010–2015 project proposal]. Zaragoza: Hydrographic Confederation of the Ebro. Retrieved from http://www.chebro.es/contenido.visualizar.do?idContenido=4171&idMenu=3040

CHE (2011b). *Sistema Nacional de Cartografía de zonas inundables en la Demarcación Hidrográfica del Ebro: Evaluación preliminar del riesgo de inundación* [National mapping system of floodable areas in the Ebro Hydrographic Demarcation: Preliminary assessment of the risk of flood]. Zaragoza: Hydrographic Confederation of the Ebro. Retrieved from http://www.chebro.es/contenido.visualizar.do?idContenido=23881&idMenu=3940

Domingo Barrado, L. (2010). *La cuenca del Ebro: una visión social, económica y ambiental* [The Ebro basin: A social, economic and environmental vision]. *Revista de Economía Aragonesa, 41,* 107–134.

European Union (1991a). Council Directive of 21 May 1991 concerning urban waste water treatment. Official Journal of the European Communities, L 135, 30 May, 40–52.

European Union (1991b). Council Directive 91/676/EEC of 12 December 1991, concerning the protection of waters against pollution caused by nitrates from agricultural sources. Official Journal of the European Communities, L 375, 31 December.

European Union (2000). Directive 2000/60/EC of the European Parliament and of the Council of 23 October 2000 establishing a framework for Community action in the field of water policy. Official Journal of the European Communities, L 327, 1–8, 22 December.

European Union (2007). Directive 2007/60/EC of the European Parliament and of the Council, of 23 October 2007, regarding the assessment and management of the risks of flood. Official Journal of the European Communities, L 288/27, 6 November, 27–34.

Fernández, P., Mateos, C., & Estrela, T. (2003). *Evaluación del balance hídrico futuro mediante la utilización conjunta de modelos climáticos e hidrológicos* [Assessment of the future water balance by means of the combined use of climate and hydrological models]. Paper presented at the 11th World Water Congress of the International Water Resources Association, Madrid.

García Vera, M. A., Abaurrea, J., Asín Lafuente, J., & Centelles-Nogués, A. (2002). *Evolución de las precipitaciones en la cuenca del Ebro: caracterización espacial y análisis de tendencias* [Precipitation trends in the Ebro basin: spatial characterization and trend analysis]. In J. M. Cuadrat, S. M. Vicente & M. A. Saz (Eds.), *La información climática como herramienta de gestión ambiental* [Climate information as an environmental management tool] (pp. 99–108). Zaragoza: VII Reunión Nacional de Climatología.

García Vera, M. A., Coch Flotats, A., Gallart, F., Llorens, P., & Pintor, M. C. (2003). *Evaluación preliminar de los efectos de la forestación sobre la escorrentía del Ebro* [Preliminary assessment of the effects of the forestation on the Ebro runoff]. Paper presented at the 11th World Water Congress of the International Water Resources Association, Madrid.

García Ruiz, J. M., & López Bermúdez, F. (2009). *La erosión del suelo en España* [Soil erosion in Spain]. Zaragoza: Spanish Geomorphological Society.

IPCC (2007). *Climate change 2007: synthesis report*. Intergovernmental Panel on Climate Change. Plenary XXVII. Valenci.

Lecina, S., Isidoro, D., Playán, E., & Aragüés, R. (2009). *Efecto de la modernización de regadíos sobre la cantidad y la calidad de las aguas: la cuenca del Ebro como caso de estudio* [Effect of the modernization of irrigated areas on the quantity and quality of water: The Ebro basin as a case study] (INIA monographs, Serie agrícola No. 26–2009). Madrid: INIA.

López-Moreno, J. I., Vicente-Serrano, S. M., Moran-Tejeda, E., Zabalza, J., Lorenzo-Lacruz, J., & García-Ruiz, J. M. (2010). Impact of climate evolution and land use changes on water yield in the Ebro basin. *Hydrology and Earth System Sciences, 7*, 2651–2681.

MARM (2010). *Preliminary version of the National Water Reuse Plan*. Madrid: Ministry of the Environment and Rural and Marine Affairs. Retrieved from http://www.magrama.gob.es/es/agua/participacion-publica/pnra.aspx

MARM-CEDEX (2011). *Assessment of the impact of the climate change in the water resources in natural regime*. Retrieved from http://www.marm.es/es/agua/temas/planificacion-hidrologica/planificacion-hidrologica/EGest_CC_RH.aspx

MIMAM (2000). *Technical documentation for the preparation of the National Hydrological Plan: Analysis of hydraulic systems*. Ministry of the Environment. Unpublished report.

Omedas Margelí, M. (2010). *La energía ante el nuevo plan hidrológico de la cuenca del Ebro* [Energy before the new Ebro Basin Hydrological Plan]. In A. Embid (Ed.), *Agua y Energía* (pp. 391–420). Zaragoza: Civitas Ediciones.

Ruiz García, J. M. (1999). *Modelo distribuido para la Evaluación de Recursos Hídricos* [Distributed model for the assessment of water resources] (CEDEX monograph No. M-67). Madrid: Ministry of Public Works.

Saladie, O., Brunet, M., Aguilar, E., Sigró, J., & López, D. (2004). *Variacions i tendencia de la precipitació a las terres de l'Ebre durant el segle XX*, Paper presented at the 4th Iberian Congress on Water Management and Planning, Tortosa.

Samper, F. J., Huguet, Ll., Ares, J., & García Vera, M. A. (1999). *Manual del usuario del programa Visual Balan V1.0: código interactivo para la realización de balances hidrológicos y la estimación de la recarga* [User manual for the program Visual Balan V1.0: Interactive code for the performance of hydrological balances and recharge estimation] (Technical Publication ENRESA 5/99). Madrid: Edita: Empresa Nacional de Residuos S.A.

UN Framework Convention on Climate Change (2007). *Quinta comunicación de España*. Retrieved from http://unfccc.int/resource/docs/natc/esp_nc5.pdf

Measures against climate change and its impacts on water resources in Greece

Evangelos A. Baltas

Department of Hydraulics, Soil Science and Agricultural Engineering, School of Agriculture, Aristotle University of Thessaloniki, Greece

This paper examines the actions toward the reduction of greenhouse gas emissions to the atmosphere that Greece has implemented to comply with international conventions and the Kyoto Protocol. It also concerns the analysis and processing of climate variables and the assessment of the impact of climate change on water resources in Northern Greece and on some critical water management issues, such as reservoir storage and water supply for agriculture and domestic use. Initially, a monthly conceptual water balance model was applied to estimate runoff values in the entrance of the Polyfyto reservoir under the UKHI equilibrium scenario referring to the year 2100. It was found that the mean annual runoff, mean winter runoff and summer runoff values will be reduced. Increases of the risks associated with the annual quantities of water supply have been observed.

Introduction

Global climate change caused by increase in the atmospheric concentration of carbon dioxide and its associated impacts has received a great deal of attention from researchers in a variety of fields (Baltas & Mimikou, 2005; Huntington, 2006; McCarthy, Canziana, Leary, Dokken, & White, 2001; Richardson, 2002). Climate change is one of the main factors which influence the hydrological regime (Bates, Kundzewicz, Wu, & Palutikof, 2008; Myles & Ingram, 2002). Climate warming observed over the past several decades is consistently associated with changes in a number of components of the hydrological cycle and hydrological systems, such as changing precipitation patterns, intensity and extremes; widespread melting of snow and ice; increasing atmospheric water vapour; increasing evaporation; and changes in soil moisture and runoff.

The assessment of impacts of climate change on environmental and socio-economic systems is subject to a range of uncertainties (New & Hulme, 2000) due to inadequate information or understanding about biophysical processes or a lack of analytical resources available for impact assessment, the inherent unpredictability of the earth system, and the inability to forecast future socio-economic and human behaviour in a deterministic manner. Uncertainties about future socio-economic trends have resulted in the wide range of predicted future greenhouse gas (GHG) emissions.

Climate change and water resources availability and quality are interlinked. If reduction in precipitation continues in the present century, adverse effects on the availability and quality of the water resources, creating difficulties in satisfying existing demands and increasing future water demands, will be encountered. Although the climate change and climate variability are observed and analyzed, no decision has been made so far by the state to study the effects of this on the Greek economy, social life and environment. The adoption of the European Water Framework Directive makes it necessary to take into consideration all up-to-date data and information on the climate and other data for evaluating the availability, quality and status of the surface water and groundwater resources. Since the availability and status of both resources is dependent on the prevailing climate, this offers an opportunity to initiate and carry out, on a national scale, a plan for the re-evaluation of the naturally available water resources and the projected water demand, taking into consideration the planned development of the country. Additionally, Greece has a long coastline and numerous small islands in the Ionian and Aegean Seas, and the projected sea-level rise due to global warming is expected to affect the scarce groundwater and land resources of the coastal areas and mostly of the smaller islands.

Concerning emissions of greenhouse gases, a number of measures have been taken to reduce them in coming years. These are concentrated on: (1) further penetration of natural gas in all final demand energy sectors as well as in power generation, including co-generation; (2) promotion of renewable energy sources for electricity and heat production; (3) promotion of energy-saving measures in industry and in the residential and tertiary sector; (4) structural changes in agriculture and in the chemical industry; and (5) emission reduction actions in the transport and waste management sectors.

The impact of climate change on the hydrological regime and water resources in the Ilarion basin was assessed in this research. It constitutes a part of the basin of the Aliakmon River, the largest river in Northern Greece. A monthly conceptual water balance model was calibrated using historical hydrometeorological data to determine changes in streamflow runoff under the UKHI (UK Meteorological Office High Resolution model) equilibrium scenario referring to the year 2100. The regional climate impacts on different forms of water resources were used to assess the operational reliability of the Polyfyto reservoir in Northern Greece.

Study region and data used

The climate of Greece is typically Mediterranean, with long, hot, dry summers. Precipitation varies greatly, ranging from about 400 mm/y in Athens to more than 1200 mm/y in the higher mountains. Rainfall is seasonal, most of it coming in late-fall and winter months. The rainfall in Greece is variable in space, increasing from south to north (because of the climatic conditions varying from dryer and warmer to humid and cooler because of the increase in latitude), and also increasing from east to west (because of the separation of the country into two different climatic unities by the Pindos range and its extension to Peloponessos and Crete) (Zambakas, 1992).

During the twentieth century, the climate of Greece, and specifically the two basic parameters of precipitation and temperature, show some variation, but not in line with what occurred in the other countries of Europe and the Mediterranean. The temperature showed a decrease, in contrast to the other countries, where it showed an increase; precipitation presented a reduction, but of no statistical significance. During the 1990s, the number of heat waves was three times that recorded during the previous 30-year period. The decade 1984–1994 was the worst decade for drought in both Athens and Thessalonica.

With the temperature globally increasing at a rate of 0.8 °C per 100 years, it is expected that the level of the oceans will rise due to seawater volume (thermal) expansion and the melting of the ice in some parts of world such as in Greenland and near the poles. From records and analysis it can be concluded that on the global level during the period 1880–1980 the sea level was rising at a rate of 1.8 ± 0.1 mm per year. During the last century, the sea level rose by 18 cm, with a margin of uncertainty of 2.5 cm. Most of the Mediterranean coasts have undergone similar changes, with the sea level rising at a rate of 1–2 mm per year. In the Nile Delta the rise was 4.8 mm/y; in the Thessalonica delta areas, 4.0 mm/y; and in the Venice delta, 7.3 mm/y (MEPPPW, 2006).

The global average surface temperature is projected to increase by 1.4 to 5.8 °C over the period 1990–2100, while mean sea level is projected to rise between 0.09 and 0.88 metres. The temperature in the Mediterranean region is projected to increase by 0.7 to 1.6 °C per 1 °C of global increase. Using five climatic models, New & Hulme (2000) predicted for Greece an increase in mean temperature of 3.1 to 5.1 °C, with an average of 4.3 °C. Other models give an increase of 1.5 to 2.3 °C, with more of an increase in summer than in winter. Concerning precipitation, this is more difficult to project because Greece lies in a transition zone. All models agree that precipitation will decrease in summer months and that there exists a greater probability that precipitation will increase in the northern regions of Greece. Other studies show an increase of the annual precipitation in Crete of 14.4 to 23.8 mm by the year 2030 (MEPPPW, 2006).

As of 2000, 19% of the total area of Greece is forest. (Coniferous forest represents 38% of forested land while the other 62% is broadleaf forest.) Other wooded land represents 25%, and grassland 13%. Other types of land cover, mainly used for grazing and agricultural land (including fallow land), account for 29%, including areas occupied by brushwood. Alpine areas and internal waterways account for 8% of the total area. Uncultivated land and desert make up the remaining 6%.

The study area belongs to the water district of Western Macedonia, which is joined to the water district of Central Macedonia through the provision of water to the city of Thessaloniki and to agricultural and industrial use from the Aliakmon River. The study area (see Figure 1 and Table 1) is within the Aliakmon River basin, which is in Northern Greece between 39°30'S and 40°30'N and between 20°30'W and 22°E. All required hydrometeorological monthly data for the study period 1961–90 (30 years) were acquired from a number of stations located in and near the study area, while the monthly runoff data were obtained from the archives of the Public Power Corporation of Greece. The hydrometeorological data included precipitation, snow, evaporation, wind velocity, relative humidity, sunshine duration and temperature values. Precipitation data from 50 rain gauges and rain-gauge recording stations were used. Temperature data were collected from 17 stations. Concerning the mean monthly evapotranspiration, which is a direct input to the water balance model, it is inferred from field data according to the Blaney-Griddle method.

These data were used as inputs (directly or indirectly) to the water balance model utilized for the assessment of the climate change effects on the surface runoff of the study region, as described elsewhere (Baltas & Mimikou, 2005). The inflows of the Polyfyto reservoir, located 32 km downstream of the Ilarion station, are estimated from the streamflows at the Ilarion site proportionally to the ratio of the corresponding drainage areas.

Five multipurpose reservoirs will soon be in operation along the route of the Aliakmon River to satisfy irrigation, water supply and power generation needs. These are, starting from upstream, Ilarion, Polyfyto, Sfikia, Assomata and Agia Varvara, as shown in Figure 1. Although efforts were made to model the operation of the five reservoirs as a system, that was not possible because four of the reservoirs are mainly regulating reservoirs (one-day

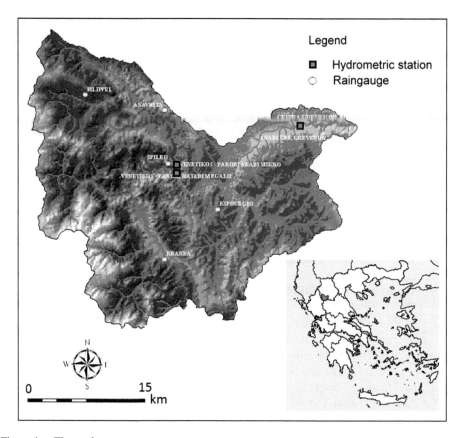

Figure 1.   The study area.

Table 1.   General characteristics of the study area.

Sub-basin	Area (km^2)	Mean elevation (m)	Mean annual historical temperature (°C)	Mean annual historical precipitation (mm)	Mean annual historical run-off (m^3/s)	Mean annual specific runoff (m^3/sec) per km^2	Sub-basin river length (km)
Ilarion	5005	917	11.0	825.1	49.0	0.0098	161.0

storage) to provide water downstream and also to contribute to power generation. Therefore, only the Polyfyto reservoir (whose technical characteristics are shown in Table 2) has been examined in this work. Regarding the operation of the Polyfyto reservoir, all relevant data have been acquired from different divisions of the Public Power Corporation and the Ministry of Agriculture of Greece. The data included inflows and outflows to and from the reservoir/plant, characteristics of the reservoir, and the hydroelectric production of the power plant, such as water level–storage capacity–water surface relationships, functions of turbines and transformers, hydraulic characteristics, etc.

Table 2. Design characteristics of the Polyfyto Reservoir.

Design head (m)	146.40
Maximum storage capacity (10^6 m^3)	1160
Minimum storage capacity (m^3)	655
Minimum (guaranteed) energy (GWh/y)	199.4
Mean (guaranteed) energy (GWh/y)	515
Firm water supply (10^6 m^3)	640
Maximum outflow capacity through the turbines (m^3/sec)	345
Number of turbines	3
Power of each turbine (MW)	125

Actions against climate change in Greece

Directive 2000/60/EU (European Commission, 2000) marks the beginning of a new era in EU environmental policy and sets the legal background for the long-term, sustainable management of water resources on a basin level in the territory of Europe. Success in the application of the directive is expected to depend on two crucial factors: on the one hand, coordination between the physical procedures and the human activities that affect the cycle of water inside the boundaries of a basin, and on the other hand, the early taking of appropriate management measures which will ensure the desired 'good condition' of the surface and underground water resources in the coming years (Baltas, 2011).

The directive aims at the establishment of a common European policy for the protection of internal, surface, transient, coastal and ground waters, in combination with protection of the environment. The basic directive trend of the European Committee for the organization of management is the principle of participation of all the interested participants up to the final user-consumer. The obligations of Greece under the UNFCC Convention (United Nations, 1992) are being fulfilled jointly with the other EU member states. For Greece, the agreed figure was a realistic objective to restrict the overall increase of CO_2 by 2000 to $+15\% \pm 3\%$ compared to 1990 levels, which was achieved. The 'burden sharing agreement' finalized during the Environment Council of the EU in June 1998 provides that Greece restricts the increase of emission of six gases to the atmosphere for the period 2008–2012 to $+25\%$ compared to 1990 levels. The major distinction between the Protocol and the Convention is that while the Convention encouraged industrialized countries to stabilize GHG emissions, the Protocol commits them to do so (http://unfccc.int/kyoto_protocol/items/2830.php). Figure 2 depicts the GHG emissions from the implementation of additional policies and measures per sector (MEPPPW, 2006). From this figure one can observe that Greece will achieve its target for the period 2008–2012.

Climate change scenario

General circulation models (GCMs) are complex gridded three-dimensional computer-based models of the climate system and constitute the base for the construction of climate change scenarios. These scenarios provide the best available means of exploring how human activities may change the composition of the atmosphere, how this may affect global climate, and how the resulting climate changes may impact upon the environment and human activities. Climate change scenarios reflecting future global increases in greenhouse gas concentrations were constructed for Europe (including Greece) at 0.5° latitude/longitude resolution by the Climatic Research Unit (CRU) of the University of East Anglia, England. The mentioned scenarios were applied in Northern Greece through the use of a conceptual physically based water balance model, which operates on a

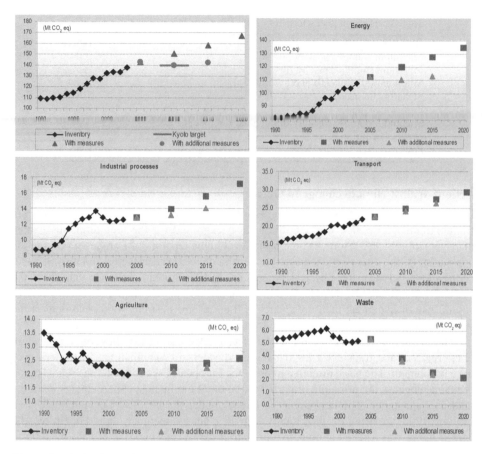

Figure 2. Projections of GHG emissions from the implementation of additional policies and measures per sector. Source: MEPPPW (2006).

monthly basis and has been used for the assessment of the regional hydrological effects of climate change.

One of the greatest concerns of future climate change is its potential impact at local to regional scales. Considerable consequences are expected for regional hydrological cycles, with subsequent effects on regional water resources, agriculture, and water and air quality. Global changes in the climate system will interact with the distinctive geographic characteristics of individual regions to produce a climate change signal unique to that region. Climate changes therefore need to be evaluated at spatial and temporal scales that make the projections relevant on a human scale (Hayhoe et al., 2008).

According to the Intergovernmental Panel on Climate Change (IPCC, 2012), observations gathered since 1950 show that it is very likely that there has been an overall decrease in the number of cold days and nights and an overall increase in the number of warm days and nights at the global scale, that is for most land areas with sufficient data. It is likely that these changes have also occurred at the continental scale in North America, Europe and Australia. In many (but not all) regions across the globe with sufficient data, there is medium confidence that the length or number of heat waves has increased. Models project substantial warming in temperature extremes by the end of the twenty-first century. It is virtually certain that increases in the frequency and magnitude of high daily temperature extremes and decreases in low extremes will occur in the twenty-first century at the global scale. It is very likely that the length, frequency, and/or intensity of warm spells or heat waves will increase over most land areas. The once-in-20-years extreme daily maximum temperature (i.e. a value that was exceeded on average only once during the period 1981–2000) is likely to increase by about 1 to 3 °C by the mid-twenty-first century and by about 2 to 5 °C by the late twenty-first century, depending on the region and emissions scenario.

It is likely that the frequency of heavy precipitation will increase in the twenty-first century over many areas of the globe. This is particularly the case in the high latitudes and tropical regions, and in winter in the northern mid-latitudes. Based on a range of emissions scenarios, a once-in-20-years annual maximum daily precipitation amount is likely to become a once-in-15-years to once-in-5-years event by the end of the twenty-first century in many regions (IPCC, 2012).

Runoff is projected with high confidence to decrease by 10 to 30% over some dry regions at mid-latitudes and dry tropics, as the result of decreases in rainfall and higher rates of evapotranspiration. There is also high confidence that many semi-arid areas (e.g. the Mediterranean Basin) will suffer a decrease in water resources due to climate change. Available research suggests a significant future increase in heavy rainfall events in many regions, including some in which the mean rainfall is projected to decrease. Increases in the frequency and severity of floods and droughts are projected to adversely affect sustainable development. In coastal areas, sea-level rise will exacerbate water resource constraints through increased salinization of groundwater supplies (IPCC, 2007).

The scenario based on equilibrium results was extracted from the gridded historical global data sets including variables such as precipitation, temperature, wind speed, sunshine hours, vapour pressure and rain-day frequencies, which were acquired by and processed at the Climatic Research Unit. The GCM output of the variables precipitation, temperature and evapotranspiration was interpolated to $0.5° \times 0.5°$ from the original GCM resolution ($3.75° \times 2.5°$ UKHI). The study area was divided into grids with dimensions $0.5° \times 0.5°$ for the application of the climate change scenarios to the basin. The precipitation, temperature and evapotranspiration values were estimated by using the provided original gridded data and through the appropriate use of a weighting coefficient associated with each grid cell constituting the basin. The weighting coefficient used for each cell was calculated according to the percentage contribution of the cell to the entire basin.

Methodology

The model used in this research work is a physically based water balance model (Baltas, 2009; Baltas & Mimikou, 2005), which operates on a monthly basis. The model was successfully calibrated using the historical hydrometeorological and hydrometric data. The input parameters used for the calibration were the maximum soil moisture parameter, the watershed lag coefficient, the groundwater reservoir coefficient, the temperature parameters (lower T_0 and upper T_1 thresholds), the minimum rain content coefficient, the melt-rate factor and the storm runoff coefficient.

More specifically, the maximum soil moisture is a basin average of the moisture-holding capacity of the upper soil zone. The watershed lag coefficient is the parameter applied on the water surplus to yield the amount of water that will eventually flow to the river course within a month, after having fulfilled the requirements of evapotranspiration and soil moisture replenishment, while the groundwater reservoir coefficient is the rate of outflow from the groundwater storage to the river course, considered to occur with a lag of one month. A simple snow melting subroutine based on temperature thresholds, minimum rain content coefficient and a melt-rate factor was applied for the calculation of the snow-melt values. Specifically, the model estimates the rain and snow from the total precipitation according to monthly average basin temperature and to the temperature thresholds (T_0 and T_1). Below the temperature T_0 the snow content of areal precipitation reaches a maximum; between T_0 and T_1 it is linearly dependent on temperature; and above T_1 precipitation falls entirely as rain. The snow tank, which is the amount of the accumulated snow at the end of each month, and the snow melt, which is the quantity of snow melting each month, are calculated through the use of the snow melting subroutine. However, it should be mentioned that, given the monthly time scale of the model (values of mean monthly temperatures are used), the produced values of snow are underestimated. A daily model would have produced more realistic snow, snow tank and snow melt values. Finally, the storm runoff coefficient determines how much of the water falling as rain flows directly as storm runoff before any other processes take place. This parameter depends on the month of the year; therefore 12 values were determined.

The final values of the input parameters were derived during the calibration phase of the model and were used in the application of the model with climate change scenario. Outputs of the model are the basin runoff and the soil moisture values. The soil moisture is the quantity of water held in the aeration zone, which can supply water for evapotranspiration when the surface water does not suffice. The Nash parameter was used as a criterion regarding the accuracy of the calibration. The calibration was performed twice, firstly by incorporating the Blaney-Criddle method and secondly by incorporating the Penman one, which was initially suggested to be applied, for the calculation of the potential evapotranspiration. Since the values of the Nash parameters obtained in the first case were higher than the values obtained in the second case, the Blaney-Criddle method was selected and used for the application of the model.

The UKHI equilibrium climate change scenario referring to 2100 was applied. For applying the scenario to the hydrometeorological data, synthetic series (from 1990 up to 2100) of precipitation, temperature and potential evapotranspiration, based on the historical data, were produced. The stochastic autoregressive models AR(1) and AR(2) were applied to the historical data of the 30-year period and a portmanteau test was used as a criterion to check their efficiency in each case. Finally, 50 synthetic series of each variable were generated to be used as inputs in the water balance model with or without the scenarios.

The climate change scenario was finally applied to the generated hydrometeorological series by correcting each monthly value using a linear interpolation between the generated values and the corresponding mean monthly historical values. Runs of the water balance model to estimate possible future runoffs for all time steps, using the already generated hydrometeorological data and considering zero climate change (no application of climate change scenarios), are referred to as base runs and were used for comparison purposes. The selection of the base runs as a basis of comparison was made for uniformity reasons and it was accepted because each base run was found to be similar to the historical record. Consequently, to evaluate the impacts of climate change on the flow regime of the Aliakmon River basin, the mean annual, winter, and summer runoffs were determined and compared.

The reservoir model that was applied for the operation of the Polyfyto reservoir was applied under different constraints concerning storage volume, outflows for domestic and agricultural use and energy production. The aim was the assessment of the risk for each time series inflow for the mean energy supply, which was estimated to be 515 GWh.

Results

To evaluate the impacts of climate change on the flow regime of the river basin and to make optimal use of all produced results, several hydrological indicators were chosen to be determined and compared, such as mean annual runoff, mean monthly runoff, and mean annual maximum and minimum runoff values. Table 3 summarizes the results of the scenario application, indicating the direction of change, using the base runs as a basis of comparison for all cases. The positive sign (+) is translated as an increase of the specific value, while the negative sign (−) represents a decrease. It is generally seen that reduction of the mean annual runoff values would occur in all cases, as well as increase of runoff for December. The minimum annual runoff values would also decrease and the maximum annual runoff values would increase.

The mean annual precipitation estimated by the application of the equilibrium climate change scenario will be reduced by 1.6%. Furthermore, it was found that the mean annual runoff will be reduced by 7.3% – more than four times the corresponding annual precipitation reduction (1.6%) – the mean winter runoff by 3.8%, and the mean summer runoff by 22.1%. Figure 3 depicts the estimated mean monthly runoff values (in mm) of the Ilarion basin for the period 1990–2100, resulting from the application of the equilibrium scenario. An increase of mean winter runoff and a reduction of summer runoff values is observed.

The mean monthly actual evapotranspiration is depicted in Figure 4, in which an increase is observed for the winter months as a result of temperature increases. A reduction is observed for the summer months. The temperature increase results in reduction of snow accumulation and decrease in spring runoff value and soil moisture. The mean annual runoff and mean summer runoff are depicted in Figures 5 and 6. The risk in the annual primary mean energy under the application of the UKHI (UK Meteorological Office High Resolution model) scenario increases, as shown in Figure 7, especially for values higher than 500 GWh.

Changes in precipitation and temperature will lead to changes in runoff and water availability. The mountain snow pack of the area that plays a crucial role in freshwater availability will be reduced and an acceleration throughout the twenty-first century is expected, leading to reductions in water availability, crop productivity and winter tourism, and extensive species losses. The changes in heat waves and snow cover will affect high-mountain phenomena such as slope instabilities, movements of mass and soil erosion.

Table 3. Summary of direction of change in percentage-application for the basin (+ for increase, − for decrease).

Hydrological indicators	1990–2100
Mean annual precipitation	−
Mean annual potential evapotranspiration	+
Mean annual actual evapotranspiration	+
Mean annual runoff	−
Mean summer runoff	−
Mean winter runoff	−
Annual max runoff	+
Annual min runoff	−
Monthly max runoff (December)	+
Monthly min runoff (August)	−

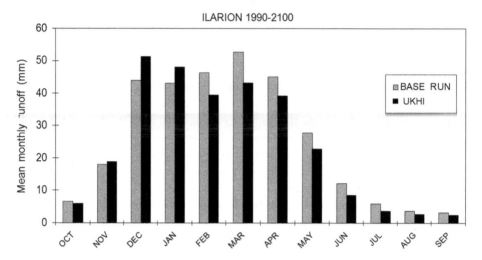

Figure 3. Mean monthly runoff of the Ilarion Basin, 1990–2100, estimated by applying the UKHI equilibrium scenario.

The changes in heavy precipitation will affect landslides. The changing seasonality of flows and the reduction of the hydropower potential are also important.

The increased temperature will further affect the physical, chemical and biological properties of freshwater lakes and rivers, with predominantly adverse impacts on many individual freshwater species, community composition and water quality. Large increases in irrigation-water demand as a result of the increased temperatures are projected.

Climate change is also projected to increase the health risks due to heat waves and the frequency of wildfires. Droughts will intensify in the twenty-first century, as a result of reduced precipitation and/or increased evapotranspiration. A reformation of the water policy should be made towards the reduction of water-demanding cultivations and the

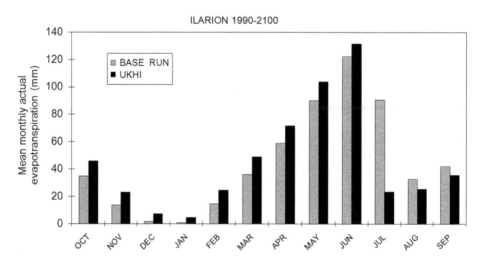

Figure 4. Mean monthly actual evapotranspiration of the basin, 1990–2100, estimated by applying the UKHI equilibrium scenario.

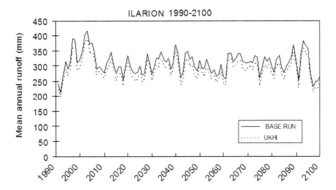

Figure 5. Mean annual runoff of the basin, 1990–2100 estimated by applying the UKHI equilibrium scenario.

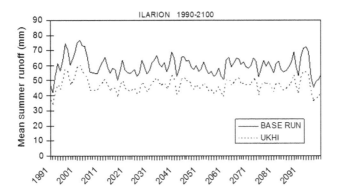

Figure 6. Mean summer runoff of the basin, 1990–2100, estimated by applying the UKHI equilibrium scenarios.

installation of supply-measurement devices. Regarding the supply of potable water, actions aiming at the sensitization of users for the consideration of water as a good should be made.

The objectives regarding the new possible planning and management practices are (Baltas, 2009):

- Works of infrastructure aiming at the reservation of surface water. These structures will supply water during the prolonged dry period and will also provide protection against extreme storm events.
- Works of artificial recharge in aquifers. These works are especially important because the future escalated evapotranspiration does not affect the vast amounts of groundwater.
- Suitable new irrigation infrastructure for the efficient watering of cultivations, characterized by low evaporation losses.
- Works of infrastructure aiming at conservation, such as reforestations, redistributions, regulations and flood structures.
- Systematic and reliable recording and evaluation of the physical and artificial water systems from a quantitative and qualitative point of view. Measurements of hydrologic, meteorological, hydrogeological and qualitative parameters should be regularly performed.
- Combined management of land reclamation works.

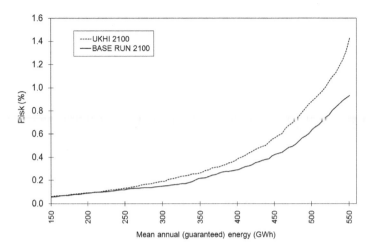

Figure 7.   Risk in the mean annual primary energy.

Concerning the effect of climate change on the design of future drainage and water-related structures, special care should be given to elements which depend on parameters affected by climate change, such as a power plant's installed capacity, the size of a reservoir or the corresponding dam height. Increased variability of the inflow will require a larger reservoir for the same guaranteed production (Guillaud, 2006). The design of a hydraulic structure mainly depends on the trend of river flow. More specifically, for example, the spillway size should be determined based on pessimistic evaluation of the trend for extreme floods, for the conditions that are expected to prevail in the mid-future (15 to 20 years). The spillway should be designed in such a way that it would be easy to increase its capacity in the future. After 10 to 15 years of operation and project monitoring, the trend of parameters related to climate change is re-evaluated, the optimization of the project is reviewed and necessary adjustments are recommended, which may consist of increasing dam height, spilling capacity, etc. (Guillaud, 2006).

Conclusions

The uncertainties are not so severe that they invalidate the results. It is important to attempt to quantify change as soon as possible so that resulting problems can be addressed in advance. The extreme conditions of flood and drought are of particular concern because it is possible that, even if there is only a small shift in average conditions, there may be larger, more significant changes in the extremes. Coping with increased flood magnitudes or reduced low flows may require long-term planning and be very costly.

The impact of climate change on the hydrological regime and the water resources in the basin will be substantial. The application of the UKHI scenario resulted in reduction of mean winter and summer runoff values, increase of maximum annual runoff and decrease of minimum annual runoff values. Additionally, an increase of potential and actual evapotranspiration was noticed as a result of temperature increase. Thus, a reduction of snow accumulation and a decrease in spring runoff values and soil moisture are expected.

The reduction in mean annual runoff is more than four times the reduction in mean annual precipitation when applying the UKHI scenario. Additionally, the risk in the annual primary energy of the Polyfyto reservoir under the application of the UKHI scenario increases, especially above 500 GWh.

A reduction of the mean annual runoff and prolongation of the dry period could severely affect the regional economy, given that it is mainly based on agriculture and pastoral farming. A reformation of the water policy should be made to follow the above possible future changes. The appropriate measures should focus on the operation of a monitoring mechanism of water uses and measurement of the water quantity that is utilized in each use (agricultural and domestic), with the corresponding application of cost accounting of water.

References

Baltas, E. A. (2009). Climate change and associated implications for the water policy framework in the basin of Venetikos. *International Journal of Water Resources Development, 25*(3), 491–506.

Baltas, E. A. (2011). The associated risks on water resources in Western Macedonia under climate change. *Journal of Water and Climate Change, 2,* 44–55.

Baltas, E. A., & Mimikou, M. A. (2005). Climate change impacts on the water supply of Thessaloniki. *International Journal of Water Resources Development, 21*(2), 341–353.

Bates, B. C., Kundzewicz, Z. W., Wu, S., & Palutikof, J. P. (Eds.). (2008). *Climate change and water.* (Technical Paper of the Intergovernmental Panel on Climate Change) Geneva: IPCC Secretariat.

European Commission (2000). Directive 2000/60/EC of the European Parliament and of the Council establishing a framework for the Community action in the field of water policy. *Official Journal* (OJ L 327) 22 December 2000.

Guillaud, C. (2006). Coping with uncertainty in the design of hydraulic structures: Climate change is but one more uncertain parameter. *EIC Climate Change Technology,* doi: 10.1109/ EICCCC.2006.277263.

Hayhoe, K., Wake, C., Anderson, B., Liang, X. -Z., Maurer, E., ... Zhu, J. (2008). Regional climate change projections for the Northeast USA. *Mitigation and Adaptation Strategies for Global Change, 13,* 425–436.

Huntington, T. G. (2006). Evidence for intensification of the global water cycle: Review and synthesis. *Journal of Hydrology, 319,* 83–95.

IPCC (2007). *Climate change 2007: Synthesis report* (assessment of the Intergovernmental Panel on Climate Change). Geneva: IPCC.

IPCC (2012). *Managing the risks of extreme events and disasters to advance climate change adaptation: A special report of Working Groups I and II of the Intergovernmental Panel on Climate Change.* Cambridge: Cambridge University Press.

McCarthy, J. J., Canziana, O. F., Leary, N. A., Dokken, D. J., & White, K. S. (2001). *Climate change 2001: Impacts, adaptation, and vulnerability. Contribution of Working Group II to the Third Assessment Report of the Intergovernmental Panel on Climate Change (IPCC).* Cambridge: Cambridge University Press.

MEPPPW (Ministry for the Environment, Physical Planning and Public Works) (2006). *4th national communication to the United Nations Framework Convention on Climate Change.* Athens: Hellenic Republic. Retrieved from http://unfccc.int/resource/docs/natc/grenc4.pdf

Myles, M. R., & Ingram, W. J. (2002). Constraints on future changes in climate and the hydrologic cycle. *Nature, 419,* 224–232.

New, M., & Hulme, M. (2000). Representing uncertainty in climate change scenarios: A Monte Carlo approach. *Integrated Assessment, 1,* 203–213.

Richardson, D. (2002). Flood risk: The impact of climate change (Proceedings of ICE). *Civil Engineering, 150*(5), 22–24.

United Nations. (1992). *United Nations framework convention on climate change.* Geneva: UNEP/WMO.

Zambakas, J. (1992). *General climatology.* Athens: Department of Geology, National & Kapodistrian University of Athens.

STATE-OF-THE-ART REVIEW

Water and disasters: a review and analysis of policy aspects

Chennat Gopalakrishnan

Department of Natural Resources and Environmental Management, University of Hawaii at Manoa, Honolulu, USA

Recent years have witnessed a significant increase in the human and economic impacts of water disasters. During 2000–2010, they accounted for almost 90% of all natural disasters, 96% of the people affected (2.4 billion) and 76% of the economic damages (approximately USD1 trillion) caused by natural disasters globally. It is ironic that despite the centrality of water disasters, relatively little attention has been paid to them in the discourse on water resources. Against this backdrop, five broad groups of water policies – risk management, vulnerability assessment, capacity building and resilience, disaster risk reduction-development linkage and institutional design – were examined to determine their adequacy and effectiveness in successfully dealing with water disasters. It was found that most policies have serious shortcomings that need to be addressed. Drawing on this study, a number of specific policy recommendations are offered to correct these deficiencies. The study has further found that there is an urgent need to generate research-grounded data to support informed policy making on water disasters. With this in view, five priority research areas have been identified.

Modern society has distinct advantages over those civilizations of the past that suffered or even collapsed for reasons linked to water. We have great knowledge, and the capacity to disperse that knowledge to the remotest places on earth. We are also beneficiaries of scientific leaps that have improved weather forecasting, agricultural practices, natural resources management, disaster prevention, preparedness and management.... But only a rational and informed political, social and cultural response – and public participation in all stages of the disaster management cycle – can reduce disaster vulnerability, and ensure that hazards do not turn into unmanageable disasters. (Kofi Annan, 2004)

Introduction

An aspect of water resources management that has received relatively little attention in the discourse on water pertains to water and disasters. The destructive potential of water has been well recorded in history, going as far back as biblical times. Recent years have seen instance after instance of the catastrophic consequences of floods and droughts throughout the world. The most recent of these disasters, Hurricane Sandy, hit the US East Coast in October 2012, causing unprecedented hardships to millions of residents in 17 states. Preliminary estimates put economic losses from the hurricane at a staggering USD70 billion (Artemis, 2012). Perhaps the most dramatic of these disasters was the earthquake-triggered tsunami that ravaged Japan in March 2011, causing a phenomenal economic cost of USD235 billion (The World Bank, 2011) and an estimated 19,300 deaths (*The Herald*

Sun, 2012). Another recent example of huge economic losses is the Thailand floods of October 2011, costing USD40 billion (The Economist, 2012). The massive 2010 floods in Pakistan resulted in total economic impact estimated at USD43 billion and over 2000 deaths (Rise Pakistan, 2010). Other examples include the Indian Ocean tsunami of 2004 (RMS, 2006) and Hurricane Katrina of 2005 (The Economist, 2012). While the former inflicted economic losses to the tune of USD10 billion, the latter accounted for almost USD144 billion in damages. The corresponding human casualties were 174,500 and 1322. Hurricane Mitch, which devastated many countries in Central America in 1998 (NCDC, 2009), and the catastrophic floods that have affected China (The Economist, 2012), parts of the US (Missouri and Mississippi) in the 1990s (Larson, 1996), England and Wales in 2000–2002 (Environment Agency, 2009), and Bangladesh in 2004 (TerraDaily, 2004) are additional instances. Another major disaster was the crippling drought that affected the Sahel in Africa from 1972 to 1984, resulting in human casualties estimated at 100,000. It also impacted 750,000 people who had to rely completely on external food aid during the crisis (UNEP, 2002). All of these attest to the colossal destructive potential of water disasters.

The goal of this paper is to identify, review and analyze water policies that have been in place in different parts of the world over the years, especially in the last decade, and offer policy insights and specific recommendations to significantly improve their efficiency and effectiveness. Based on a historical survey, I have identified five broad categories of water policies for the purposes of this paper: risk management; vulnerability assessment; capacity building and resilience; disaster risk reduction–development linkage; and institutional design. In examining the adequacy and effectiveness of these policies, I have looked at a variety of factors such as the state of economic development, development policies, environmental issues, demographic factors, climate change impacts, proximity of major cities and urban centres to the coast, concentration of people and capital in vulnerable areas, and land use practices.

This paper is organized as follows. After the introduction, an overview of the trends in natural disaster occurrences worldwide during the past decade is presented. This is followed by a discussion of water-related disasters and their human and economic costs. The broader socio-economic consequences of water disasters are then examined. The following section provides a critical appraisal of the adequacy and effectiveness of current water policies in meeting the difficulties and challenges of water disasters. The next section, the central part of this paper, focuses on revamping the current system and toward this end offers specific policy insights and recommendations. Priority areas for research based on the findings from this analysis are identified and briefly discussed in the section that follows. The final section presents conclusions and recommendations.

Natural disasters – an overview

A review of the trends in natural disasters (Tables 1–4) points to a significant increase in the scale and scope of their human and economic costs in most regions of the world in the past decade. People globally have become increasingly vulnerable to extreme weather events, which have grown in frequency and intensity with accompanying adverse impacts.

Table 1 shows the scope and dimensions of natural disasters globally between 2000 and 2010. The recorded number of disasters during this period was 4241. The number of people affected was approximately 2.5 billion, with more than 1 million fatalities. The estimated total damage amounted to approximately USD1 trillion, with 2010 alone

Table 1.   Disasters by year, 2000–2010.

Year	Number of disasters	Total fatalities	Total affected (millions)	Total damage (USD billions)	Damage covered by insurance (USD billions)
2000	413	9,686	173.2	45.7	5.4
2001	379	30,981	108.7	27.0	6.6
2002	421	12,380	638.0	52.0	10.9
2003	360	109,991	254.9	69.8	12.6
2004	354	241,635	161.7	136.2	42.8
2005	432	89,192	160.2	214.2	92.3
2006	401	23,491	126.0	34.1	7.1
2007	414	16,940	211.3	74.4	22.7
2008	351	235,287	220.9	190.5	30.9
2009	343	11,082	198.7	48.7	12.3
2010	373	296,818	207.7	109.5	21.8
Total	4,241	1,077,683	2,481.5	1,002.4	265.4

Source: The above table is adapted from UN/ISDR (2011, p. 31).

Table 2.   Disasters by type, 2000–2010.

Disaster type	Number of disasters	Total fatalities	Total affected (millions)	Total damage (USD billions)	Damage covered by insurance (USD billions)
Drought	188	1,159	765.9	27.0	0
Earthquake (seismic activity)	313	680,351	89.6	215.7	15.5
Extreme temperature	250	147,952	85.5	37.9	2.8
Flood	1,910	62,131	1,127.4	203.9	25.6
Mass movement– dry*	8	282	0.004	0	0
Mass movement– wet**	220	10,891	4.0	2.0	0.2
Storm	1,137	173,587	405.3	491.4	214.2
Volcano	66	560	1.6	177.9	0
Wildfire	149	770	2.2	24.1	7.1
Total	4,241	1,077,683	2,481.5	1,002.4	265.4

Source: The above table is adapted from UN/ISDR (2011, p. 30).
*Rockfall, landslide, avalanche and subsidence.
**Wet mass movement consists of water-saturated rock fall, landslide, avalanche and subsidence.

accounting for almost USD110 billion. It is worth noting that only 26% of the total economic losses were covered by insurance, imposing severe economic hardships on millions of affected people.

A look at Table 2 shows that disasters triggered by weather-related events (drought, flood, extreme temperature, storm and mass movement–wet) are the most frequent disaster types, outnumbering all other natural disasters combined and collectively accounting for over 87% of all natural disasters, with the widest impacts on people. A closer look reveals that droughts, floods and storms combined affected the largest number of people (2300 million), resulting in total economic losses of USD722.3 billion, 72% of the total losses. Next to water disasters, earthquakes accounted for 63% of total fatalities, 4% of total

Table 3.   Disasters by continent, 2000–2010.

Continent	Number of disasters	Total fatalities	Total affected (millions)	Total damage (USD billions)	Damage covered by insurance (USD billions)
Africa	711	15,550	159.4	9.9	0.07
Americas	1,016	247,970	82.7	448.3	198.6
Asia	1,684	674,106	2,227.9	390.7	23.2
Europe	661	138,764	10.1	135.3	33.9
Oceania	169	1,293	1.2	18.1	9.6
Total	4,241	1,077,683	2,481.5	1,002.4	265.4

Source: The above table is adapted from UN/ISDR (2011, p. 31).

Table 4.   Water disasters by type, 2000–2010.

Disaster type	Number of disasters	Total fatalities	Total affected (millions)	Total damage (USD billions)	Damage covered by insurance (USD billions)
Drought	188	1,159	765.9	27.0	0
Extreme temperature	250	147,952	85.5	37.9	2.8
Flood	1,910	62,131	1,127.4	203.9	25.6
Mass movement–wet*	220	10,891	4.0	2.0	0.2
Storm	1,137	173,587	405.3	491.4	214.2
Total	3,705	395,720	2,388.1	762.2	242.7

Source: The above table is adapted from UN/ISDR (2011, p. 30).
* Wet mass movement consists of water-saturated rock fall, landslide, avalanche and subsidence.

affected, and 22% of total damages. It is particularly noteworthy that only one-third of the economic losses from all disaster types were covered by insurance.

Table 3 presents data on total fatalities, total affected and total economic losses by continent for the period 2000–2010. We notice that the most severe human impacts, in terms of both fatalities and number affected, were inflicted on Asia. Thus, 63% of the total fatalities and 90% of total affected were in Asia, with other continents experiencing significantly smaller fatalities and impacts. As for total economic losses, the Americas sustained the heaviest damages (because of the large number of expensive built structures affected), followed by Asia.

Water disasters

General trends

Table 4 provides a breakdown, by category, of the total fatalities, the people affected and the economic losses caused by water-related natural disasters globally. (For the purposes of this study, "water disasters" include drought, extreme temperature, flood, mass movement–wet and storm.) It shows that storms are responsible for the most fatalities (closely followed by extreme temperature) and economic losses. Flood constitutes another important type of water disaster of critical concern owing to its sheer enormity in terms of people affected and economic damages inflicted. The destructive potential of droughts is also significant, as demonstrated by the number of people affected.

Table 5.   Water Disasters as a Percentage of Total Natural Disasters, 2000–2010.

	Number of disasters	Total fatalities	Total affected (millions)	Total damage (USD billions)	Damage covered by insurance (USD billions)
Natural disasters	4,241	1,077,683	2,482	1,002	265
Water disasters	3,705	395,720	2,388	762	243
Water disasters as percentage of total disasters	87%	37%	96%	76%	91%

Source: developed by the author based on information from UN/ISDR (2011).

Table 5 reveals that water-related disasters accounted for almost 90% of natural disasters that occurred during 2000–2010, a compelling testimony to the primacy of water-related disasters on a continuing basis.

Human and economic losses

Human losses

A review of Table 5 shows that water-related disasters were responsible for a staggering 96% of the total victims of natural disasters during 2000–2010. A closer scrutiny of the types of water disasters (see Table 4) indicates that droughts, floods and storms together contributed to 87% of the total water disasters during this period; these collectively resulted in 60% of the fatalities and 96% of the victims. Water disasters continued to take a heavy toll, in terms of both human and economic losses, in 2011. Cases in point are the Japanese earthquake-induced tsunami of March 2011, the massive floods in Thailand, Australia and China, and the hurricanes, tornadoes and floods in the US (The Economist, 2012). They provide further evidence of the colossal destructive potential of water disasters.

Economic losses

The information reported in Table 5 confirms the enormous devastation caused by water disasters as measured by economic losses. Thus, during the 2000–2010 period, water disasters resulted in 76% of the total economic losses from all disasters combined. A significant part of the economic losses resulted from the massive storm systems that ravaged a number of countries during this period, including the Indian Ocean tsunami of 2004 and Hurricane Katrina of 2005. The same trend continued in 2011 with massive water disasters buffeting different parts of the globe (see previous paragraph). The UN Council on Sustainable Development estimates the cost of disasters globally, since 2000, at USD1.4 trillion (UNCSD, 2012).

Socio-economic impacts

Socio-economic impacts and the resulting damages from water disasters have shown a significant increase globally over the years. For instance, according to the Overseas Development Institute (ODI 2005) the reported global cost of natural disasters showed a 15-fold increase from the 1950s to the 1990s. Natural disasters in Latin America and the Caribbean during the period 1973–2007 contributed to total damages estimated at USD148.5 billion (Zapata & Madrigal, 2009). As noted earlier, the Indian Ocean tsunami of 2004, Hurricane Katrina of 2005, and the 2011 earthquake-triggered tsunami of Japan all resulted in huge economic losses and substantial human casualties.

The social impacts of natural disasters have demographic, psychological, political and economic consequences (National Research Council, 2006). The demographic effects include massive displacement of population, involving immigration from and emigration to the affected areas. The psychological impacts involve "a wide range of negative psycho-social responses" (National Research Council, 2006, p. 78), while political impacts involve "community conflict resulting in social activism and political disruption during recovery periods" (p. 83).

Economic impacts can be grouped into "direct" and "indirect" impacts. The former occur immediately during or after the disaster and consist of impacts on assets – infrastructure, capital and stocks. Indirect damages include effects on flows (production, reduced income, increased expenses) and are observed after the phenomenon for weeks to months (Le-Huu, 2005).

The economic losses from the Japanese earthquake and tsunami of March 2011 were unprecedented. The World Bank (2011) has estimated that the total economic cost could reach as high as USD235 billion, 2.3–4% of Japan's GDP. Private insurance is expected to cover only between USD14 billion and USD33 billion, with a significant part of the balance to come from the Japanese government.

The massive floods that swept Pakistan in July 2010 provide a vivid illustration of the severity and magnitude of the socio-economic impacts of water disasters. The economic impacts included severe destruction of the infrastructure of Pakistan, resulting in extensive damage to homes, roads, bridges, irrigation and agricultural production. Almost 17 million acres of farmland were destroyed by the floods. The World Bank estimated crop losses at USD1 billion, not including the effects of soil erosion on agriculture. The total cost of rebuilding the country after the floods has exceeded USD43 billion (Ismail, 2010).

The social impacts included major demographic disruptions resulting in the displacement of nearly 20 million Pakistanis, 30% of the population. The health impacts included thousands of documented cases of dengue and malaria (WHO, 2010).

Also worth noting are the differential impacts of socio-economic disruptions on the GDP of the affected countries. For instance, the 1997–98 El Niño event cost the United States USD1.96 billion or 0.03% of its GDP. In sharp contrast, economic losses from this event accounted for 14.6% of Ecuador's GDP (Maplecroft, 2010). The loss from natural disasters during 1989–96 is estimated to have caused an annual impact of 3.9% on China's GDP. More recently, the 2011 floods in Thailand resulted in economic losses of USD40 billion, costing the country nearly 13% of its GDP (CRED, 2012). Clearly, this provides additional supporting evidence of the increasing burden of socio-economic impacts on countries with low income and lower rates of development.

In summary, most analysts forecast that major water disasters are likely to occur with increasing frequency and intensity in the years ahead. If past experience is any guide, a major share of the social and economic impacts of these disasters will occur in less developed and densely populated low-income countries. Given this prospect, special attention has to be paid in crafting policies designed to reduce the severity of these impacts on less developed countries.

Reasons for increasing impacts of water disasters

As we have seen, the human and economic impacts of natural disasters in general, and water disasters in particular, have been increasing at a rapid rate worldwide during the past decade (Tables 1 and 4). The human (96%) and economic (76%) impacts water disasters have unleashed have been staggering (Table 5). It is critical, therefore, to gain an understanding of the factors that have contributed to this situation, so that appropriate policy measures can be crafted to effectively address them.

The UN Office for Disaster Risk Reduction has identified a number of reasons for the increasing impacts of natural disasters.

> Key factors include environmental degradation, settlements in marginal hazard-prone lands, inadequate buildings and water management systems, lack of risk awareness and information, poverty and low capacities for prevention, preparedness and early warning, and lack of political and institutional commitment to reducing risks (UN–ISDR, 2008a, p. 3).

Additional reasons for rapid increase include: settlements by political and social refugees on land that is vulnerable, such as floodplains (Kron & Thummerer, 2002); changes in land use and increasing concentration of people and capital in vulnerable areas, for example in coastal regions exposed to windstorms and in fertile river basins exposed to floods (Mileti, 1999); and a possible link between climate change and high rates of precipitation, as in many parts of the Northern Hemisphere, resulting in major floods (WMO, 2004).

Other contributing factors are: inappropriate land management practices; human encroachment on wetlands, marshes and other natural barriers, as in the Gulf Coast region of the United States; structural weaknesses (e.g. the collapse of levees in New Orleans in the wake of Hurricane Katrina); lack of integration of disaster risk reduction into development plans; and institutional impediments (the last two points are discussed in detail later in this paper).

Water disaster management: policy aspects

Review and critique of current policies

In this section, five policy areas germane to water disaster management are identified and their adequacy in effectively meeting the challenges of water disaster management is reviewed. The five areas identified are risk management, vulnerability assessment, capacity building and resilience, disaster risk reduction–development linkage, and institutional design.

Although there have been some achievements in the field of *risk management*, an overall evaluation suggests that there is significant room for further improvement in policies in this area. A careful study of the data pertaining to risk management in different parts of the world provides many examples of repeated failures in the implementation of disaster risk management projects, leading to widespread destruction. This is evidenced by the relentless damages from floods, droughts and windstorms (88.5% of the 1000 most disastrous events) that have continued to ravage many parts of the world, most notably Asia (Adikari & Yoshitani, 2009). As our review has confirmed, water-related disasters continue to result in substantial death toll and property damages, pointing to a poor record of risk management (Tables 4 and 5).

Most recent forecasts suggest the likelihood of further worldwide increases in the intensity and frequency of water disasters in the years ahead. There is growing recognition that anthropogenic global climate change is contributing to the increasing impacts and losses. The Intergovernmental Panel on Climate Change (IPCC) projects that changes in rainfall amounts, intensity and frequency in many parts of the world will continue to add to water-associated risks, including severe droughts and possible sea-level rise (Bates et al.,

2008). Thus, all things considered, there is considerable room for improvement in risk management policies.

Another important policy area has to do with *vulnerability assessment.*

> Vulnerability is the pre-event characteristic of systems that create the potential for harm or the differential ability to recover following an event. Vulnerability is a function of the exposure (who or what is at risk) and the sensitivity of the system (the degree to which people and places can be harmed). (Cutter, 2008, p. 3)

A major factor that has contributed to the exacerbation of disaster impacts in the form of human casualties, economic losses and environmental disruptions is vulnerability. This is particularly true in the case of water disasters. Compelling recent examples are the Indian Ocean tsunami in 2004, Hurricane Katrina in 2005, Cyclone Nargis in Myanmar in 2008, massive floods in Pakistan in 2010 and in Thailand in 2011, and major Chinese floods in the 1990s and continuing into the first decade of this century and beyond.

A review of the measures taken to address vulnerability in the context of water disasters in a number of developed and developing countries shows that only limited attention has been paid to this aspect. Cases in point include the continued presence of low-lying, impoverished farm areas in many countries, especially in the Third World, which have borne the brunt of major floods and famines, as in India, Pakistan, Bangladesh and Myanmar, among others. Disasters such as Hurricanes Katrina and Andrew (2005) and the Mumbai floods (2005) demonstrate the vulnerability of urban areas to catastrophic disasters (Gopalakrishnan & Okada, 2007). These examples point to the need to re-examine current practices and policies.

Another important policy area in water disaster risk management consists of the closely intertwined concepts of *capacity building and resilience* in communities that are prone to disaster risks. Capacity building involves the development of the different sectors in a country such as the policy and legal domains, technological and scientific capabilities, institutions broadly defined, and human resources and managerial expertise (see UNDP, 1991).

Resilience refers to the ability of a country to bounce back and achieve stability after being subjected to serious economic and human losses resulting from natural disasters. Although there have been sporadic references in the past to the concept of resilience in water disaster management, a systematic analysis and discussion of the concept has been lacking until recently.

The concept of disaster resilience gained prominence in the wake of the adoption of the *Hyogo Framework for Action 2005–2015: Building the Resilience of Nations and Communities to Disasters* (Manyena, 2006). This has resulted in a shift in focus from vulnerability reduction to developing community resilience. However, there is a limited understanding of the concept of disaster resilience among disaster policy makers. This appears to be the main reason for the paucity of concrete examples of the adoption of resilience-enhancing measures by many countries and regions ravaged by water disasters.

Another crucial policy area pertains to the *linkage between disaster risk reduction and development.* However, the link between disaster risk reduction and specific development goals has not been recognized in most of the current plans, e.g. the Millennium Development Plan and the Hyogo Framework. A review of the impacts of recent water disasters has shown that significant development gains of the previous decades have been eroded by damages and losses to infrastructure and other community assets. To lessen the impact of water disasters on sustainable development, it is crucial to develop new policies clearly acknowledging the link between disaster risk reduction and development.

The final area of concern in water disaster policy relates to the role of *water institutions*. Concerns have been voiced over the years about the lack of efficient and flexible institutional arrangements that facilitate disaster preparedness, mitigation, recovery and reconstruction. Mileti (1999, p. 53) has made a convincing case for "flexible local institutions with the ability to take action on issues affecting long-term sustainability". Weak institutional and legal arrangements have been identified as a major bottleneck to effective natural disaster management in El Salvador (Nicholls, 2001). In spite of the growing recognition of the potential impact of global climate change on "weather extremes, disease outbreaks, and global and local environmental destruction, decision-making institutions have not, for the most part, incorporated global climate change in their policies and planning efforts" (Zimmerman & Cusker, 2001, p. 9–1). The World Bank has recognized the centrality of institutional arrangements, especially in multijurisdictional settings, in effectively coping with disaster management in large urban areas (Kreimer, 2002; Sharafudeen, 2002).

Historical data and empirical evidence gleaned from national and international sources point to several instances of dysfunctional institutions dealing with water disasters at the global, regional, national, state and local levels. These include a lack of inter-agency coordination and jurisdictional overlapping; duplication of responsibilities among management agencies at different levels; and the minimal role played by local entities. This situation has a significant detrimental effect on efficient and effective implementation. The availability of and access to information are also adversely affected. This leads to problems with enforcement and also to a lack of accountability. There is limited provision for factoring in unique local conditions and the cultural context (Gopalakrishnan & Okada, 2007, 2012).

Revamping the current system – suggested policy changes

In this section, specific suggestions to improve the efficiency and effectiveness of water disaster management policies are presented and discussed based on the review in the previous section. The policy insights included in this section are grounded in a comprehensive survey and synthesis of important work in the field and reflect recent advances in policy discourse.

At this point, however, a cautionary note is in order. The success of the policy recommendations that follow depends heavily on a major exogenous force: the quality of water governance. This is the big unknown which has the potential to either make or break the proposed reforms. As Biswas and Tortajada (2010, p. 130) pointed out in an insightful paper, "There have got to be radical changes in the governance processes and the institutions responsible for water to cope with the immediate challenges, potential future changes, and uncertainties both from within the sector and around the sector."

Risk management

Risk from natural disasters has shown a dramatic increase in recent years.

> Between 1970 and 2010, the proportion of the population living in flood-prone river basins increased by 114 per cent, and on cyclone-exposed coastlines by 192 per cent. The 2011 floods in Thailand cost USD40 billion and led to an estimated 2.5 per cent drop in global industrial production . . . . The risk of economic loss is increasing. Since 2000, disasters have cost over USD1.4 trillion. Annual losses have risen to over USD200 billion, with the highest cost in 2005, the year of Hurricane Katrina in the United States. The Great East Japan earthquake and tsunami sent a clear message that both developed and developing countries are exposed to high risks." (UNCSD, 2012, p. 1).

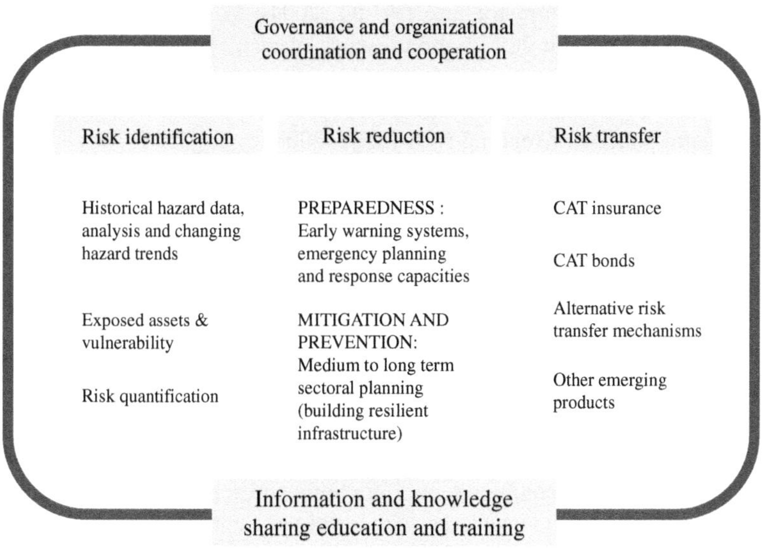

Figure 1. Governance and organizational coordination and cooperation. Source: World Meteorological Organization (2004).

Given this dire situation, the case for developing comprehensive and effective disaster risk management policies becomes compelling. This will involve risk identification and assessment, development of disaster management plans and specific mitigation measures, evaluation of the effectiveness of the proposed strategies in reducing risk exposure, widespread dissemination of mitigation information to stakeholders, and effective implementation of the proposed policies. A very useful framework for disaster risk management, anchored in governance and organizational coordination and cooperation and developed by the World Meteorological Organization (WMO), is presented in Figure 1. It frames disaster risk management under three main areas: risk identification, risk reduction, and risk transfer.

Risk identification involves analysis of historical hazard data and changing hazard trends, review of exposed assets and vulnerability, and risk quantification (WMO, 2004). Significant advances in risk analysis, projection, and planning and management have occurred in recent years. Some examples include the development of highly sophisticated prediction models for sea level rise, flooding and Temperature variability due to climate change. Flood decision-support system architecture using the latest advances in remote sensing, geographic information systems (GIS), hydrologic models, numerical weather prediction, information technology and decision theory has been developed and successfully applied. Rapid economic assessment of flood-control failure can now be made through the use of an innovative combination of satellite imagery, GIS and economic methods, thereby avoiding major potential flood risks (Sheng et al., 2007). Detailed projections of climate change scenarios have been made by the IPCC, the US National Academy of Sciences, and many other scientific research institutes globally. As a result, risk identification associated with climate change can be more effectively undertaken.

Risk reduction includes two key elements: preparedness; and mitigation and prevention. The former includes early-warning systems and emergency planning and response capacities, while the latter focuses on medium-to-long-term sectoral planning such as building resilient infrastructure (WMO, 2004). Water-related disaster risk has received only scant attention despite the presence of many parties involved in the field. Possible contributing factors include fragmented institutional systems lacking in effective mechanisms to ensure coordination and cooperation, lack of political will and commitment, and paucity of funding (UN-ISDR, 2008a).

The third area is risk transfer, which includes catastrophe (CAT) insurance, CAT bonds and alternative risk transfer mechanisms (WMO, 2004). Some examples are innovative risk management policies such as flood insurance, technically efficient irrigation systems, and new tools like the rainfall index contract (Zeuli & Skees, 2007) to reduce flood and drought risk.

Governance is at the core of effective implementation of risk management policies. The hallmark of governance that enhances the effectiveness of implementation is flexibility. Absent flexibility, quick, appropriate and timely implementation is almost impossible. In disaster situations, as we well know, time plays a critical role. Thus, flexibility, the freedom from the chain of command in decision making, is an absolute must. Similarly, political ideologies rooted in ethnic and religious rivalries and factions, and economic disparities that leave large sections of people marginalized, are examples of governance that would add considerably to the difficulties of successful implementation of disaster management and mitigation. These are issues that need to be examined carefully and critically in our deliberations on the role of governance in policy implementation (Gopalakrishnan & Okada, 2012).

Aside from natural water disasters, water disasters resulting from human error have begun to assume prominence, as evidenced by the 2010 disaster in the Gulf of Mexico from the explosion of the oil-drilling platform owned by Transocean Ltd. and leased by British Petroleum (BP) (Levy & Gopalakrishnan, 2010). The human, economic and environmental impacts from this catastrophe are of staggering scale and scope, even dwarfing major natural water disasters such as the Indian Ocean tsunami and Hurricane Katrina. Clearly, this points to the need for advance planning and readiness to cope with potential human-induced disasters. Had appropriate policies been in place, the magnitude and severity of the consequences of this disaster could have been significantly lessened.

Specific recommendations to enhance the effectiveness of risk management follow.

- A comprehensive disaster risk management policy, including identification, assessment, reduction/mitigation and transfer, must be made an integral part of water policy.
- An effective early-warning system that can alert all concerned parties in a timely fashion at the onset of a disaster should be in place.
- A coordinated plan involving local, state and national agencies to implement at short notice the search, rescue and evacuation of all disaster victims should be developed.
- A comprehensive flood insurance system designed to ensure adequate coverage and to minimize economic losses should be accorded high priority in risk management plans.
- Comprehensive water disaster risk policies involving diverse stakeholders from all relevant sectors, including civil defence and the military, environment, health, education, land use and development planning, need to be developed.
- Efforts to develop policies to effectively deal with water disasters resulting from human error should be undertaken.

Vulnerability assessment

In the context of disaster risk management, the concept of vulnerability deserves careful consideration (Benson & Clay, 2004; Golding, 2001; Leichenko & O'Brien, 2002; Wisner, Blaikie, Cannon, & Davis, 2003). In essence, "vulnerability draws attention to the intersections of society, culture and nature that become expressed in the disaster process" (Oliver-Smith & Hoffman, 2002, p. 17). To explore this theme, it is necessary to study the relationship between society and nature from the perspective of vulnerability, the impacts of the process through cultural, economic and political factors underlying vulnerability and how "disasters are inscribed in the environment" (p. 17).

It should be noted that the larger implication of these cultural approaches is that natural disasters are as much "social constructions" as they are environmental disruptions. This thesis is supported by studies that have shown "the high correlation between disaster proneness, chronic malnutrition, low income and famine potential, which led to the conclusion that the root causes of disasters lay more in society than in nature" (Oliver-Smith & Hoffman, 2002, p. 27).

Wisner et al. (2003) have made an important contribution to the study of vulnerability in the context of disaster risk management. They challenge the conventional wisdom about natural disasters as an aberration and argue that vulnerability is the catalyst transforming a hazard into a disaster. Based on this premise, they have developed two analytical models which attempt to explain vulnerability in a new light. The first of these is what they call a pressure-and-release (PAR) model. In this model they identify the root causes, the dynamic pressures and the unsafe conditions associated with vulnerability. The root causes of vulnerability are explained by the authors in terms of limited access to power, structures and resources, and ideologies consisting of political systems and economic systems. The dynamic pressures identified include lack of local institutions, training, appropriate skills, local investments, local markets, freedom of the press, and ethical standards in public life. Equally important are macro forces such as rapid urbanization, rapid population growth, debt repayment schedules, deforestation, and decline in soil productivity. Under unsafe conditions, four categories are listed: fragile physical environment, fragile local economy, vulnerable society, and public actions (Wisner et al., 2003).

The access model is an elaboration of the factors discussed in the PAR model. The model, as its name suggests, focuses on how differences in access to political or economic resources influence the capacity of households to deal with disasters. A review of recent disaster events in a number of developing countries provides indisputable evidence that the most vulnerable households were the ones with the least access to resources. Diminished access to resources, in effect, translates itself into increased vulnerability. To alter the situation, this imbalance in access to resources has to be corrected. As St. Cyr (2005, p. 4) points out, "The central premise behind the Access Model is that risk and vulnerability of social groups can be minimized by identifying the intervention points through which enhancements in the allocation of additional assets and resources can be made."

Other contributing causes of vulnerability have been identified in the UN Water Series as: poverty; unplanned urbanization; environmental degradation; fragmented institutional structures; imbalance between prevention and response resources; lack of understanding of risk and vulnerability; and insufficient public awareness programs (UN Water Series, 2007).

The UN Development Programme (2011) has drawn attention to the risk posed by earthquakes of magnitude 7 or higher to many of the world's major cities, with populations ranging from 2 to 15 million. It goes on to point out that a number of densely populated cities such as Tokyo, Mexico City, Port-au-Prince, Istanbul and Kathmandu are located near fault zones with a potential to trigger earthquakes. The resulting social and economic losses could be staggering. A telling example is the 2010 earthquake in Haiti, which cost the country 100% of its GDP.

It is important to note (McGranahan et al., 2007) that more than two-thirds of the world's large cities are located in areas vulnerable to global warming and rising sea levels, potentially putting in excess of 634 million people at risk of being swamped by flooding and intense storms. Examples of major cities likely to be affected are: Tokyo (32.5 M), Mumbai (19.2 M), Shanghai (16.7 M), New York (19.8 M), Lagos (13.5 M), Los Angeles (15.3 M), Kolkata (15.1 M) and Dhaka (11 M). (These population figures are for the year 2010.) Thus, in crafting disaster management policies, special attention must be paid to reducing the risk posed by the exposure and vulnerability of urban areas.

The use of a carefully constructed vulnerability index can be helpful in vulnerability assessment. A *vulnerability index* is a policy planning tool designed to measure the impact of exposure to a hazard or disaster on the population in the affected area. It is a "composite of multiple quantitative indicators that via some formula, delivers a single numerical result" (Vulnerability index, 2012).

As currently conceived, the vulnerability index has a number of limitations.

> The sparse amount of data available globally, their tendency to reduce human beings to numbers, the problems inherent in comparing small countries such as Fiji with the largest such as China, the problem of autocorrelation among the various indicators of risk vulnerability, the major difference between indicators and costs and the question of who the users are and why an index might be constructed in the first place are all factors that must be carefully examined and weighed before opting to use a Vulnerability Index. (Gopalakrishnan & Okada, 2007, p. 369).

Significant work is currently underway to address these issues and thus it has the clear potential to serve as a very effective tool in vulnerability assessment.

Measures for vigorously enforcing vulnerability assessment are long overdue. Four specific suggestions follow.

- Vulnerability assessment and reduction should be made a mandatory part of risk assessment associated with water disasters.
- Vulnerability measurement using new techniques, including a carefully constructed vulnerability index, has to be carried out periodically in disaster-prone areas.
- The critical role of human factors in causing vulnerability has to be considered in vulnerability assessment.
- Assessment of vulnerability of coastal mega-cities due to extreme climate events (e.g. sea-level rise) should be made a key component of emerging water policy.

Capacity building and resilience

Capacity building and resilience are closely intertwined and both play important roles in the context of disaster risk management. Typically, there is a positive correlation between the two, with the resilience of a country in bouncing back from the impact of natural disasters increasing proportionately with the ability of the country to build its capacity.

The UNDP (1991) considers capacity building as a dynamic, ongoing, long-term process involving all stakeholders in a country. The UNDP has identified three areas central to the building (development) of capacity: (1) policy and legal domains; (2) institutions (with provision for community-level participation by women); and (3) human resources and managerial capabilities. It should contribute to a reduction in vulnerability and an enhancement in resilience.

Capacity building calls for an effective and steady mobilization of the resources of a country at all levels – individuals, groups, organizations and institutions (private as well as public) – to ensure its sustained, uninterrupted growth as envisioned and set forth in its development plans. This process should embrace all sectors (e.g. infrastructure, institutions, legal frameworks, science and technology, governance) and all stakeholders (ADB, 2004).

In recent years, capacity building as it relates to disaster management has broadened in scope to include the ability of countries to prevent hazards from developing into full-blown disasters (McBean & Rodgers, 2010). Furthermore, in post-disaster situations it is crucial to develop the "psychosocial capacity" of disaster responders to assist survivors in restoring their ability to deal with their emotional and psychological trauma (Miller, 2012).

There is no single definition of the term "resilience". It is generally used to denote the ability of a system, physical or social, to bounce back to its original condition after being subjected to a hazard or disaster. According to Holling (1973), resilience of an ecosystem is the measure of the ability of an ecosystem to absorb changes and still persist.

The concept of resilience has moved far beyond the confines of ecology in recent years. It is now commonly used in the context of disaster risk management. For example, Timmerman (1981) defines resilience as a measure of a system's, or part of a system's, capacity to absorb and recover from a hazardous event (Klein, 2003). According to Rose (2004, p. 308), resilience refers to "post-disaster conditions and response, which are distinguished from pre-disaster activities to reduce potential losses through mitigation". Mayunga (2007, p. 3) points out that "there is an agreement among researchers that the notion of disaster resilience should be associated with the capacity/ability of people, a group of people, a community or a society to cope with disasters."

A more recent (2008) approach to the concept of resilience is the one developed by the Multidisciplinary Center for Earthquake Engineering Research (MCEER) at the State University of New York at Buffalo. The centre developed a conceptual framework that defines

> disaster resilience as the ability of social units (e.g., organizations, communities) to mitigate hazards, contain the effects of disasters, and carry out recovery activities in ways that both minimize social disruption and mitigate the effects of future disasters. Resilience reduces the likelihood and consequences of failures – and the time required to recover from failures – among critical infrastructure in disasters." (NEHRP, 2008, p. 1).

Resilience and capacity building have assumed heightened importance in the context of climate change–induced uncertainty and the hazards triggered by it. Cases in point are the potential impacts of sea-level rise on densely populated coastal cities and the wide-ranging consequences of drought conditions on all water-using sectors. Given this situation, there is growing recognition of the need to integrate capacity building and resilience as essential components of development policies, especially because water is recognized to be central to the achievement of many of the UN's Millennium Development Goals.

In summary, the goal of future water policies should be to bring about substantial reduction in the casualties and property damage that inevitably accompany major water disasters. Toward this end, six specific steps to promote resilience are given by Gopalakrishnan (2007); see also Levy and Gopalakrishnan (2007):

- Provide timely and convenient access to disaster information (educating stakeholders) and livelihood recovery assistance (health care, food assistance).
- Improve ecological integrity (preserving coral reefs and mangrove forests), promote institutions for disaster prevention (schools, training, etc.), and address poverty.

- Foster appreciation for the local cultural context.
- Harness recent technological innovations in disaster detection, modelling and warning (e.g. high-resolution digital bathymetric maps of continental shelf areas).
- Integrate early warnings into a multi-hazard system and increase the preparedness of coastal communities.
- Provide effective community consultation and participation that empower stakeholders and stimulate meaningful dialogue.

Capacity building and disaster resilience have been grossly neglected in disaster management policies. Some specific suggestions to alter the situation follow:

- Development policies must include concrete plans that help facilitate capacity building and resilience with special reference to water disasters.
- High priority has to be accorded to developing and implementing measures to speedily respond to climate change–induced impacts in vulnerable areas.
- Make provision to closely monitor the development of physical, economic, social and human capacity during a given planning period.
- Shift the focus of future water disaster management policies from conventional structural measures to non-structural approaches to enhance community resilience.

Disaster risk reduction-development linkage

It is now well understood that natural disasters can significantly slow socio-economic development if explicit provision is not made in national, regional and international development plans for disaster risk reduction (Askew, 1997). Given the increasing frequency and intensity of water disasters in recent years, the case for designing and integrating disaster risk reduction policies in development plans has taken on a new urgency.

The link between disaster risk reduction and development is made clear by the UN International Strategy for Disaster Reduction:

> Water risks and water-related disasters ... are an integral part of social and economic development. They can become serious impediments to achieving the Millennium Development Goals (MDGs) by 2025, since disasters can quickly destroy accumulated development gains, in terms of damage and losses to infrastructure and other assets and frustrated social and economic progress." (UN-ISDR, 2008b, p. 24)

Water-related disasters impact the development plans of less-developed and developing countries even more drastically than developed countries. For instance, the Intergovernmental Panel on Climate Change (IPCC 2001) reports that 65% of deaths worldwide from natural disasters between 1985 and 1999 took place in nations whose incomes were below USD760 per capita. This situation continues to prevail to this day. Figure 2 shows a disproportionate distribution of natural disasters by region during 2001–2010, with 40% of the disasters occurring in Asia alone, along with 89% of the mortality and 38% of the economic costs (Guha-Sapir et al., 2012). In numbers, this translates into an annual average of approximately 208 million deaths in Asia. It is worth noting that this grossly unequal share of the deaths caused by such environmental stressors as earthquakes, floods, cyclones, hurricanes and extreme temperature events is borne by people in a region with a preponderance of less-developed countries. A review of the development plans of many of the countries in Asia shows that little or no attention was paid to disaster risk reduction strategies by the planning agencies.

The link between development and disaster risk is further amplified in a study by Kahn (2005). He concludes, in his analysis using a comprehensive data set spanning 73 countries, that "if a nation with a population of 100 million experienced a GDP per capita

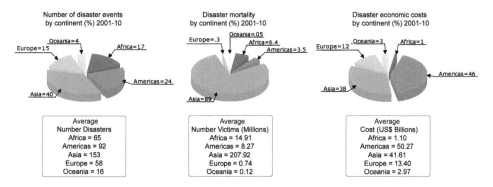

Figure 2.   Regional impacts of natural disasters, 2001–2010 (average). Source: developed by the author using data from Guha-Sapir et al. (2012).

increase from USD2,000 to USD14,000, that nation would suffer 764 fewer natural-disaster deaths a year" (p. 283).

Disaster risk reduction has to be viewed as an integral part of national planning policies, taking into account the dangers of building large cities in disaster-prone areas exposed to flooding, earthquakes and tropical cyclones. Likewise, disaster risk reduction measures should be accorded high priority in water resource programs and projects funded by international development agencies such as the World Bank and the Asian Development Bank.

The disaster risk reduction–development linkage clearly needs strengthening. Three suggestions follow.

- Water disaster risk reduction has to be made an integral part of development plans through specific earmarking of funds toward this end.
- Disaster risk reduction policies and measures need to be designed in such a way that they are consistent with long-term development objectives and implementation plans.
- The inclusion of specific policies for water disaster risk reduction should be made mandatory in development plans.

Institutional design

Water institutions play a pivotal role in the context of water disaster management. "Water institutions", for the purposes of this paper, consist of three elements: water laws, political processes, and water administration (Gopalakrishnan, 2005). However, as noted earlier in this paper, a review of the performance of water institutions clearly suggests that they have been largely ineffective in addressing the challenges of water disasters. Examples of water institutions in dire need of major reforms to increase their efficiency abound in the literature on institutions. Cases in point are water institutions in India (Saleth, 1996; Vaidyanathan, 1999), Sri Lanka (Gunatilake & Gopalakrishnan, 2002), the Middle East (Beaumont, 2005), and China (Nickum, 2005), among others.

The Katrina debacle, the more recent Chinese floods, and the 2011 Japanese earthquake and tsunami all further reinforce the concerns that have been articulated about institutional impediments. For instance, the excruciatingly slow delivery of much-needed assistance by the Federal Emergency Management Agency (FEMA) to the residents of New Orleans and other Gulf Coast areas after the disaster struck has been singled out by many observers and analysts as the major contributing factor to the widespread devastation that followed.

Likewise, in the case of the great Indian Ocean tsunami, the absence of a tsunami warning system was largely responsible for the extensive destruction in the Indian Ocean countries. Robust institutions for disaster risk management are, thus, essential to the timely implementation of disaster warning, evacuation, emergency relief, mitigation and post-recovery efforts. The case for a thorough overhaul of the institutional component of disaster risk management policies as currently conceived is thus compelling.

I argue that a major factor that has resulted in institutional ineffectiveness historically is what I would call "institutional entropy". I use this term to refer to the "progressive decrease in effectiveness and efficiency (of institutions) in performing the goals and objectives as originally envisioned and set forth" (Gopalakrishnan, 2005, p. 3).

I identify here the constraints that might lead to institutional entropy. It should be noted that this is a preliminary assessment and is not meant as a definitive account of all possible contributory factors.

> First, as changes in politics, economics, technology and lifestyle occur in a society, the institutions embedded in it must have the flexibility or adaptability to cope with these changes. Without such flexibility, the ability for effective performance will be compromised. Second, a key feature or attribute of an effective institution is autonomy. The institution should be free from internal as well as external pressures to manipulate water policy. Lack of autonomy, thus, will force institutions to stray from the optimal decision-making path and lead to undesirable outcomes. Third, full and free access to all pertinent information and data that might have a bearing on making efficient and equitable decisions is an indispensable attribute of optimal institutions. In terms of both quality and quantity, the empirical and policy data should be reliable, verifiable and timely. Lack of access to such information inevitably leads to the onset of institutional entropy. A fourth feature of institutional entropy is a gradual erosion in what I would call "cultural calibration". By this term I mean that the institutions must be firmly anchored in the local cultural milieu in order to effectively capture and absorb the aspirations, preferences and unique sensibilities of the multiple stakeholders in the given community, of which the institution is an integral part (Gopalakrishnan, 2005, pp. 3–4).

Based on experience, there is ample evidence to suggest that resource management institutions originally designed to function at top efficiency have failed to make adequate and appropriate adjustments to accommodate the many changes – political, technological, legal and cultural – that inevitably come about with the passage of time. I attribute this to an incremental accumulation of entropy; and I hypothesize that this would make the institutions increasingly dysfunctional. There are some extreme cases where institutions have become obsolete due to the encroachment of entropy.

What specific attributes must be incorporated in designing institutions to effectively address "institutional entropy"? Based on a detailed literature review, eight key elements, central to designing effective institutions for integrated disaster risk management, were identified: awareness/access, autonomy, affordability, accountability, adaptability, efficiency, equity and sustainability (Gopalakrishnan & Okada, 2007). In order to revamp water institutions, considering these key elements, six approaches are suggested: institutional integration, public-private partnership, information sharing and technology transfer, disaster diagnosis, legislative revamping and "cultural calibration." (For a comprehensive discussion elaborating on these ideas, see Gopalakrishnan & Okada, 2007.)

For institutional revamping, the following recommendations are offered.

- Significant effort is to be directed toward the reduction of "institutional entropy" through the inclusion of greater flexibility and adaptability, autonomy, full and free access to information, and cultural sensitivity in building and operating water institutions.

- Collaborative arrangements between public agencies and private groups have to be developed and fostered to meet the challenges of water disasters.
- In designing new water institutions, special attention has to be paid to incorporate features that enhance their robustness, among them, accountability, efficiency and equity.
- In order to revamp current water institutions using the above design features, specific approaches compatible with them, as described earlier, have to be developed and implemented.

Priority areas for research

Based on the information and insights gained from the policy analysis presented in this paper, I suggest *five priority areas* for comprehensive and in-depth research in the near future. These are. (1) a reliable database; (2) mainstreaming disaster risk reduction policies; (3) climate-induced vulnerability; (4) Capacity building and resilience; and (5) effective implementation policies grounded in new institutions. A brief discussion of each suggested area follows.

Development of an *accurate and reliable database* on water disasters is critical. At present, we have very few reliable data sources on natural disasters such as EM-DAT, Swiss Re and Munich Re. We need to significantly augment the database to include rigorous methodology to estimate direct and indirect economic losses, their short-term and long-run impacts on GDP, and estimates of the cost of rebuilding. Estimation of the full range of social impacts is equally important. Comprehensive information based on credible data sources is indispensable for crafting credible disaster management policies.

The link between *disaster risk reduction and overall development policies* of countries vulnerable to water disasters is now well acknowledged. Nevertheless, policies and mechanisms to effectively bring about this integration are conspicuous by their absence. Important new research needs to be initiated for "mainstreaming" the risk reduction policies into the overall development plans.

Another area that calls for further research has to do with *climate-induced vulnerability*. Although much work has been done in this field, the threat of sea-level rise posed by global warming has given new urgency to additional research because a large number of densely-populated megacities globally are located in coastal areas (e.g. Tokyo, Mumbai, Shanghai, New York, Lagos, Los Angeles, Kolkata and Dhaka). Given the magnitude of potential human casualties and economic losses that could result in the event of sea-level rise, it is prudent to initiate new research to effectively address this threat.

Capacity building and resilience have assumed a new importance in the context of planning for disaster management. The goal of tomorrow's water policies should be to bring about substantial reduction in the casualties and property damage that inevitably accompany major water disasters. Given this situation, comprehensive new research to integrate capacity building and resilience as an integral part of development policies has to be undertaken, with special emphasis on the Millennium Development Goals.

Even the best of policies designed to address water disasters will be of limited value if they cannot be implemented effectively. A global survey of disaster management policies clearly reveals that they have been of limited use because of the inability to implement them in a timely and efficient manner. Immediate new research, including conceptual and theoretical discussions and case studies, to develop a robust body of knowledge on *successful implementation* of disaster management policies needs to be launched. Special attention has to be given in this context to assessing the role of *institutions* in enhancing the viability of implementation strategies.

Conclusions and recommendations

Recent years have witnessed a significant exacerbation of disaster impacts in the form of human casualties, environmental disruptions and economic losses. Of special interest in the context of this study is the fact that water-related disasters have resulted in a significant share of these disasters. The human and economic impacts unleashed by water disasters have been colossal, with the former accounting for 96% of the people affected and the latter contributing to 76% of the total economic losses during 2000–10. Also to be noted is the fact that Asia and Africa together accounted for 95% of the total human casualties from water disasters during 2001–10. Furthermore, only 23% of the economic losses sustained by Asia and Africa in 2000–2010 were insured, in sharp contrast to the much higher share for the developed countries. A dramatic increase in the socio-economic impacts from water disasters has occurred in recent years, with a large proportion of them occurring in densely populated developing countries.

It is ironic that despite the rapidly growing threats posed by water disasters, little attention has been paid to them in the discourse on water resource management. Against this backdrop, five broad categories of water policies (risk management, vulnerability assessment, capacity building and resilience, disaster risk reduction–development linkage and institutional design) were examined with a view to determine their adequacy and effectiveness in successfully dealing with water disasters. It was found that the current policies have serious limitations in many respects that need to be addressed. Our study has further found that there is an urgent need to generate research-grounded data to support informed policy making on water disasters. Toward this end, five priority research areas have been identified.

Drawing on this study, a number of specific policy recommendations are offered to improve the current system. These include a comprehensive disaster risk assessment policy, an effective early-warning system, a carefully crafted vulnerability assessment and reduction system, capacity building and resilience enhancement measures, integration of water disaster risk reduction policies into development plans at all levels, and revamping of water institutions through "institutional entropy" reduction measures. There is significant potential for success in meeting the challenges of water disasters in the years ahead with the effective implementation of these measures as part of the policy process. The only caveat is that ultimately, the success of these innovations will, in large measure, depend on the quality of water governance in place.

Acknowledgements

The author gratefully acknowledges the financial support received from the Institute for Water Policy of the National University of Singapore in conducting this study. Special thanks to Asit K. Biswas for his insightful comments on earlier versions of this paper and to Cecilia Tortajada for her understanding and support throughout the long revision process.

References

Adikari, Y., & Yoshianti, J. (2009). *Global trends in water-related disasters: an insight for policymakers*. Paris, France: UN World Water Assessment Programme.

Annan, K. (2004). Message to World Water Day, 22 March, Bangkok (United Nations Conference Centre, Bangkok).

Artemis (2012). Economic losses from hurricane Sandy heading northwards to USD70 billion. 28 November. http://www.artemis.bm/blog/2012/11/28/economic-losses-from-hurricane-s andy-heading-northwards-to-70-billion/

Asian Development Bank (ADB) (2004). Briefing paper. Manila, Philippines: ADB Secretariat.

Askew, A. J. (1997). Water in the international decade for natural disaster reduction. In G. H. Leavesley, H. F. Lins, F. Nobilis, R. S. Parker, V. R. Schneider & F. H. M. Van de Ven (Eds.), *Destructive water: water-caused natural disasters, their abatement and control* (pp. 3–11). Wallingford, UK: IAHS Press.

Bates, B. C., Kundzewiez, Z. W. & Palutikof, J. P. (Eds.). (2008). *Climate change and water* Technical paper of IPCC. Geneva: IPCC Secretariat.

Beaumont, P. (2005). Water institutions in the middle east. In C. Gopalakrishnan, C. Tortajada & A. K. Biswas (Eds.), *Water institutions: policies, performance and prospects*. Berlin: Springer.

Benson, C., & Clay, E. J. (2004). *Understanding the economic and financial impacts of natural Disasters*. Washington, DC: World Bank Publications.

Biswas, A. K., & Tortajada, C. (2010). Future water governance: problems and perspectives. *International Journal of Water Resources Development, 26*(2), 129–139.

CRED (2012). *CRED Crunch newsletter (February)*. Brussels, Belgium: Université catholique de Louvain.

Cutter, S. L. (2008). *A Framework for measuring coastal hazard resilience in New Jersey communities*. Monmouth, NJ: Urban Coast Institute.

The Economist (2012). Counting the cost of calamaties. Jan. 14.

Environment Agency (2009). *Flooding in England: a national assessment of flood risk*. Bristol: Environment Agency.

Golding, D. (2001). Vulnerability. In A. S. Goudie & D. J. Cuff (Eds.), *Encyclopedia of global change: environmental change and human society*. Oxford: Oxford University Press.

Gopalakrishnan, C. (2005). Water ownership, allocation, and management in Hawai'i: A case of institutional entropy. In C. Gopalakrishnan, C. Tortajada & A. K. Biswas (Eds.), *Water institutions: policies, performance and prospects* (pp. 1–23). Berlin: Springer.

Gopalakrishnan, C. (2007). *Natural disasters and extreme climate events: Impacts and implications for water resources management*. Paper presented at the Seventh Annual IIASA-DPRI Conference on Integrated Disaster Risk Management, September 15–22, 2007, Stresa, Italy.

Gopalakrishnan, C., & Okada, N. (2007). Designing new institutions for implementing integrated disaster risk management (IDRM): key elements and future directions. *Disasters, 31*(4), 353–372.

Gopalakrishnan, C., & Okada, N. (2012). Reflections on implementation science. *Journal of Natural Resources Policy Research, 4*(1), 79–88.

Guha-Sapir, D., Vos, F., Below, R., & Ponserre, S. (2012). *Annual Disaster Statistical Review 2011* Centre for Research on the Epidemiology of Disaster (CRED). Brussels, Belgium: Université catholique de Louvain.

Gunatilake, H. M., & Gopalakrishnan, C. (2002). Proposed water policy for Sri Lanka: the policy versus the policy process. *International Journal of Water Resources Development, 18*, 547–564.

The Herald Sun (2012). Japan tsunami death toll at 19,300. January 11.

Holling, C. S. (1973). Resilience and stability of ecological systems. *Annual Review of Ecology and Systematics, 4*, 1–23.

IPCC (Intergovernmental Panel on Climate Change) (2001). *Third Assessment Report – Climate Change 2001*. Geneva: IPCC Secretariat.

Ismail, A. (2010). Pakistan Floods Unleash Desperate Economic Crisis. *World Socialist Web Site*. 26 August. Available at: http://www.wsws.org/articles/2010/aug2010/pkst-a26.shtml (accessed 5 August 2012).

Kahn, M. E. (2005). The death toll from natural disasters: The role of income, geography, and institutions. *Review of Economics and Statistics, 87*(2), 271–284.

Kreimer, A. (2002). 'Disaster management in metropolitan areas'. World Bank Metropolitan Governance Series. 25 April. http://www.Worldbank.org.WBI/B-SPAN/docs/metro-governanceI.pdf

Kron, W., & Thumerer, T. (2002). Water-related disasters: Loss trends and possible countermeasures from a (re-)insurer's point of view. Germany: Munich Reinsurance Company. Available at: http://www.mitchec.net/workshop3/Papers/paper_thumerer.pdf (accessed 5 August 2012).

Larson, L. W. (1996). Destructive Water: Water-Caused Natural Disasters – Their Abatement and Control. IAHS Conference, June 24–28, 1996, Anaheim, California.

Le-Huu, T. (2005). *Assessment of socio-economic impacts of hydro-meterological disasters: recent experiences & developments*. Bangkok, Thailand: UNESCAP (United Nations Economic and Social Commission for Asia and the Pacific).

Leichenko, R. M., & O'Brien, K. (2002). The dynamics of rural vulnerability to global change: the case of southern Africa. *Mitigation and Adaptation Strategies for Global Change, 7*(3), 1–18.

Levy, J. K., & Gopalakrishnan, C. (2007). Promoting disaster-resilient communities: The great Sumatra-Andaman earthquake of 26 December 2004 and the resulting Indian Ocean Tsunami. In C. Gopalakrishnan & N. Okada (Eds.), *Water and disasters* (pp. 51–70). London and New York: Routledge.

Levy, J. K., & Gopalakrishnan, C. (2010). Promoting ecological sustainability and community resilience in the US Gulf Coast after the 2010 Deepwater Horizon Oil spill, *Journal of Natural Resources Policy Research, 2*(3), 297–315.

McGranahan, G., Balk, D., & Anderson, B. (2007). The rising tide: assessing the risks of climate change and human settlements in low elevation coastal zones. *Environment and Urbanization, 19*(1), 17–37, (Sage Publications).

Manyena, S. B. (2006). The concept of resilience revisited. *Disasters, 30*(4), 433–450.

Maplecroft (2010). Haiti and Mozambique most vulnerable to economic losses from natural disasters. *Maplecroft.com.* 7 August. Available at: http://maplecroft.com/about/news/economi c_losses.html (accessed 19 November 2012).

Mayunga, J. S. (2007). Understanding and Applying the Concept of Community Disaster Resilience: A Capital-based Approach. Draft paper prepared for the Summer Academy for Social Vulnerability and Resilience Building. *July 22–28, 2007, Munich, Germany.*

McBean, G. A., & Rodgers, C. (2010). *Climate hazards and disasters: the needs for capacity building.* New York: John Wiley & Sons, Ltd.

Mileti, D. (1999). *Disasters by design: a reassessment of natural hazards in the United States.* Washington, DC: Joseph Henry Press.

Miller, J. L. (2012). *Psychological capacity building in response to disasters.* New York: Columbia University Press.

National Climatic Data Center (NCDC), NOAA (2009). *Mitch: the deadliest Atlantic Hurricane since1780.* (Asheville, North Carolina).

National Research Council (2006). *Facing hazards and disasters: understanding human dimensions.* Washington, DC: The National Academies Press.

NEHRP (Natural Earthquake Hazards Reduction Program), FEMA (2008). MCEER research: enabling disaster-resilient communities. *Seismic Waves Newsletter (November)* (pp. 1–2).

Nicholls, N. (2001). CDB Disaster Management Programme: Lessons of experience. Presentation at Caribbean Disaster Preparedness Seminar, 9–10 January 2001, Montego Bay, Jamaica.

Nickum, J. E. (2005). Uphill flow of reform in China's irrigation districts. In C. Gopalakrishnan, C. Tortajada & A. K. Biswas (Eds.), *Water institutions: policies, performance and prospects* (pp. 81–98). Berlin: Springer.

ODI (Overseas Development Institute) (2005). *Aftershocks: natural disaster risk and economic development policy.* London, UK: Overseas Development Institute.

Oliver-Smith, A., & Hoffman, S. M. (2002). Why anthropologists should study disasters. In S. M. Hoffman & A. Oliver-Smith (Eds.), *Catastrophe and culture: the anthropology of disaster.* Santa Fe, NM: School of American Research Press.

Rise Pakistan (2010). *2010 Floods in Pakistan.* (Chicago, Illinois).

Risk Management Solutions, Inc. (RMS) (2006). *Managing tsunami risk in the aftermath of the 2004 Indian Ocean earthquake & tsunami.* (Newark, California).

Rose, A. (2004). Defining and measuring economic resilience to disasters. *Disaster Prevention and Management, 13*(4), 307–314.

Saleth, R. M. (1996). *Water institutions in India: economics, law, and policy.* New Delhi: Commonwealth Publishers.

Sharafudeen, T. (2002). *Disaster management in metropolitan areas.* World Bank Metropolitain Governance Series, 25 April. Available at http://www.Worldbank.org.WBI/BSPAN/docs/m etro-governanceI.pdf (accessed 5 August 2012).

Sheng, Z., Sturdivant, A., Michelsen, A., & Lacewell, R. (2007). Rapid economic assessment of flood control failure along the Rio Grande: A case study. In C. Gopalakrishnan & N. Okada (Eds.), *Water and disasters* (pp. 86–106). London and New York: Routledge.

St. Cyr, J. F. (2005). At risk: natural hazards, people's vulnerability and disasters. *Journal of Homeland Security and Emergency Management, 2*(2), Available at http://www.geo.mtu.edu/rs 4hazards/links/Social-KateG/Attachments%20Used/AtRiskReview.pdf.pdf (accessed 5 August 2012).

TerraDaily (2004). *Death toll in Bangladesh floods rises to 185, more than 19 million affected.* 23 July.

Timmerman, P. (1981). *Vulnerability, resilience and the collapse of society: a review of models and possible climatic applications* Institute for Environmental Studies. Toronto: University of Toronto.

UNCSD (United Nations Conference on Sustainable Development) (2012). Fact Sheet, 20–22 June 2012. (pp. 1–2).

UNDP (United Nations Development Program) (2011). Briefing by Eric Calais, 20 April, 2011, New York.

UNDP (United Nations Development Program) (1991). *Supporting capacity building the UNDP approach.* New York: UNDP Secretariat.

UNEP (United Nations Environmental Program) (2002). Africa Environment Outlook. Past, present and future perspectives. Nairobi, Kenya: UNEP Headquarters.

UN/ISDR (International Strategy for Disaster Reduction) (2011). *Disaster Through a Different Lens.* Geneva: UN/ISDR Secretariat.

UN/ISDR (International Strategy for Disaster Reduction) (2008a). *Water-related disaster risk reduction: policy issues and guidance* (pp. 3.) Geneva: UN/ISDR Secretariat.

UN/ISDR (International Strategy for Disaster Reduction) (2008b). *Guidelines for reducing flood losses* (pp. 24. Geneva: UN/ISDR Secretariat.

UN Water Series (2007). Water Hazard Risks. Geneva: United Nations.

Vulnerability index (2012). In *Wikipedia*. Retrieved November 10, 2012, from http://en.wikipedia.org/wiki/Vulnerability_index

Vaidyanathan, A. (1999). *Water resource management: institutions and irrigation development in India.* New Delhi: Oxford University Press.

Wisner, B., Blaikie, P. M., Cannon, T., & Davis, I. (2003). *At Risk: natural hazards, People's vulnerability and disasters, 2nd edition.* London: Routledge.

WHO (2010). News Release. Geneva, August 3, 2010.

WMO (World Meteorological Organization) (2004). *Sustainable development in the information age: annual report 2004.* (Geneva, Switzerland).

World Bank (2011). The recent earthquake and tsunami in Japan: Implications for East Asia. *East Asia and Pacific Economic Update* (pp. 1–2).

Zapata, R., & Madrigal, B. (2009). *Economic impact of disasters: Evidence from DALA assessments by ECLAC in Latin America and the Caribbean.* Mexico City: ECLAC Subregional Office.

Zeuli, K. A., & Skees, J. R. (2007). Rainfall insurance: A promising tool for drought management. In C. Gopalakrishnan & N. Okada (Eds.), *Water and disasters.* London and New York: Routledge.

Zimmerman, R., & Cusker, M. (2001). "Institutional decision-making," Chapter 9 & Appendix 10. In C. Rosenzweig & W. D. Solecki (Eds.), *Climate change and a global city: the potential consequences of climate variability and change. Metro east coast.* pp. 9–1 to 9–25 and A11-A17, July New York, NY: Columbia Earth Institute & Goddard Institute of Space Studies.

STATE-OF-THE-ART REVIEW

Managing drought risk in water supply systems in Europe: a review

Giuseppe Rossi and Antonino Cancelliere

Department of Civil and Environmental Engineering, University of Catania, Italy

The frequent occurrence of drought and the increasing severity of its impacts make the traditional emergency approach inadequate and call for a risk-management approach, particularly in order to reduce water shortages in water supply systems. This paper attempts to provide a review of criteria, methods and tools for the management of drought risk in water systems, beginning with a discussion of legislative and institutional frameworks for coping with drought; objectives and contents of drought-planning instruments (at strategic, tactical and emergency levels) are then discussed. The review focuses on: 1. the drought indices to be used for an effective monitoring and early warning system; 2. the methods for assessing the risk of water shortage due to drought; and 3. the measures for reducing societal vulnerability to droughts and mitigating their impacts. Better coordination of drought-preparedness planning tasks, adaptive operation of water supply systems to prevent severe shortages, and more extensive use of early drought warning are suggested. Further research needs are identified.

Introduction

In recent decades, frequent and severe droughts have occurred in several countries of the world under nearly all climatic regimes, so that drought is in first place on the list of disasters in terms of affected population and often of economic losses (Wilhite, 2000). These drought events have caused large direct economic damages, especially in rainfed and irrigated agriculture and in municipal and industrial supply sectors, with heavy consequences on economy, health, and social well-being. Occurrences of droughts have also increased the conflicts among the competitive users of water in arid and semi-arid countries. Furthermore, the quality of water worsens during and soon after drought episodes, due to the higher concentration of contaminants in all water bodies and to the growing sea-water intrusion in coastal aquifers following the over-exploitation of groundwater.

Drought risk is expected to increase in the near future as a result of the expected changes in climate that could lead to precipitation reduction and temperature increase in several regions (IPCC, 2007). Furthermore, other global changes, such as population growth, population shift from humid to more arid regions, urbanization, touristic development and pollution, are likely to increase the vulnerability of many regions to water scarcity and drought.

In the view of Wilhite and Pulwarty (2005), the increase in social and economic vulnerability to drought, as exemplified by the rise in magnitude and complexity of impact, can be considered the most significant factor to explain the growing interest in drought preparedness by policy makers and water resources managers.

The fight against drought has traditionally been carried out following a reactive approach, i.e. by implementing emergency measures after a severe drought has already been recognized as a natural disaster. A shift toward a proactive (or risk-management) approach with measures planned in advance has been progressively advocated (Rossi, 1990; Wilhite, 1987; Yevjevich, Hall, & Salas, 1983). Today, such a shift is emphasized in policy instruments adopted in some more drought-prone countries, such as Australia (see Botterill & Wilhite, 2005) and USA (see Wilhite, 2000). It is also suggested by almost all the findings of recent research on drought (e.g. European research projects as ASTyDA, DSS-DROUGHT, WAM-ME, MEDROPLAN, PRODIM and ARIDE, as analyzed by XEROCHORE's final documents [2011]). Unfortunately, it is less evident in local, national and international policy agendas on drought issues as well as in the legislation and institutional frameworks of water resources management.

The objective of this paper is to review the development of criteria, methods and tools for managing drought risk, particularly in water supply systems. The focus of the review is on the planning instruments for coping with drought, and particularly on: 1. drought indices to be used for effective monitoring; 2. methods to assess the risk of water shortage due to drought in water systems; and 3. drought preparedness and mitigation measures. The paper is organized as follows. After this introduction, the shift from the emergency approach to the risk-management approach is discussed. Then, a framework of drought management, in terms of legislation and institutions, is examined, with particular focus on the European Union context; the objectives and contents of the drought planning instruments at strategic, tactical and emergency levels are discussed as well. Methods for the assessment of water-shortage risk are also analyzed for both the planning and operation of water systems, followed by a review of the measures proposed to improve drought preparedness and mitigate drought impact. Finally, a few concluding remarks are drawn and a list is provided of further research to improve the resilience of water systems as well as that of society to drought threat.

Drought management: from reactive to risk-management approach

A severe drought can be considered a natural disaster, and, similarly to other disasters, its impacts on society depend on the vulnerability of affected sectors and the preparedness to implement appropriate mitigation measures. However, drought risk management presents some peculiarities with respect to other disasters: 1. the strategic measures to be planned for improving drought preparedness are generally more complex, since the spectrum of potential long-term actions is large; and 2. the operational measures, to be implemented once a drought begins, require an adaptive response to the dynamic character of drought, considering the uncertainty in the evolution of drought, namely a duration and severity different from the one considered in the planning of preventive actions.

Broadly speaking, the nature of the response to drought events can be divided into two main categories (Rossi, 2000). The *reactive approach* (or *emergency management*) consists of measures conceived and implemented once a drought occurs and its impacts are perceived. It includes the measures taken during and after the drought event to minimize the drought impact. Often it is termed a *crisis management* approach because it is not based on specific plans prepared in advance. Although the reactive approach still represents the most common response to drought, there is an increasing awareness of its weaknesses in that it implies last-minute decisions that generally lead to expensive actions, with unsustainable environmental and social impacts.

Conversely, the *proactive approach* (or *risk management*) consists of measures conceived and prepared according to a planning strategy rather than within an emergency framework. Such measures are devised and implemented before, during, and after the drought event on the basis of a comprehensive drought management plan.

Legislation and institutional framework of drought management in Europe

The risk-management approach, as mentioned above, is becoming the new paradigm for all natural disasters at the international level. In particular, within the Hyogo Framework for Action of the UN International Strategy for Disaster Reduction (UNISDR, 2007) the following principles are stated:

- Dissemination of long-term benefits and effectiveness of preparedness and mitigation
- Incorporation of long-term mitigation and preparedness activities into the disaster response and recovery process
- Enhancement of stakeholder participation and ownership
- Assessment of the capacity of local communities to implement the strategy
- Clear distinction of responsibility among authorities for action implementation
- Increase of investments in natural hazard preparedness and mitigation.

The core of the risk-management approach consists of the development of appropriate planning tools, including assessment of drought vulnerability, establishment of a drought warning system, and development of programmes of preparedness and mitigation measures oriented toward preventing or reducing economic losses and social and environmental impacts. Many countries have developed planning legislation to cope with drought, referring to principles either from the UN Convention for Combating Desertification (UN Secretariat General, 1994) or to the Integrated Water Resources Management (IWRM) paradigm, introduced at the 1977 UN Conference on Water in Mar del Plata and one of the leading themes in subsequent years at several international water events such as World Water Forums.

Several countries affected by the repeated occurrence of severe droughts have developed national drought policies in recent decades. Particularly interesting is the comparison of the drought policies carried out in Australia, South Africa and the United States. The analysis of Wilhite, Botterill, and Monnik (2005) concerning the evolution of the drought planning processes in these countries shows, despite the differences among national approaches, a common goal of reducing societal vulnerability to drought and a very similar emphasis on risk management, including monitoring and early warning, risk assessment, and preparedness planning.

Until recent years, European water policies did not devote particular attention to drought issues in terms of technical and financial instruments and legislative acts, in spite of large costs due to droughts experienced. The European Commission (EC, 2007a) estimated such costs as at least €100 billion over the last 30 years, besides the physical direct consequences of drought on rivers and environment as well as the social impacts, in terms of exposure to stresses, job losses, etc. The Water Framework Directive 2000/60 (WFD, 2000) – which started a complex water resources planning process at the basin level, aimed at preserving or improving water quality to safeguard human uses and ecosystem protection – dealt marginally with drought. Indeed, drought mitigation is only mentioned among the directive's objectives and drought events are considered exceptional circumstances that enable the derogation of requirements of good ecological status of water bodies. In order to overcome these weaknesses in EU water policy, the EU Water Scarcity and Drought Expert Network has developed a guidance document on drought preparedness and mitigation (EC, 2007b) with the proposal of drafting a drought management plan (DMP) as an annex to the river basin management plan (RBMP). Such a DMP should be prepared by the same body responsible for basin planning, i.e. the river basin or district authority. Although the DMP is not mandatory for member states, it aims at extending the goals and criteria of the WFD to improve drought management and in particular to reduce the vulnerability of the water supply systems and mitigate drought impact. Its specific objectives are: (1) to guarantee sufficient water availability to cover essential human needs to ensure the population's health and life; (2) to avoid or minimize negative drought impact on water bodies; and (3) to minimize negative effects on economic activities (see Rossi, 2009).

On the basis of the successive work of the EU Water Scarcity and Drought Expert Network, recently the Report from the Commission to the European Parliament and the Council on these issues (EC, 2011) has suggested to review the related European policy including some specific topics listed in Table 1.

At the EU level, discussions are ongoing on how member states should incorporate climate change considerations into the implementation of EU water policy to minimize vulnerability to future climate changes and to fight possible emergencies by preparing specific response actions. According to the Commission of the European Communities White Paper, *Adapting to Climate Change: Towards a European Framework for Action* (CEC, 2009), one of the strategies proposed to increase resilience to climate change consists in the improvement of the management of water resources. With specific reference to water scarcity, such water management should promote further measures to enhance water efficiency in agriculture, households and buildings. Also, it is expected that the revision in 2012 of the WFD and of the water scarcity and droughts strategy will include options to increase drought resilience. Furthermore, revisions of the river basin

Table 1.   Main topics to revise European policy on water scarcity and drought (from EC, 2011).

Improving water efficiency
- Introducing water-saving devices and practices in buildings and improving water-efficient construction
- Reducing water leakages in supply distribution systems
- Improving efficiency in agricultural use of water

Achieving better planning and preparedness to deal with droughts
- Integrating actions against water scarcity and drought into other sectorial policies (agriculture, households, industry)
- Assessing the adequacy of the river basin management Plans on water scarcity and drought issues
- Further developing the prototype of an observatory and early-warning system on drought
- Defining a more comprehensive list of indicators on water scarcity, drought and vulnerability of water resources

Developing adequate implementation instruments of financing, water pricing, water allocation research and education
- Encouraging EU funding of natural risks through Cohesion Policy, Regional Policy, Solidarity Fund and Economic Recovery Plan, and reforming Common Agricultural Policy
- Making the national rules more restrictive that authorize water abstractions
- Developing new research projects on vulnerability and increased drought risk
- Introducing new educational programmes and awareness-raising campaigns

management plan (due in 2015 and 2021 according to the WFD) are indicated as a concrete occasion to incorporate climate changes within basin planning, through analysis of the pressures on the water bodies, definition of the phenomena to be monitored and verification of the resiliency of the action programme to climate changes.

As part of the actions included in the White Paper, Guidance Document No. 24 under the Common Implementation Strategy for the WFD (EC, 2009) examined ways to ensure that river basin management plans are climate-proof. This document suggests both actions to monitor and detect climate-change effects on water resources and to develop adaptation measures to water scarcity and drought. In particular, the following principles have been emphasized: (1) to handle available scientific knowledge and uncertainties about climate change; (2) to develop strategies that build adaptive capacity for managing climate risks; (3) to integrate adaptive management within key steps of the RBMP of the WFD; (4) to address the specific challenge of managing future flood risk; and (5) to address the challenge of managing water scarcity and drought. The same document, in order to revise the traditional concept of water resources planning, suggests some actions concerning institutional, water supply management, and interdisciplinary aspects:

- To strengthen the institutions in charge of water management to prepare them for the challenges that lie ahead
- To build robustness into water resources systems by integrating multiple sources of supply and water demands in conjunctive systems and by improving and enlarging the water transportation and distribution infrastructure to achieve the best possible allocation of available resources
- To discuss adaptation measures related to water scarcity and droughts in a transboundary and interdisciplinary context.

As a follow-up step to this, the expected 2012 EU water revision (*Blueprint to Safeguard European Waters*), also on the basis of the analysis of all plans for river basin districts, will assess achievements and identify further requirements towards long-term sustainable water use across the EU. For this process a better harmonized approach on drought risk management at all levels of governance (EU, national, regional, river basin) is proposed in order to integrate drought management policy into water resources management (Kampragou, Apostolaki, Manoli, Froebrich, & Assimacopoulos, 2011).

Objectives and contents of planning instruments for drought management

In general terms, risk-based drought management requires the following main steps: planning; monitoring; implementation of planned measures to avoid the most severe impacts; management of emergency situations; and recovery from damages due to drought.

The severity of drought impact on a water supply system and consequently on the socio-economic sectors is mainly connected to the vulnerability of the different sectors involved. The risk of shortage in water supply systems differs from basic drought risk because the water shortage results from an imbalance between water supply and demand, which is caused by a meteorological phenomenon but affected by other time-varying factors such as demand development, supply infrastructures and management strategies.

Different levels of drought planning are necessary with regard to the need to take into account the legislative and institutional framework of each country, and particularly to consider the sharing of the competences among the different institutions involved in (1) the general planning of the measures to cope with drought risk at the basin level; (2) the planning of preventive actions for drought management within the water supply system operation; and (3) the planning of emergency measures during a drought event which is recognized as a natural disaster.

Thus, depending on the level of planning and on the institution task in water resources, three different plans have been proposed to face water shortage risk due to drought (Rossi, Nicolosi, & Cancelliere, 2008b), namely the strategic drought preparedness plan (SDPP), the water supply system operation under drought conditions plan (WSSOP), and the drought contingency plan (DCP).

The general objective of the SDPP is to reduce the susceptibility of the water supply system to drought impact, and particularly to reduce the risk of water shortages due to drought. The SDPP should be prepared by the same bodies responsible for water resources planning, i.e. river basin or district authorities, according to the EU Water Framework Directive. It can be considered a "drought management (sub) plan" to be attached to the river basin management plan according to the indications given by the Water Scarcity and Drought Expert Network mentioned above. The WSSOP should include measures to be adopted by the organizations which manage water supply systems to prevent the onset of a real water emergency.

The DCP should include, among other items, short-term measures to be adopted when exceptional droughts cause considerable damage and a natural disaster is declared. The main contents of the three plans are reported in Table 2.

The first plan, at the strategic level, aims at identifying the drought-vulnerable areas within the river basin – through the analysis of past drought events and their impacts – and to estimate the water-shortage risk in water systems as preliminary stages for defining, comparing and selecting long-term measures, including procedures for information transparency and public participation. The same plan has to give general indications for drafting the other two plans.

The second plan (the WSSOP) aims at defining the best combination of long-term and short-term measures within each water supply system designed to prevent drought emergency. Finally, the DCP represents the planning tool which includes the drought indicator level for calamity declaration and defines short-term measures to be adopted to mitigate its impacts and to recover relative damage.

The proposed planning framework for drought risk management in water supply systems is reported in Figure 1, which shows the role of the main preliminary investigations necessary to draft the plans and to implement the planned measures.

Drought characterization and indices for drought monitoring

The identification and quantification of a drought and consequently the assessment of the drought vulnerability of an affected area and/or of the water supply systems can be carried out through several methodologies. An objective procedure that serves to identify the start and the end of drought, evaluating its characteristics (duration and magnitude) and assessing the probability of the event, consists in the application of "run method" on the time series of the variable of interest (Yevjevich, 1967). The "run method" has been applied for probabilistic characterization of drought through univariate, bivariate and spatial-temporal analyses (among recent reviews see Bonaccorso, Cancelliere, & Rossi, 2003; Cancelliere & Salas, 2010; Mishra & Singh, 2011).

The development of a drought monitoring system generally requires choosing appropriate indices that describe drought conditions through the measure of the anomaly from a "normal" situation for one or more meteorological or hydrological variables. The several proposed indices for drought monitoring mainly differ according to the selected

Table 2.   Main contents of drought management plans (from Rossi *et al.*, 2008b).

Plan	Responsible body	Contents

Strategic water shortage preparedness plan (SWSPP) to be annexed to the river basin management plan	Basin hydrographic district authority	• Identification of drought-vulnerable areas through the analysis of past drought events and their impacts
		• Estimation of water-shortage risk in water supply systems, taking into account:
		  - definition of priority in water allocation under shortage conditions among different uses
		  - definition of guarantee levels for different uses (expressed as time reliability and volumetric reliability)
		• Definition of appropriate long-term actions to reduce water-shortage risk
		• Comparison and selection of alternative drought-mitigation measures
		• Procedures to ensure the transparency of information during droughts and planning process and to allow public participation in decisions
		• General indications for the drafting of water supply system management plan (WSSMP)
		• Estimation of costs and financing sources
		• General indications for the drafting of drought contingency plan (DCP)

Water supply system management plan	Agencies for water supply management	• Definition of indicators and their values to define Normal, Alert and Alarm conditions with respect to drought for a given water supply system • Definition of the best mix of long-term and short-term measures to avoid emergency • Estimation of costs and financing sources for the chosen mitigation measures • Tools for fostering stakeholder participation and exchanges
Drought contingency plan	Regions or basin authorities (with the contribution of civil protection)	• Definition of indicators and their values for declaration of a drought as natural calamity • Tools for an institutional participation through a devoted task force on drought • Definition of short-term mitigation measures and their costs • Indications for the coordination of state, regional and local interventions during emergency • Tools to ensure the transparency of information on drought situation • Possible recovery from drought damages

variable, the time scale, the definition of "normal" condition, the way of measuring the anomaly (e.g. difference, ratio, etc.) and the method for standardization.

Several reviews and classifications of drought indices have been made in the last decades. Among the most recent, examples can be found in MEDROPLAN (2007) and Niemeyer (2008), and on websites such as the National Drought Information Center (http://drought.unl.edu/Planning/Monitoring/ComparisonofIndicesIntro.aspx).

Generally, drought indices are categorized as meteorological, hydrological, agricultural, or remote sensing–based. Some indices also attempt to combine different data related

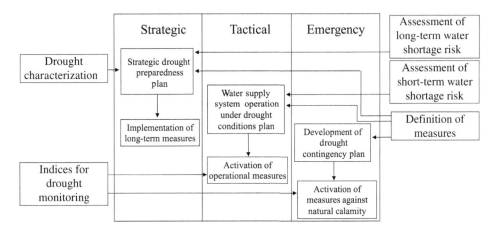

Figure 1.   Role of preliminary analyses and early warning in the drafting and implementation of drought-risk management plans (from Rossi *et al.*, 2008a).

to different variables (e.g. precipitation, soil, water content) and/or to merge the information from several indices into one value, taking into account also the status of water reserves.

Since an effective response to drought depends on early perception through reliable monitoring, the indices to be used in a drought monitoring system have to satisfy several requisites, such as: 1. representing the complex interrelation between meteorological and hydrological components of a significant reduction of water availability; 2. making use of real-time, easily available hydro-meteorological data; 3. being able to describe drought conditions even in a drought's early stages; 4. providing comparability of drought events both in time and space; 5. describing drought impact in some way; and 6. assessing the severity of the current drought as a trigger to support decision makers to activate drought mitigation actions (Rossi, Nicolosi, & Cancelliere, 2008a). Table 3 summarizes a comparison among the most consolidated indices (Palmer, SPI) and a few new indices (such as RDI and DFI) aimed at exploring strengths and weaknesses, spatial comparability, relevance as proxy of critical impact, and suitability for a monitoring system.

Assessment of water-shortage risk due to drought in water supply systems

Assessment of water-shortage risk due to drought is a key step within the strategic planning of drought preparedness measures in water supply systems. In addition, risk assessment can find useful application during the operation of a water supply system in selecting among different management alternatives. When dealing with strategic decisions, risk assessment generally has to be unconditional (not referred to a particular state or condition of the system) and aimed at selecting the best long-term measures (Bonaccorso, Cancelliere, Nicolosi, Rossi, & Cristaudo, 2007). In the case of the operation of water supply systems under drought conditions, the risk assessment has to be "conditional", i.e. taking into account the initial state/condition of the system. In this case the main problem is deciding *when* and *how* to activate adequate mitigation measures (i.e. rationing policies and/or the use of additional water resources) in order to prevent future severe shortages (Cancelliere, Nicolosi, & Rossi, 2009). Due to the uncertainty of future drought development, the decision should be taken on the basis of an assessment of shortage risk due to drought while also introducing the drought measures in the system model. In many cases, these predefined measures are implemented in different stages,

Table 3. Comparison among some of the most used drought indices (from Rossi et al., 2008a).

Index	Strengths	Weaknesses	Spatial comparability	Relevance for impact assessment	Suitability for monitoring
PHDI – Palmer Hydrological Drought Index (Palmer, 1965)	• Detailed estimate of hydrological drought based on soil moisture balance	• Classes of drought severity not consistent in terms of probability of occurrence	• Poor (empirical parameters estimated for arid regions of the USA)	• Good description of agricultural impacts	• Large use in monitoring systems (although it underestimates drought in wet regions)
SPI – Standardized Precipitation Index (McKee et al., 1993)	• Simple computation and easy interpretation • Drought categories based on probability	• Severity of drought events sensitive to aggregation timescale	• Very high for fixed timescale • Difficulties in comparing events of different durations	• Good description of severity of generic impacts	• Widely used for early warning of drought
RDI – Reconnaissance Drought Index (Tsakiris et al., 2007)	• Estimate based on precipitation and potential evapotranspiration (PET) • Able to analyze climatic change	• Necessity of data for computing PET • Drought description very similar to SPI (variability of PET lower than precipitation)	• Very high for fixed timescale	• Good description of agricultural impacts	• Use yet limited
DFI – Drought Frequency Index (Gonzalez & Valdes, 2006)	• Asymptotic estimation of return period considering persistent deviation from normal • Slightly sensitive to the selected threshold	• Complex computation under the hypothesis of randomness and time independence of considered variable	• Very high since index is slightly sensitive to threshold, timescale and characteristic (i.e. duration, cumulative deficit)	• Depends on the selected variable • Poor relevance since drought characteristics not directly representative of impacts	• Difficult application since index is oriented to probabilistic characterization of drought

according to an interactive approach, and have to be established according to the different conditions of the water system (e.g. normal, alert, alarm) (MEDROPLAN, 2007).

Different definitions of drought risk have been proposed in the literature. Some definitions, similar to the ones widely used for other natural disasters like earthquakes or floods, are based either on the probability of an extreme event or on its consequent expected damages. It can be computed by combining the probability of an adverse event (hazard) with the vulnerability of the elements affected by the drought. Regardless of the particular technique adopted for computing risk, such a conceptual definition has the advantage of attempting to take into account both the stochastic nature of drought occurrences and a drought's impacts.

The topic of the economic assessment of drought damage and of preparedness and mitigation measures has been the subject of a great deal of literature. A review of the different methodologies proposed has been carried out in two recent EC-funded projects, namely XEROCHORE (2011) and CONHAZ (2012). However, given the lack of appropriate data combined with the relative complexity of the economical assessment of damages, the analysis of water supply system management under drought conditions has traditionally been carried out assuming water shortage as a proxy of damages. Thus, drought risk has been assessed in terms of the probabilistic features of water shortages due to droughts, with reference to the different demands.

In general terms, the impact of droughts on water supply greatly depends on the characteristics of water storage facilities, their operating rules and the temporal distribution of water demands, as well as on the actions taken to reduce drought impact. It follows that a correct approach to water-shortage risk assessment should take into account both the *hazard* (i.e. drought occurrences) and the *vulnerability* of the water supply system, which depends on the physical characteristics of the system, as well as on the demands and on management factors. To this end, a Monte Carlo simulation of the system, where the probabilistic features of droughts are implicitly taken into account (making use of stochastic models to generate hydrological inputs) and where the vulnerability of the system is considered in the simulation stage, may constitute an efficient tool to assess water-shortage risk (see Figure 2).

As previously mentioned, assessment of water-shortage risk due to droughts can be carried out with reference to two distinct objectives: increasing the robustness of the system within the planning stage (including the definition of appropriate risk-mitigation strategies) and improving the performance of water supply during droughts within the operation stage.

Several procedures have been proposed to assess the long-term adequacy of a water supply system to satisfy demands during drought events since the study of Russel, Arey, and Kates (1970), who proposed to estimate the expected losses due to drought as a function of the "level of adjustment" of the water system, defined basically as a demand– supply ratio. The evaluation of the performance of a water resources system has generally been made through appropriate criteria or indices, attempting to quantify shortage amounts and occurrences through the concepts of reliability, resiliency and vulnerability (Hashimoto, Loucks, & Stedinger, 1982). More recently, the use of probabilities of shortage of different levels of severity to evaluate the different drought mitigation measures is becoming a popular procedure (Andreu, Pérez, Ferrer, Villalobos, & Paredes, 2007; Rossi, Castiglione, & Bonaccorso, 2007).

Some studies make use of the concept of "design drought", like the one by Frick, Bode, and Salas (1990), which assessed the capability of a water system to cope with drought by simulating its performance during a fixed-return-period drought derived from long hydrological generated series, taking into account the planned expansion of the system. Cancelliere, Ancarani, and Rossi (1998) studied the relationship between

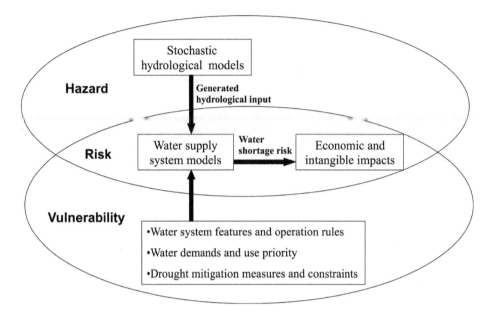

Figure 2.   Assessment of water-shortage risk due to drought in a water supply system through Monte Carlo simulation.

the severity of droughts identified through the "run method" and performance indices for a reservoir with different demand patterns by using the standard operating policy and a few hedging policies, showing that the shortage characteristics cannot be computed on the basis of a single design drought and that the use of a Monte Carlo analysis should be preferred in order to evaluate shortage risk.

Johnson and Kohne (1993) explored the possibility of using the Palmer hydrological drought index for a preliminary assessment of the susceptibility of reservoirs to drought aimed at a more detailed investigation for those more vulnerable.

When the focus of the planning of complex water supply systems under drought risk refers to the evaluation of drought mitigation measures, the decision making includes: (1) the sharing of water shortages among different users; (2) the temporal distribution of release from each source; and (3) the priority of release from various sources. In this case a decision support system (DSS) – with the purpose of helping decision makers facilitate the use of models and databases – and a multi-criteria technique, which allows for a comparison and ranking of measure alternatives to face drought and reduce shortage, can be appropriate. Many studies have been proposed to help water system managers in the planning of the drought mitigation measures through expert systems and decision support systems. Among the recent examples, a knowledge-based system to evaluate different drought-management options has been developed by Karavitis (1999), while Merabtene, Kawamura, Jinno, and Olson (2002) developed a DSS to assess the susceptibility of water supply systems to drought and to determine optimal release through the minimization of drought risk by using a genetic algorithm for a system in Japan.

A greater number of papers have been devoted to evaluating the risk of water shortage with the aim of defining operating policy or storage allocation in a single reservoir and/or complex water supply system in response to drought.

In particular, the definition of operating rules, following the approach proposed by Young (1967), has been carried out through optimization procedures for computing the optimal set of releases on the basis of a given objective function (Labadie, 2004) and by expressing the relationship between optimal release and hydrological inputs and system-state variables by means of different techniques, including but not limited to linear regressions, piecewise regressions, neural networks, and neuro-fuzzy systems. Among the several papers applying this approach for operation under drought conditions it may be worthwhile to mention Randall, Houck, and Wright (1990); Jain, Das, and Srivastava (1999); Cancelliere, Ancarani, Giuliano, and Rossi (2002); and Cancelliere, Giuliano, Nicolosi, and Rossi (2003). Other papers have focused on the operation of water systems under drought conditions by using other tools. Hirsh (1981) estimated the risk of reservoir storage falling below a certain level over a specified time horizon by using several generated streamflow series and computing the selected storage based on the current state of the reservoir and withdrawal rate. Jowitt, Howarth, and Walker (1991) presented a computer-based decision support system for group of reservoirs developed to modify the current reservoir control curve in response to drought events. In particular, a simulation model was applied, able to calculate the cumulative monthly sequences of natural inflows and/or pumped supplies from groundwater or river abstractions. Shih and ReVelle (1994) derived demand-management policy rules during droughts or impending droughts for a single reservoir. The signal used for calling for rationing is a trigger volume given in terms of the months of demand (as a volume) that are needed in storage. When the sum of actual storage plus anticipated inflow is less than the trigger volume, rationing is initiated.

Shih and ReVelle (1995) presented a mixed integer programming model that determines, in a water supply reservoir, the triggers which activate several phases of rationing under the objective of maximizing months without rationing, given a limit on the number of months with a second phase of rationing. Lund (2006) developed storage allocation rules among reservoirs which are part of a system operated under drought conditions in order to reduce evaporative and seepage losses, thus demonstrating that balancing storage among reservoirs, a common practice where each reservoir is filled to a similar percentage of its overall capacity, does not minimize water losses during droughts. Some studies focus on integrating early-warning system information within drought management of water supply systems. Huang and Yuan (2004) developed a color-coded early-warning system for drought management on the real-time multi-reservoir operation. Huang and Chou (2008) introduced a risk-based decision process integrated into a drought early-warning system for reservoir operation. Cañón, Gonzáles, and Valdés (2009) used the drought frequency Index (DFI) as a drought indicator–triggering mechanism for multi-reservoir system operations during drought through a multilevel nonlinear optimization procedure designed to reduce water deficits in irrigation districts. Nicolosi, Cancelliere, and Rossi (2009) used a heuristic multi-objective approach based on genetic algorithms and Monte Carlo simulation in order to define triggering levels to activate mitigation measures, and which thereby verify the performance of the procedure using observed and generated series.

Rossi, Nicolosi, and Cancelliere (2011) proposed a methodology for managing water supply systems during droughts based on the assessment of conditional risk of future shortages and on the consequent activation of mitigation measures. More specifically, the methodology is based on the computation of an indicator of shortage probability caused by drought through Monte Carlo simulation of the behaviour of the water supply system within a short-term horizon starting from its current condition making use of several stochastically generated streamflow series.

Definition of drought preparedness and mitigation measures

In the literature, several classifications of drought mitigation measures are available. A consolidated classification of drought mitigation measures distinguishes three main categories of measures oriented towards (1) increasing water supply; (2) reducing water demands; and (3) minimizing drought impacts (Yevjevich et al., 1983). Other traditional classifications are based on the typology of approach to the drought phenomenon, either reactive or proactive or in relation to the timing of their implementation, differentiating between *long-term* measures aimed at improving drought preparedness (and which includes a set of structural and non-structural adjustments to an existing water supply system) and *short-term* measures defined within a contingency plan, designed to mitigate drought events when they have already started through actions oriented toward improving water supply through new sources or reducing water demand (Dziegielewski, 2000). In Tables 4 and 5, a list of short- and long-term mitigation measures is reported, with reference to the main categories of actions mentioned above and to the different sectors of application (urban, agricultural, industrial and recreational). More recently, the EU Water Scarcity and Drought Expert Network (EC, 2007b) proposed different drought measures, distinguishing between: (1) preventative/strategic measures to be applied during normal status; (2) operational (tactic or emergency) measures, including actions on demands, on supply and on environment; (3) organizational measures to be activated during pre-alert, alert and emergency conditions; (4) drought management plan follow-up measures; and (5) restoration measures, with the deactivation of supply actions and restrictions.

A different classification of measures, set up for the mitigation of general natural hazards, drought included, has been recently proposed within the CONHAZ project (CONHAZ, 2012). It distinguishes the following categories: (1) risk-management planning and adaptation plans; (2) hazard modification; (3) infrastructures; (4) mitigation measures, *stricto sensu*; (5) communication; (6) monitoring and early warning; (7) emergency response; (8) financial incentives; and (9) risk transfer. Regardless of the adopted classification, after a set of potential mitigation measures are identified, selection of the best combination should be based on a comparison and ranking of the performance of each measure in mitigating any negative impact of drought as well as of the main economic, environmental and social consequences of the adopted measure. To this end, multi-criteria approaches have been proposed since the pioneering work by Duckstein (1983), who described the multiple viewpoints to be adopted in a multi-criteria approach and has discussed the set of available specific multi-criteria methods such ELECTRE, compromise programming, etc. The NAIADE model has been applied to different complex water systems, in order to rank the alternative combinations of long-term and short-term measures for reducing shortage risk (see Munda, Parrucini, & Rossi, 1998; Rossi, Cancelliere, & Giuliano, 2005).

Conclusions

Managing drought risk in water supply systems is a complex task: it requires one to consider drought as a natural hazard and at the same time to take into account the features of the water systems themselves and their operation rules, rules that affect the vulnerability to the natural phenomenon, as well as the set of measures to be adopted for reducing drought impacts within the legislative and institutional framework. This paper has discussed the main steps of a risk-management approach, based on a set of planning instruments able: (1) to assess the risk of water shortage due to drought; (2) to identify the measures to prevent and mitigate economic and social impact; and (3) to define the

WATER MANAGEMENT AND CLIMATE CHANGE

Table 4. Long-term drought mitigation measures (modified from Rossi, 2000).

Category	Long-term actions	Affected sectors*			
Demand reduction	Economic incentives for water saving	U	A	I	R
	Agronomic techniques for reducing water consumption		A		
	Dry crops instead of irrigated crops		A		
	Dual-distribution network for urban use	U			
	Water recycling in industries			I	
Water supply increase	Conveyance networks for bidirectional exchanges	U	A	I	
	Reuse of treated wastewater		A	I	R
	Inter-basin and within-basin water transfers	U	A	I	R
	Construction of new reservoirs or increase of storage volume of existing reservoirs	U	A	I	R
	Construction of farm ponds		A		
	Desalination of brackish or saline waters	U	A		R
	Control of seepage and evaporation losses	U	A	I	
Impact minimization	Education activities for improving drought preparedness and/or permanent water saving	U	A	I	
	Reallocation of water resources based on water quality requirements	U	A	I	R
	Development of early-warning systems	U	A	I	R
	Implementation of a drought contingency plan	U	A	I	R
	Insurance programmes		A	I	

* U = urban; A = agricultural; I = industrial; R = recreational

indicators in an early-drought-warning system and related triggers to implement the mitigation measures.

Based on the review of several methods and applications cases, the following conclusions can be drawn.

First, in general terms, effective drought management in water supply systems requires an integrated approach which includes the same list of elements proposed by Grigg (2008) to improve water resources management, namely policy sectors, water sectors, government units, organizational levels, functions of management, geographic units, phases of management, disciplines and professions. However, drought management can be considered a more difficult challenge due to several specific weaknesses and gaps affecting the planning, organization and implementation of the drought preparedness and mitigation actions.

A conceptual misinterpretation still exists between *water scarcity* (i.e. a permanent imbalance between available water resources and demands) and *drought* (i.e. a natural temporary negative deviation from the normal precipitation amount for a significant duration and extension, which leads to a temporary water shortage in a supply system). In addition, a need for complex institutional structure in order to cope with drought risk is not fully recognized. The river basin or district authority cannot, in many countries, cover all specific tasks necessary for drought mitigation and recovery and it appears necessary to entrust the bodies responsible for the operation of each water supply system to prepare, in advance, measures to face water-shortage risk as well as to develop early-warning systems based on drought indices and triggers. Furthermore, the criteria for declaring drought a natural disaster should be defined at the national level while, at the regional and local levels, emergency management organizations (e.g. civil protection agencies in European countries) should intervene within a predefined emergency plan. Therefore,

Table 5. Short-term drought mitigation measures (modified from Rossi, 2000).

Category	Short-term actions	Affected sectors*			
Demand reduction	Public information campaign for water saving	U	A	I	R
	Restriction in some urban water uses (e.g. car washing, gardening)	U			
	Restriction of irrigation of annual crops		A		
	Pricing	U	A	I	R
	Mandatory rationing	U	A	I	R
Water supply increase	Improvement of existing water systems efficiency (e.g. leak detection programmes, new operating rules)	U	A	I	
	Use of marginal waters for quality or cost	U	A	I	R
	Over-exploitation of aquifers or use of groundwater reserves	U	A	I	
	Increased diversion by relaxing ecological or recreational use constraints	U	A	I	R
Impact minimization	Temporary reallocation of water resources	U	A	I	R
	Public aid to compensate income losses	U	A	I	
	Tax reduction or delay of payment deadline	U	A	I	
	Public aid for crop insurance		A		

* U = urban; A = agricultural; I = industrial; R = recreational

a more complex "governance" is necessary to overcome the institutional barriers to integrated or adaptive drought management.

Second, despite the interesting outcomes of several research projects on drought, a list of future research challenges could be proposed in order to improve the resilience to drought of water systems and society. Very briefly, the categories of research that seem to have priority cover the following topics:

- Better modelling of drought occurrences and characterization, both in terms of their stochastic nature as well as of their links with global atmospheric circulation patterns, especially when the analysis should take into account climatic changes
- More frequent and thorough analysis of past experiences in drought monitoring and mitigation which could lay the basis for defining best practices in drought management
- Advanced assessment of economic, environmental and societal impacts of droughts and of the effects of alternative drought mitigation policies in reducing such impacts, based on multi-criteria tools
- Development of appropriate models and an integrated package of techniques which can be easily understood and applied by decision makers responsible for drought preparedness planning to take advantage of the more advanced results in specific drought-related topics (e.g. stochastic hydrology for drought characterization; economics and environmental sciences for comprehensive impact evaluation; social sciences for selecting the way to reduce user conflicts)
- The development of advanced tools for "adaptive" drought management in water supply systems, including an early drought warning system and a reliable monitoring and forecasting system, as well as an advanced DSS, using the improved computer facilities (in terms of computational power and user-friendly interface) available within water utilities and regulators, in order to implement the most appropriate short-time drought mitigation actions on the basis of reliable triggering mechanisms tested through simulation.

Acknowledgements

This paper is partially based on the results of research projects carried out at the University of Catania, Department of Civil and Environmental Engineering: SEDEMED (Interreg IIIB-MEDOCC Programme); MEDROPLAN (MEDA Water); PRODIM (Interreg IIIB-ARCHIMED); PRIN MIUR 2005, 2008. The author would like to thank B. Bonaccorso, L. Castiglione and V. Nicolosi, who cooperated on the projects, and particularly L. Castiglione for help in preparing this paper.

References

Andreu, J., Pérez, M. A., Ferrer, J., Villalobos, A., & Paredes, J. (2007). Drought management decision support system by means of risk analysis models. In G. Rossi, T. Vega, & B. Bonaccorso (Eds.), *Methods and tools for drought analysis and management* (pp. 195–216). Dordrecht: Springer.

Bonaccorso, B., Cancelliere, A., Nicolosi, V., Rossi, G., & Cristaudo, G. (2007). Methods for risk assessment in water supply systems. *Options Méditerranèennes, 58*, 115–127.

Bonaccorso, B., Cancelliere, A., & Rossi, G. (2003). An analytical formulation of return period of drought severity. *Stochastic Environmental Research and Risk Assessment, 17*, 157–174.

Botterill, L. C., & Wilhite, D. A. (Eds.). (2005). *From disaster response to risk management: Australia's national drought policy*. Dordrecht: Springer.

Cancelliere, A., Ancarani, A., Giuliano, G., & Rossi, G. (2002). A neural networks approach for deriving irrigation reservoir operation rules. *Water Resources Management, 16*, 71–88.

Cancelliere, A., Ancarani, A., & Rossi, G. (1998). Susceptibility of water supply reservoirs to drought conditions. *Journal of Hydrologic Engineering, 3*(2), 140–148.

Cancelliere, A., Giuliano, G., Nicolosi, V., & Rossi, G. (2003). Optimal short-term operation of multipurpose reservoirs systems under limited water supply. In G. Bloschl, *et al.* (Eds.), *Water resources systems: Hydrological risk, management and development* (pp. 200–207), No. 281. Wallingford, UK: IAHS Press.

Cancelliere, A., Nicolosi, V., & Rossi, G. (2009). Assessment of drought risk in water supply systems. In A. Iglesias, *et al.*, (Eds.), *Coping with drought risk in agriculture and water supply systems* (pp. 93–109). Dordrecht: Springer Science+Business Media.

Cancelliere, A., & Salas, J. D. (2010). Drought probabilities and return period for annual streamflows series. *Journal of Hydrology, 391*, 77–89.

Cañón, J., González, J., & Valdés, J. (2009). Reservoir operation and water allocation to mitigate drought effects in crops: A multilevel optimization using the drought frequency index. *Journal of Water Resources Planning and Management, 135*(6), 458–465.

CEC (2009). *White paper. Adapting to climate change: Towards a European framework for action* (COM(2009) 147 Final). Brussels: Commission of the European Communities.

CONHAZ (2012). Costs of natural hazards. Retrieved from http://www.conhaz.org

Duckstein, L. (1983). Trade-offs between various mitigation measures. In V. Yevjevich, L. Da Cunha, & E. Vlachos (Eds.), *Coping with droughts* (pp. 203–215). Littleton, CO: Water Resources.

Dziegielewski, B. (2000). Drought preparedness and mitigation for public water supply. In D. A. Wilhite (Ed.), *Drought: a global assessment, vol. 2*. London: Routledge.

EC. (2007a). Addressing the challenge of water scarcity and droughts in the European Union: Impact assessment. Second interim report. Retrieved from European Commission: http://ec.europa.eu/environment/water/quantity/pdf/comm_droughts/impact_assessment.pdf

EC. (2007b). *Drought management plan report including agricultural, drought indicators and climate change aspects* Water Scarcity and Drought Expert Network technical report 2008-023. Luxembourg: European Commission.

EC (2009). *River basin management in a changing climate*, Guidance document No. 24, technical report 2009-040, Common Implementation Strategy for the Water Framework Directive (2000/60/EC).

EC (2011). *Water scarcity and droughts in the European Union*, Report from the Commission to the European Parliament and the Council. SEC(2011) 338.

Frick, D. M., Bode, D., & Salas, J. D. (1990). Effect of drought on urban water supplies. II: Water supply analysis. *Journal of Hydrological Engineering, 116*(6), 754–764.

Gonzáles, J., & Valdés, J. B. (2006). New drought frequency index: Definition and comparative performance analysis. *Water Resources Research, 42*, 1–13.

Grigg, N. S. (2008). Integrated water resources management: Balancing views and improving practice. *Water International, 33*(3), 279–292.

Hashimoto, T., Loucks, D. P., & Stedinger, J. R. (1982). Reliability, resilience, robustness and vulnerability criteria for water resources systems. *Water Resources Research, 18*(1), 14–20.

Hirsh, R. M. (1981). Stochastic hydrological model for drought management. *Journal of Water Resources Planning and Management, 107*(2), 303–313.

Huang, W. C., & Chou, C. C. (2008). Risk-based drought early warning system in reservoir operation, *Advances in Water Resources, 31,* 649–660.

Huang, W. C., & Yuan, L. C. (2004). A drought early warning system on real-time multireservoir operations, Water Resources Research, 40, W06401. doi:10.1029/2003WR002910.

IPCC (2007). Climate change: the physical science basis. Summary for policymakers. Retrieved from Intergovernmental Panel on Climate Change: http://www.ipcc.ch/publications_and_data/ar4/wg1/en/contents.html

Jain, S. K., Das, A., & Srivastava, D. K. (1999). Application of ANN for reservoirs inflow prediction and operation. *Journal of Water Resources Planning and Management (ASCE), 125*(5), 263–271.

Johnson, W. K., & Kohne, R. W. (1993). Susceptibility of reservoirs to drought using Palmer index. *Journal of Water Resources Planning and Management, 119*(3), 367–387.

Jowitt, P. W., Howarth, D. C., & Walker, S. (1991). Development of a knowledge-based system for drought management. *Water Resources Management, 5*(3–4), 187–198.

Kampragou, E., Apostolaki, S., Manoli, E., Froebrich, J., & Assimacopoulos, D. (2011). Towards the harmonization of water-related policies for managing drought risk across the EU. *Environmental Science & Policy, 14,* 814–824.

Karavitis, C. (1999). Decision support systems for drought management strategies in metropolitan Athens. *Water International, 24,* 10–21.

Labadie, J. W. (2004). Optimal operation of multireservoir systems: State-of-the-art review. *Journal of Water Resources Planning and Management, 128*(5), 93–111.

Lund, J. R. (2006). Drought storage allocation rules for surface reservoir systems. *Journal of Water Resources Planning and Management, 132*(5), 395–397.

McKee, T. B., Doesken, N. J., & Kleist, J. (1993). The relationship of drought frequency and duration to time scales. Paper presented at 8th Conference on Applied Climatology, American Meteorological Society, Anaheim, CA, 17–22 January 1993.

MEDROPLAN (2007). *MEDROPLAN: Drought management guidelines and examples of application in Mediterranean countries,* Retrieved from http://www.iamz.ciheam.org/medroplan.

Merabtene, T., Kawamura, A., Jinno, K., & Olson, J. (2002). Risk assessment for optimal drought management of an integrated water resources system using a genetic algorithm. *Hydrological Process, 16,* 2198–2208.

Mishra, A. K., & Singh, V. P. (2011). Drought modelling: A review. *Journal of Hydrology, 403,* 157–175.

Munda, G., Parrucini, M., & Rossi, G. (1998). Multi-criteria evaluation methods in renewable resources management: Integrated water management under drought conditions. In E. Beinat & P. Nijkamp (Eds.), *Multicriteria analysis for land-use management* (pp. 79–93). Dordrecht: Kluwer.

Nicolosi, V., Cancelliere, A., & Rossi, G. (2009). Reducing risk of shortage due to drought in water supply systems using genetic algorithms. *Irrigation and Drainage, 58,* 171–188.

Niemeyer, S. (2008). New drought indices. In A. Lopez-Francos (Ed.), *Drought management: Scientific and technological innovations* (*Options méditerranéennes, series A, no. 80*), pp. 267–274.

Palmer, W. C. (1965). *Meteorological drought* Research paper no. 45. Washington, DC: Weather Bureau, US Department of Commerce.

Randall, D., Houck, M. H., & Wright, J. R. (1990). Drought management of existing water supply system. *Journal of Water Resources Planning and Management, 116*(1), 1–20.

Rossi, G. (1990). Siccità: dalla gestione dell'emergenza alla gestione del rischio [Drought: From emergency management to risk management]. *Protecta, 4*(4), 79–83.

Rossi, G. (2000). Drought mitigation measures: a comprehensive framework. In J. V. Vogt & F. Somma (Eds.), *Drought and drought mitigation in Europe* (pp. 233–246). Dordrecht: Kluwer.

Rossi, G. (2009). European Union policy for improving drought preparedness and mitigation. *Water International, 34*(4), 441–450.

Rossi, G., Cancelliere, A., & Giuliano, G. (2005). Case study: Multi-criteria assessment of drought mitigation measures. *Journal of Water Resources Planning and Management, 131*(6), 449–457.

Rossi, G., Castiglione, L., & Bonaccorso, B. (2007). Guidelines for planning and implementing drought mitigation measures. In G. Rossi, T. Vega, & B. Bonaccorso (Eds.), *Methods and tools for drought analysis and management* (pp. 325–347). Dordrecht: Springer.

Rossi, G., Nicolosi, V., & Cancelliere, A. (2008a). Recent methods and techniques for managing hydrological droughts. In A. Lopez-Francos (Ed.), *Drought management: Scientific and technological innovations (Options méditerranéennes, series A, no. 80)*, pp. 251–265.

Rossi, G., Nicolosi, V., & Cancelliere, A. (2008b). Strategic water shortage preparedness plan for complex water supply systems. In G. Tsakiris (Ed.), *Proceedings of international symposium "Water Shortage Management"* (pp. 65–81). Athens: CANAH-NTUA.

Rossi, G., Nicolosi, V., & Cancelliere, A. (2011). Operational drought management via risk-based conjunctive use of water. *Proceedings of XIVth IWRA Congress*, Porto de Galinhas, Recife, Brasil, 25–29 September 2012.

Russell, C. S., Arey, D. G., & Kates, R. W. (1970). *Drought and water supply: Implications of the Massachussetts experience for municipal planning.* Baltimore: Johns Hopkins Press.

Shih, J. S., & ReVelle, C. (1994). Water supply operations during drought: A continuous hedging rule. *Journal of Water Resources Planning and Management, 120*(5), 613–629.

Shih, J. S., & ReVelle, C. (1995). Water supply operations during drought: A discrete hedging rule. *European Journal of Operational Research, 82*, 163–175.

Tsakiris, G., Pangalou, D., & Vangelis, H. (2007). Regional drought assessment based on the Reconnaissance Drought Index (RDI). *Water Resources Management, 21*(5), 821–833.

UNISDR (2007). *Drought risk reduction framework and practices: Contributing to the implementation of the Hyogo Framework for Action.* Retrieved from United Nations Office for Disaster Risk Reduction: http://www.unisdr.org/files/3608_droughtriskreductionpdf.

UN Secretariat General. (1994). *United Nations convention to combat drought and desertification in countries experiencing serious droughts and/or desertification, particularly in Africa.* Paris.

WFD (2000). Directive 2000/60/EC of the European Parliament and of the Council of 23 October 2000 establishing a framework for Community action in the field of water policy, *Official Journal* (OJ L 327), 22 December 2000.

Wilhite, D. A. (1987). The role of government in planning for drought: Where do we go from here? In D. A. Wilhite, W. E. Easterling, & D. A. Wood (Eds.), *Planning for drought* (pp. 425–444). Boulder: Westview Press.

Wilhite, D. A. (Ed.). (2000). *Drought: A global assessment, vols. 1 and 2.* London: Routledge.

Wilhite, D. A., Botterill, L., & Monnik, K. (2005). National drought policy: lessons learned from Australia, South Africa and the United States. In D. A. Wilhite (Ed.), *Drought and water crises* (pp. 137–172). Boca Raton, FL: Taylor & Francis.

Wilhite, D. A., & Pulwarty, R. S. (2005). Drought and water crises: Lessons learned and the road ahead. In D. A. Wilhite (Ed.), *Drought and water crises* (pp. 389–398). Boca Raton, FL: Taylor & Francis.

XEROCHORE (2011). *An exercise to assess research needs and policy choices in areas of drought.* EU-FP7 Support Action Project. Guidance documents on 1. Natural systems and droughts; 2. Environmental effects of droughts; 3. Economic and social effects; 4. Drought policy and management. Retrieved from http://www.feem-project.net/xerochore/index.php.

Yevjevich, V. (1967). *An objective approach to definitions and investigations of continental droughts* Hydrological Paper 23. Fort Collins, CO: Colorado State University.

Yevjevich, V., Hall, W. A., & Salas, J. D. (1983). *Coping with droughts.* Littleton, CO: Water Resources.

Young, G., K. Jr. (1967). Finding reservoir operating rules. *Journal of Hydraulic Division, ASCE, 93*(6), 297–321.

Index

Note: Page numbers in **bold** type refer to **figures**
     Page numbers in *italic* type refer to *tables*
     Page numbers followed by 'n' refer to notes

abcd model 36, 39, 41, **42**, 44, 45, **46**
adaptive management framework 23
African countries: agriculture 8
agriculture: African countries 8; climate
    variability 5–6; crop yield **10**; dominance **6**;
    rainfed 11; small scale farmers 5; societal
    water supply 7
Aragón (Spain) 86, **87**, 89
aridification 11–12; global warming 11; rainfed
    agriculture 11
Arizona 35, **35**; Verde River basin 34–5, 48, 49
Arreguín-Cortés, F.I.: and López-Pérez, M.
    52–63
Atlantic rivers 73
atmospheric circulation: water deficiency 9
atmospheric forcing variables 65
Atmospheric-Ocean Coupled General
    Circulation Models (AOGCM) 83, 85, 94
Australia 23, 7; community 26; context 28;
    CSIRO 21, 24; dollar 25; dry-climate 6;
    floods 27; IPCC 28, **28**; Murray Darling
    Basin Authority (MDBA) 22; Murray Darling
    Basin Commission (MDBC) 18, 19, 20–1,
    22; Murray Darling Basin (MDB) 25, 26,
    24, 30; National Hydrological Modelling
    Strategy 27; National Plan for Water Security
    (2007) 19–20; National Water Initiative
    (NWI) 17–18, 20; National Water Market
    System 26; rainfall 21–2; risk management
    framework 27; South East Australia Climate
    Initiative 22; Water Act (2007) 22, 26; *Water
    for the Future* (2008) 20–1; water policy
    17–31
Australia Day: speech (2007) 19
Australian government 26, 27; CSIRO 21

Baltas, E.A. 117–29
Ban Ki-Moon 81
Barnett, T.: et al. 34
Barrera, A.: and Llasat, M. 104

baseflow 41
basins *see* river basins
Bates, C.: et al. J. 107
biophysical processes 118
blue water: competition 6–7, **6**; problems 8;
    scarcity modes 6
Botterill, L.C.: Monnik, K. and Wilhite, D.A.
    154

Cabezaz, F.: Estrada, F. and Estrela, T. 106
California 7
Cancelliere, A.: and Rossi, G. 152–69; Rossi,
    G. and Nicolosi, V.163
Cancún Climate Change Convention (2010) 60
Cañón, J.: Gonzáles, J. and Valdés, J. 163
capacity building and resilience: disaster
    management 137, 142–3, 147
Caribbean Sea 56
CHE (Confederation of the Ebro) 104, 105
China: water disaster 131
Chou, C.: and Huang, W. 163
climate: regional 65, 84, 94; solar activity 33
climate change adaptation: tool and
    hydrological planning 99–114; water scarcity
    7–8
climate change models 21
climate change projections 93; Couple Model
    Intercomparison Projects (CMIP) 87;
    downscaled over Spain 81–98; Iberian
    Peninsula streamflow 64–80; research
    projects 86; Spain 81–98; uncertainty 95
climate models: downscaling algorithm
    82–5; predictions 33–4; projections for US
    extremes 32–51; state-of-the-art 32–51,
    83–4
climate system: physical processes 83
climate-induced vulnerability: disaster risk
    management 147
Cohn, H.: and Lins, T. 45–8
Colorado river basin 34

Commonwealth 19
Commonwealth Water Holder (CEWH): direct water purchasing 23
community: remote and indigenous 27–8; water management 95
Conference of Ibero-America Director Generals of Water (CODIA) 60
Couple Model Intercomparison Projects (CMIP) 8 /
crisis management: drought 153
critical responses 13
crop yield **10**
CRU TS 1.2 database 66
CSIRO 21, 24
cyclones: Mexico 54

demand management policies 28
demand and supply strategies: IPCC 29
Dialog for Water and Climate Change (D4WCC) 61
direct water purchasing 23; overallocation 23–4
disasters: natural 131–3, *132*, 144, **145**; and water - policy analysis 130–51, *see also* water disaster management policy; water disaster risk management; water disasters
dollar: Australian 25
Dominguez, F.: et al. 32–51
downscaling procedure **65**
drainage and treatment: Ebro Basin Plan (2010–15) 109
drought 10, 24, *165*; categories 164; characterization and monitoring 157–9; crisis management 153; damage 161; definition 161; Ebro Basin Plan (2010–15) 112; economic damages 152; episodes and water deficiency 9; and floods 107–9, 128; intensity versus duration **38**; interannual 10–11, **11**, 12; periods 23; proactive approach 154; reactive approach 143; research categories 166; response categories 153; risk management 153–4, 164–5; water supplies risk in Europe 152–68;
drought frequency index (DFI) 163
drought management: Europe 152–67; planning techniques 156–7; risk 153–4, 164–5
drought management plan (DMP) 155, *158*
drought-risk management plans **159**
drought-sensitive countries **8**
dry-climate countries: societal water security 3–16
dryspells: interseasonal 9–10

Earth Summit (Rio, 1992) 59
earth system processes: uncertainty 85
Ebro basin 99–116; annual discharge 101; climate change effects 101–9; effects on flows 104–6; estimated flows **101**; Hydrographic Confederation of the Ebro (CHE) 100;

hydrological planning tool 99–116; location (Spain) **100**; precipitation 103, **105**; reduced flows 101; temperature trends 103; water consumption 101; water development boards *104*; water output **102**; water quality 109
Ebro Basin Plan (2010–15) 100, 109–13, *110*; drainage and treatment 109; drought 112; energy production 112; floods 113; food-farm complex 111; irrigation areas 111; pollution problems 110; regulatory infrastructure 112; research projects 113; river and riverbank restoration projects 109; riverbeds and watercourses 113; urban water supply 111; water intake control 109
economic development: adverse effects 17
economic losses: water disasters 148
electrical conductivity: Zaragoza **108**
emissions scenarios: IPCC 88–9
energy: primary 128
energy production: Ebro Basin Plan (2010–15) 112
environmental flow reserve 6–7
Estrada, F.: Estrela, T. and Cabezaz, F. 106
Estrela, T.: Cabezaz, F. and Estrada, F. 106; Mateos, C. and Fernández, P. 106
Europe 77, 152–67; drought risk management and water supplies 152–69; Southern 74; water availability 76
European Commission: Water Framework Directive (2000/60) 154–6
European policy: Greece 121; water scarcity and drought *155*
European Union (EU) 156
evaporitic materials 108
evapotranspiration (ET) 36, 37, 39, 44, 69, 70, 125, **126**

Falkenmark, M. 3–16
farmers: small scale 5
farms: small-hold 9
Fernández, P.: Mateos, C. and Estrela, T. 106
flooding: water resource management 29
floods: Australia 27; and droughts 107–9, 128; Ebro Basin Plan (2010–15) 113
Food and Agriculture Organization (FAO) 13–14
food-farm complex: Ebro Basin Plan (2010–15) 111
forest areas: rainfall 105
freshwater: consumption 74–8

García-Vera, M.Á. 99–116
Garmendia, C.: García-Codron, J.C. and Rasilla, D.F 64–80
general circulation models (GCMs) 48, 64, 65; Greece 121–3; predications 33
geographical information systems (GIS) 139
global climate models 83

global warming: aridification 11; climate change scenarios 66; Iberian Peninsula 71, 78
Global Water and Adaptation Action Alliance (GWAA) 60
Gonzáles, J.: Valdés, J. and Cañón, J. 163
Gopalakrishnan, C. 130–51
Gray, D.: and Sadoff, C. 5
Greece 117–29; climate change 121–3; Climate Research Unit (CRU) 121; and European Committee 121; European policy 121; general circulation models (GCMs) 121–3; greenhouse gases (GHG) **122**; Polyfyto reservoir 119, 120; precipitation 123; snow 124; temperature 119; temperature extremes 122–3; UNFCC Conventions 121; water balance model 119, 124; water resources 117–29; woodlands area 119
greenhouse gases (GHG) 52; emissions 82, 117; Greece **122**
Grigg, N. 165
gross domestic profit (GDP) 135
groundwater 41

Hadley Centre: Had3CM (Coupled model) 69, 71; regional climate model 94
Hague: Ministerial Declaration 5
hailstorms: Mexico 54
Hamon, W. 69
Hargreaves, G. 36, 39, 45
Horne, J. 17–31
Howard, J. 19
Howarth, D.C.: Walker, S. and Jowitt, P.W. 163
Huang, W.: and Chou, C. 163; and Yuan, L. 163
Hurricane Katrina 131, 135
Hurricane Sandy 130–1
Hurst phenomenon 33
Hurst-Kolmogorov processes 33
Hydrographic Confederation of the Ebro (CHE) 100
hydrologic simulations 39–45; variables **42**, **43**
hydrological basin plans 100
hydrological cycle: Mexico 52–63
hydrological models: abcd 36; parameters 68; reliability 68; SIMPA 94
hydrological planning: climate change adaptation tool use in Ebro basin 99–114; Spain 106; water management 99
hydrological variables: measurements 53
hydrology: US South-West 34
hydrometry 14
Hyogo Framework for Action (2005–15) 137

Iberian Peninsula: Aragón 86, **87**, 89; global warming 71, 78; monthly runoff changes **71**; streamflows 64–80
Ilarion basin 125, **126**

India 131; interannual droughts 1, 10
indigenous community 27–8
industrialization: nineteenth century 77
information and science: importance of 21–2
infrastructure operation 28
institutional design 145–7
institutional entropy 146
interannual droughts 10–11, 12; India 1, 10; Zimbabwe 10, **11**
Intergovernmental Panel on Climate Change (IPCC) 39, 41, 53, 82, 84, 86, 122; Australian context 28, **28**; climate change and water conclusions 28–30; demand and supply strategies 29; emissions scenarios 88–9; Fourth Assessment Report (AR4) 54; knowledge and research 30; management policies 29; operation of infrastructure 28; recommendations 58; report (2007) 64; uncertainty 85; water disaster management 136; water resource management 29–30
international initiatives 94
international organizations 13
International Water Management Institute (IWMI) 14–15
interseasonal dryspells: rainfall 9; small-hold farms 9; water deficiency 9–10; yield reduction 9
irrigation areas: Ebro Basin Plan (2010–15) 111
irrigation infrastructure 24–6; first programmes 24; Murray Darling Basin (MDB) 24; *Water for the Future* 25
irrigation-dependant countries 13

Japan: water disasters 135
Johnson, W.: and Kohne, R. 162
Jowitt, P.W.: Howarth, D.C. and Walker, S. 163

Kohne, R.: and Johnson, W. 162
Kolmogorov, A. 33
Koutsoyiannis, D. 33
Kundzewicz, Z.W. 33; et al. 107
Kyoto Protocol 59, 82–3

Lins, T.: and Cohn, H. 45–8
Llasat, M.: and Barrera, A. 104
López-Pérez, M.: and Arreguín-Cortés, F.I. 52–63
Lund, J. 163

McCabe, G.: and Wolock, D. 34
management: community 95
Mann-Kendall test 37
MARM-CEDEX 107
Martín, J.M.: et al. 81–98
Mateos, C.: Fernández, P. and Estrela, T. 106
Maya Version 1 database (Mexico) 56
Mexico: achievements 59–61; Cancún Climate Change Convention (2010) 60; Caribbean

Sea 56; cyclones 54; Earth Summit (Rio, 1992) 59; General Law on Climate Change (2012) 59, **59**; hailstorms 54; hydrological cycle 52–63; impacts of climate change 53; Kyoto Conference (1997) 59; Maya Version 1 database 56; National Development Plan (2007–12) 56; National Resources Strategy Climate Change Adaptation 57; National Resources Strategy on Climate Change Adaptation (2010) 57; National Water Commission (CONAGUA) 52, 57, 60, 61; National Water Programme (NWP, 2007–12) 52; precipitation 54, **55**; public policy 56–9; Special Programme on Climate Change (PECC) 57, 58, 59; temperature 54, **55**; vision (2050) 58; water per capita 54; water resources 61; water scarcity 56

Mileti, D. 138
Millennium Development Goals (MDGs) 144
Milly, P.: et al. 33
Ministerial Declaration (The Hague) 5
modern society 130
mountains: snow 125; watersheds 73
Murray Darling Basin Authority (MDBA): Basin Plan 22
Murray Darling Basin Commission (MDBC) 18, 19, 20–1, 22
Murray Darling Basin (MDB) 30; irrigation infrastructure 24; plan 25, 26; rivers 24; sustainability 25

natural disasters: by continent *133*; by type *132*; by year *132*; overview 131–3; regional impacts 144, **145**
Nicolosi, V.: Cancelliere, A. and Rossi, G. 163
nineteenth century: industrialization 77

overallocation: direct water purchasing 23–4; overuse 23

Pakistan 135
PCM model 68, 69, 71–2
Petisco, E.: et al. 81–98
physical processes: climate system 83
planning: and management 19, 127
pollution: Ebro Basin Plan (2010–15) 110
Polyfyto reservoir (Greece) 119, 120
population growth 7
potable water 127
potential evapotranspiration (PET) 39
precipitation **44**, 48, **92**, 125; change in days 93; downscaled annual projection **92**; Ebro basin 103, **105**; ensemble and average projection **40**; evapotranspiration (ET) 70; Greece 123; hailstorms 54; heavy contribution index 93; Mexico 54, **55**; Spain 104, 106; Standardized Precipitation Index (SPI) 36–7, **38**; and

temperature 93; temporal variability 0, 93; uncertainty **89**, 90; water balance 69
pressure and release (PAR) model 141
primary energy 128
Productivity Commission (2011) 27
projections *see* climate change projections
public policy: Mexico 56–9
public water domain: Spain 100
Pulwarty, R.S.: and Wilhite, D.A. 153
purchasing: water 23

rainfall 22, 73; Australia 21–2; interseasonal dryspells 9; new forest areas 105; Spain 86; temperature drop 57; variability 8, **8**, 12; water deficiency 9
rainfed agriculture: and aridification 11
Rajagopal, S.: et al. 32–51
Ramos, R.: et al. 81–98
Rasilla, D.F.: Garmendia, C. and García-Codron, J.C. 64–80
regional climate 84
regional climate models (RCMs) 65, 84; Hadley Centre 94
regional policy dialogue **60**
remote and indigenous community: water supply 27–8
research projects: climate change projections 86; Ebro Basin Plan (2010–15) 113
reservoir 119
resilience 142–3; disaster risk management 143
ReVelle, C.: and Shih, J.S. 163
rich countries 7
rich and emerging economies 11
risk assessment: water shortage 159–64
risk management: Australian framework 27; disaster 136, 142–3; drought 153–4, 164–5
risk reduction and development 137
risk transfers 140
river basins 7, 73, 165; Colorado 34; flow regime 125; hydrological plans 100; Ilarion 125, **126**; locations **107**; management 14; Verde 34–5, 48, 49, *see also* Ebro basin; Murray Darling Basin (MDB)
river and riverbank restoration projects: Ebro Basin Plan (2010–15) 109
riverbeds and watercourses: Ebro Basin Plan (2010–15) 113
rivers: Arizona 35, **35**; Atlantic 73
Rodríguez, E.: et al. 81–98
Rose, A. 143
Rossi, G.: and Cancelliere, A. 152–69; et al. *160*; Nicolosi, V. and Cancelliere, A. 163
runoff: annual 128; average 106–7, *108*; summer 125, **127**

Sadoff, C.: and Gray, D. 5
Salt River Project 35, **35**, 49
Santander (Spain) 78

savannas 12
science: importance of 21–2
Seager, R.: et al. 34
security: societal water in dry-climate countries 3–16
Serrat-Capdevila, A.: et al. 32–51
Shih, J.S.: and ReVelle, C. 163
SIMPA hydrological model 94
small scale farmers: agriculture 5
small-hold farms 9
snow: Greece 124; mountains 125; temperature 124; water 73–4, **76**
snowpack 73–4
social constructions: pressure and release (PAR) model 141; water disaster management 141
social learning 13
societal problems 12
societal water security: dry-climate countries 3–16
societal water supply 7
soil moisture 41, 125; watershed lag coefficient 123
solar activity 33
South East Australia Climate Initiative 22
Spain 76, 77, 94; Aragón **87**, 89; downscaled climate change projections 81–98; hydrological planning 106; National Climate Change Adaptation (PNACC) 82, 83; precipitation 104, 106; public water domain 100; rainfall 86; Santander 78; water management 99, *see also* Ebro basin
Spanish mountains 73
Spanish State Meteorological Agency (AEMET) 87, 88
Standardized Precipitation Index (SPI) 36, 37–9, **38**; gamma distribution 36
state-of-the-art climate models 83–4
streamflow 22, 41
streamflow (Iberian Peninsula) 64–80, **67**, **74**, **75**; data *66*; gauge time series 66; inter-annual variability **68**; regime **72**
summer runoff: UKHI equilibrium 125, **127**
surface storage 14
surface water: Murray Darling Basin (MDB) 23
sustainability 21, 25
sustainable diversion limits 22–3

temperature 57, 69, **69**, 125; Ebro basin 103; extremes (Greece) 122–3; Greece 119, 122–3; Mexico 54, **55**; precipitation 93; snow 124
temporal variability: precipitation 70, 93
Thornwaithe, C. 65–6
Timmerman, P. 143
twentieth century: water consumption 77

UKHI equilibrium **126**, **127**, 128; summer runoff **127**

uncertainty 94, 117; climate change projections 95; earth system processes 85; IPCC 85; precipitation **89**, 90
United Nations (UN): Climate Change Conference (Bali, 2007) 82; Development Plan (UNDP, 2011) 141; Framework Convention on Climate Change (UNFCCC) 52, 81, 121; Office for Disaster Risk Reduction 136; Secretary General 81
United States of America (USA) 34; East Coast and Hurricane Sandy 130–1; South-west extremes 32–51
urban water supply: Ebro Basin Plan (2010–15) 111

Valdés, J.B.: Cañón, J. and Gonzáles, J. 163; et al. 32–51
variability: climate 5–6; rainfall 12, 13
variable infiltration capacity (VIC) 36–7, 44, **47**, 48
Verde River basin (Arizona) 34–5, 48, 49
Vörösmarty, C.: et al. 5
vulnerability: assessment in water disaster management 141–4; blue water problems 8; climate change 54–6; climate-induced and disaster risk management 147; index 142; Programme on Climate Change (PECC) 58; water supply system 161

Walker, S.: Jowitt, P.W. and Howarth, D.C. 163
Water Act (Australia, 2007) 22, 26; whole-of-basin focus 22
water availability 23, 24, 25; CSIRO 24; Europe 76; extremes 49
water balance 65–6; evapotranspiration (ET) 69; Had3CM model 69; modifications 69–71; precipitation 69
water balance model (Greece) 119, 124
water consumption: Ebro basin 101; freshwater 74–8; Santander (Spain) 78; Spain 77; twentieth century 77
water cycle 53–4
water deficiency 8–12, 9; atmospheric circulation 9; drought episodes 9; interseasonal dryspells 9–10; rainfall 9
water development boards: Ebro basin *104*; location **103**
water disaster management policy 136–47; capacity building and resilience 137; changes 138; geographical information systems (GIS) 139; Hyogo Framework for Action (2005–15) 137; IPCC 136; recommendations 140; risk management policy 136; risk reduction and development 137; risk transfers 140; social constructions 141; vulnerability assessment 141–4; World Meteorological Organization (WMO) 139

water disaster risk management: capacity
building and resilience 142–3, 147; and
climate-induced vulnerability 147; database
147; development 144–6; development
linkage suggestions 145; five priority
research areas 147; implementation 147–8;
institutional design 145–7; institutional
entropy 146; Millennium Development Goals
(MDGs) 144; resilience definition 143
water disasters 130–51; by type *133*; China
131; economic losses 134, 148; general
trend 133–4; global examples of 131; gross
domestic profit (GDP) 135; human losses
134; Hurricane Katrina 131, 135; impacts
135–6; India 131; Japan 135; modern society
130; natural disasters percentage *134*;
Pakistan 135; socio-economic impact 134–5;
UN Office for Disaster Risk Reduction 136
water extremes: in US South-west 32–51
water intake control: Ebro Basin Plan (2010–
15) 109
water management: community 95;
hydrological planning 99; poor 9; Spain 99;
user needs 93–5
water planning: adaptive management
framework 23
water policy 131, 143; Australia 17–31; reform
26–7; societal problems 12; urban 27–8
water quality 107–9
water resource management 130; flooding 29;
IPCC 29–30
water resources: climate change effects 99;
Greece 117–29, 123; Mexico 61; US
basins 34
water scarcity 7–8, 56, 165; types 6

water scarcity and drought: European
policy *155*
water shortage 165; risk assessment
159–64
water storage **12**, 14
water supply: remote and indigenous
community 27–8; societal 7; urban and
industrial 7
water supply systems: Europe drought
risk management 152–67;
vulnerability 161
water-balance models 93
watershed lag coefficient:
soil moisture 123
watersheds: mountains 73
well-developed countries 7
wet periods: intensity versus duration
37–9, **39**
Wilhite, D.A.: Botterill, L.C. and Monnik, K.
154; and Pulwarty, R.S. 153
Wisner, B. 141
Wolock, D.: and McCabe, G. 34
Wong, P. 21
woodlands area: Greece 119
World Health Organization (WHO) 77
World Meteorological Organization (WMO)
139
World Wildlife Fund (WWF) 61

yield reduction: interseasonal
dryspells 9

Zaragoza (Spain): electrical conductivity
108–9, **108**
Zimbabwe 10

For Product Safety Concerns and Information please contact our EU
representative GPSR@taylorandfrancis.com Taylor & Francis Verlag GmbH,
Kaufingerstraße 24, 80331 München, Germany

Batch number: 08158490

Printed by Printforce, the Netherlands